The Maryland 400
in the Battle of
Long Island, 1776

The Maryland 400 in the Battle of Long Island, 1776

LINDA DAVIS RENO

McFarland & Company, Inc., Publishers
Jefferson, North Carolina, and London

The present work is a reprint of the illustrated case bound edition of The Maryland 400 in the Battle of Long Island, 1776, *first published in 2008 by McFarland.*

LIBRARY OF CONGRESS CATALOGUING-IN-PUBLICATION DATA

Reno, Linda Davis.
The Maryland 400 in the Battle of
Long Island, 1776 / Linda Davis Reno.
p.   cm.
Includes bibliographical references and index.

ISBN 978-0-7864-7735-7
softcover : acid free paper ∞

1. Long Island, Battle of, New York, N.Y., 1776. 2. Maryland — History — Revolution, 1775–1783 — Regimental histories. 3. Soldiers — Maryland — History — 18th century.
I. Title. II. Title: Maryland Four Hundred in the Battle of Long Island, 1776.
E241.L8R46 2014   973.3'32 — dc22   2008017043

BRITISH LIBRARY CATALOGUING DATA ARE AVAILABLE

© 2008 Linda Davis Reno. All rights reserved

No part of this book may be reproduced or transmitted in any form or by any means, electronic or mechanical, including photocopying or recording, or by any information storage and retrieval system, without permission in writing from the publisher.

Cover illustration: *Departure of Smallwood's Command from Annapolis to Join General Washington, July 10, 1776,* by Wordsworth Thompson

Manufactured in the United States of America

*McFarland & Company, Inc., Publishers
Box 611, Jefferson, North Carolina 28640
www.mcfarlandpub.com*

To the good people of Brooklyn, New York, who have
never forgotten the sacrifice of the men of The Maryland 400
and who strive to keep the memory alive.

To Kathleen McDonagh and the
Brooklyn Irish American Parade Committee;
Michael A. Rawley American Legion Post #1636;
Joe Ferris, parade historian; and Kim Maier, executive director,
and the Board of Directors of the Old Stone House:
a simple thank you is insufficient.

Acknowledgments

The author gratefully acknowledges the following individuals for their assistance in developing various aspects of this book: Joyce Bennett, Tom Jennings, Shirley Middleton Moller, Shirley Platt, Bill Simon, Mary Simmons, John Willis Barlow, Father Joseph M. Doyle, June Feder, Aimee Curry, Roy Fluharty, Richard Prall, Kathy Alvis Patterson, Marilyn Pettit, Bill Parry, Bob Lyons, Barry McKown, Ann Jensen, David Cummins, Mary McCleary, Nancy Kurtz, Christine Senese, the staff of the Maryland Military Monuments Commission and the Maryland Historical Trust, Carolyn Billups (former president, William Thomas Chapter, Maryland Daughters of the American Revolution), Rev. Christou Christos, Jr. (former president, Maryland Society, Sons of the American Revolution), Ernie Irish (former president, Maryland Society, Sons of the American Revolution), the Maryland National Guard, and Joseph Balkoski (former command historian, Maryland National Guard). A special thanks to Joe Ferris and Kim Maier of the Old Stone House who have been so gracious and supportive.

Table of Contents

Acknowledgments	vi
Preface	1
Introduction	3
Storm Clouds Brew	7
The Marylanders March	12
Lapse of Leadership	18
The Battle	20
Aftermath of the Battle	30
Colonel William Smallwood	36
Lord Stirling	42
The Men of The Maryland 400	44
Mordecai Gist	48
First Company	51
Second Company	75
Third Company	95
Sixth Company	115
Ninth Company	130
Unsung Heroes	157
The Marylanders Fight On	167
Epilogue	170
Chapter Notes	173
Bibliography	187
Index	193

Preface

In early 2004 while researching military records for another project, I happened upon the story of The Maryland 400. These young men had willingly placed themselves in harm's way to allow the retreat of the defeated American army at the Battle of Long Island on August 27, 1776. Had it not been for them, the Revolution would have ended that day.

Vastly outnumbered and outgunned, they successfully held off thousands of British and Hessian soldiers with nothing more than their bayonets and courage so that their fellow Americans could escape to fight another day. Tradition says that of the 400 men, 256 were killed, and the rest, with the exception of nine, were taken prisoner. It is from their service that day that Maryland took her nickname as the "Old Line State."

> Maryland earned the nickname "Old Line State" in the American Revolution. The Maryland Line, Maryland's regiments of regulars, achieved a reputation as the saviors of the Continental Army and the cause of independence. References to the "Old Line" are a tribute to the Maryland Line, but more specifically, to the first incarnation of the Maryland Line, the men who first mobilized in December 1775 and early 1776 and fought at Long Island on 27 August 1776, serving under William Smallwood, Francis Ware, Thomas Price, and Mordecai Gist. The battle-worn survivors of this regiment ostensibly reorganized in December 1777, continuing their enlistments "for three years or during the war." But by the close of 1777, few remained from the original line Washington witnessed at Long Island. Bled weak by fighting in the vanguard of the war, they received reinforcements from the Maryland companies of the Flying Camp, and earned recognition for their sacrifices in the form of a nickname.[1]

It wasn't the first time I had heard the tale, and I had vaguely wondered who these men might have been. This time I decided to find out. My first task was to locate a listing of the men. While a plethora of information has been published about the battle, there is very little personal information available. While searching the Internet, I found an article about a week-long event held in Brooklyn, New York, in August every year to honor the men, and eventually I located Joe Ferris, one of the organizers, who mailed me a listing of the soldiers whose names were read each year at the opening ceremonies.

When I received the list and began going through it, I found that names were misspelled; one entire company was misidentified; and one company listed only surnames and first initials. I volunteered to clean up the obvious errors and Mr. Ferris accepted my offer. At the same time, I called Ernie Irish, an old friend and now president of the Maryland Society, Sons of the American Revolution (MDSAR), who provided their listing. An e-mail to the web site of the Maryland Society, Sons of the American Revolution generated a response from Christou Christos, Jr., then president, who took time out of his extremely busy schedule to review and draw up a revised listing, eliminating duplicate names, and so forth. Now I had three lists, all similar, but none completely matching.

What I thought initially would be a simple task took almost two months to complete, and left me with many unanswered questions and a hunger to know more.

In August of that year I decided to attend opening ceremonies in Brooklyn, taking Michael, my youngest grandson, with me. We arrived at the Michael A. Rawley Post, just a few doors away from where it is believed the mass grave of the 256 soldiers who perished in the battle lies. We were warmly greeted, and I couldn't help being deeply touched by the obvious dedication of these good people who refuse to allow the memory of these men to die. As we walked into the courtyard, the first thing I saw was the Maryland state flag proudly flying and, as a Marylander to the bone, my heart swelled with pride.

After brief introductory remarks, the names of the men were read by various members of the group, and I was honored to be asked to participate. At the end of the ceremony, the entire contingent, led by the bagpiper and color guard, solemnly marched to the Old Stone House, the site of the battle, where a commemorative wreath was laid just outside the front door and where, incidentally, the Maryland flag flies every day. Proclamations from New York City mayor Michael Bloomberg and Martin O'Malley, then mayor of Baltimore, were also read.

Many people attended, including some from New Jersey, Pennsylvania, New York, and many local residents of Brooklyn. It was, however, disappointing to note that Michael and I were apparently the only ones there from Maryland.

Now I knew their names, but I wanted to know more. Upon returning home, my research began in earnest. I hungrily devoured every book and document I could locate on the subject. A vague interest had now become a commitment not only to correctly identify each and every one of these men but to know more about them than just their names. Although unfortunately the loss of records of all kinds across the years has been a barrier to fully completing my quest and, although we still have only the names for some, the search continues.

While I could have told this story in my own words, the letters, newspaper articles, obituaries, pension applications, and other documents written by the participants themselves or those who were living at the time make a much more fascinating story. Therefore, I have chosen to be more of a narrator.

Introduction

On July 4, 1776, our fledgling country, then calling itself the United Colonies, declared its independence from England, one of the greatest military forces in the world at that time. England, for her part, was determined to squelch these rebel upstarts once and for all.

Six weeks later, on August 27, 1776, the first major battle of the Revolutionary War took place in Brooklyn, New York. Known as the Battle of Long Island (also known as the Battle of Brooklyn), the Revolution would have ended on that day had it not been for approximately 400 Marylanders who held back overwhelming numbers of British soldiers to allow the rest of the defeated Americans to escape to safety. This was the largest battle of the war until the British surrendered at Yorktown in 1781 and it was the bloodiest of any of them.

Both sides in this conflict knew the strategic importance of the port of New York. By taking New York, the British, in theory, could divide the colonies by isolating New England and blockading shipments to the southern colonies.

The British had come prepared with nearly 32,000 seasoned, professional soldiers transported by the largest fleet assembled since the Spanish Armada. Approximately 17,000 of these men were Hessians — bought from their German princes and paid for by the British for $800,000. George Washington remarked "Many of them were ignorant, brutal, and blood-thirsty, were hated by the patriots, and despised even by the regular British army."[1]

Meanwhile, the colonies were still scrambling to fill the quotas set for them by the Continental Congress. They had amassed 11,000 men, only about 3,000 of whom had any training whatsoever. The enlistees lacked arms, ammunition, tents, blankets, and uniforms. State militia companies would often have to combine resources to allow just one company to march. This lack of resources, coupled with poor planning and leadership, led to a disaster at Brooklyn, and it is not surprising that within a few short hours the British had outflanked and surrounded the American soldiers. The Brooklyn battleground soon became a killing field.

> All over the field, many who tried to surrender were slaughtered and stragglers were shot down or bayoneted when they could not escape. Hessians with leveled bayo-

nets formed circles around terrified groups of Americans in the woods; methodically these rings would close until all life within them was extinguished. Earlier, the British had made a point to spread the rumor in the Hessian ranks that the Americans practiced cannibalism on defeated enemies, noting, as evidence, the tomahawk each man carried.[2]

General Washington, observing the carnage from a nearby hill, ordered a retreat. Simultaneously, he ordered the Pennsylvania, Delaware, and Maryland troops to provide cover for the fleeing soldiers. The Pennsylvania, Delaware, and many of the Maryland troops were soon overrun and Washington ordered their retreat as well. Blocking their way was a stone house, held by the British who were showering gun and cannon fire on the soldiers as they fled across the Gowanus Swamp to safety.

General William Alexander (also known as Lord Stirling) kept 400 Marylanders with him while the rest were ordered to retreat. They were to undertake the last mission of this battle. They were to take the house from the British and hold it until the rest of the American army escaped.

The Marylanders charged the house six times, closing ranks after each assault over the bodies of their dead and dying comrades. General Washington, observing from Cobble Hill, wrung his hands and cried out, "Good God! What brave fellows I must this day lose."

The mortal remains of 256 of these men are said to lie in a mass grave beneath the concrete on Third Avenue between Seventh and Eighth Streets in Brooklyn. There is no uniformed sentry to guard their final resting place — no stone to mark their tomb. They lie in relative obscurity, forgotten except for a few dedicated residents of Brooklyn who gather together each year on the Sunday closest to the anniversary of their deaths to pay tribute.

Who were these men who sacrificed themselves that day? Over the years various lists have been compiled of The Maryland 400, but the names of the men are often misspelled, the companies in which they served are identified incorrectly, and further research indicates that, in some cases, although a soldier was listed, he was not present the day of the battle. There is no listing of who was actually killed that day, and almost nothing is known about the lives of these brave men.

As a group, the Marylanders have often been described as wealthy young gentlemen from some of the finest families in Maryland. Well-equipped, well-trained, well-armed, and resplendent in their scarlet and buff uniforms, they have been eulogized and romanticized. Poems by such luminaries as Walt Whitman have attested to their bravery and sacrifice.[3]

Some of what has been written is fact, but not all. Little is known about the men themselves. Colonel William Smallwood was in charge of all Maryland troops, but he was absent at the onset of the battle, having been ordered by General Wash-

The romanticized version of the story of The Maryland 400 is that the men wore these uniforms into battle. Officers may have worn them, but not the enlisted men, who wore hunting shirts.

ington to conduct a court-martial. In his absence, Colonel Smallwood placed Major Mordecai Gist in command of the Maryland troops.

Most of those who survived the battle or captivity immediately reenlisted. Most went on to fight in later battles where a number of them were subsequently killed or wounded.

Some of these soldiers were so crippled by the wounds they received at the Battle of Brooklyn that they could no longer support themselves or their families. Others pushed on, regardless of missing limbs and unhealed damage, not wanting to apply for a pension, which they considered charity, doing the best they could as long as possible.

After the war ended, many of them faded into obscurity while others went on to achieve fame and greatness. A few lived long enough to apply for pensions and to tell a little about what happened to them that day. They were not boastful or grandiose in their descriptions — they simply related their stories.

The quest of this writer has been to determine who they were, where they were from, and as much about their lives as possible. In many cases, the stories of some of the survivors will be told in their own words.

Heroes? Yes, they were. They were sent on a suicide mission that day and they knew it. It would be 400 Marylanders with nothing but their bayonets and guts against at least 10,000 British soldiers who would save the American army. It would be 400 Marylanders who would provide the impetus for the Americans to fight on.

John J. Gallagher writes: "This sacrifice was to be remembered throughout the war. According to someone unidentified in any history book: 'The Declaration of Independence that was signed in ink in Philadelphia was signed in blood in south Brooklyn.'"[4] Gallagher concludes, "The story of the Battle of Brooklyn is simple. In the first major trial of the American Army with the forces of the British Empire, the rebels with no thought-out concept of battle, were outmaneuvered and lost. The heroism of Stirling and the Marylanders, however, showed that the Americans were a force to be reckoned with. It would be an age of the 'patriot' fighting for the 'patriotic cause' from now on."[5]

Storm Clouds Brew

Maryland had stood firm with its sister colonies in opposing the various acts proposed by Parliament in the years leading up to the Revolutionary War. Marylanders readily joined in boycotting British goods such as paint, tea, glass, and paper as set forth in the Townshend Act of 1767. Most of the taxed items covered in the Townshend Act were exempted in 1770 with the exception of tea. Marylanders then refused to buy tea.

British ships were not allowed to unload their cargoes and ordered to return to England. Maryland merchants who knowingly or otherwise accepted goods and paid the taxes were dealt with swiftly. At a minimum, they lost a great deal of money as the cargo they received was often seized and destroyed. A further risk could have been the loss of their lives.

The most famous Maryland tax revolt incident involved Anthony Stewart of Annapolis. On October 15, 1774, Stewart's ship, called the *Peggy Stewart*, arrived in Annapolis loaded with, among other valuable cargo, 2,320 pounds of tea. Stewart decided to pay the tax and have the tea moved quietly ashore, but before he could do so, his plan became public knowledge. Angry crowds gathered, with some marching to Stewart's home giving him the choice of either burning the ship or being hanged at his front door. Stewart agreed to burn his ship, but he asked that he be allowed to unload the rest of the cargo. His offer was refused. Stewart himself ran the ship aground and set the *Peggy Stewart* on fire. The crowd watched and cheered as the ship burned to the water line.

Marylanders were active in resistance and figured prominently in the activities of the Continental Congress. Indeed, it was Maryland who initially proposed the idea that a representative of each colony meet in Philadelphia, despite the feelings of many Marylanders that an agreement with England could be reached, thereby averting war.

At the Second Continental Congress on June 15, 1775, it was one of Maryland's representatives, Thomas Johnson, who nominated George Washington as commander in chief of the Continental Army.

Maryland would have been even more strident had it not been for Sir Robert Eden, the royal governor of Maryland, who was well-liked and respected. He often acted on behalf of the colonists, even advising the British to repeal the tax on tea. He was the only royal governor in the colonies not forcibly ousted from office. Instead, the Maryland Council of Safety asked him to step down. He did so in June 1776 and was placed on board a ship bound for England with instructions that he was not to be molested.

In 1784 former governor Eden returned to Maryland to recover some of his property, and, while here, he died in Annapolis. His body was returned to England for burial. In 1926, his remains were returned to Maryland and he was reinterred at St. Anne's Episcopal Church in Annapolis. Governor Eden's wife, Caroline, was the daughter of Charles Calvert, 5th Lord Baltimore. Caroline County, Maryland, is named for her. This couple were the ancestors of Sir Anthony Eden, Britain's prime minister from 1955 to 1957.

Mordecai Gist would be one of those who would not wait for an official declaration of war:

> It stands upon record that while Massachusetts was preparing for the contest in the earlier days, there were men along the Chesapeake and the Potomac who took the alarm with their northern brethren. Mordecai Gist, Esq., of "Baltimore town," was among the first to snuff the coming storm, and the first to act, for he tells us that as early as December, 1774, at the expense of his time and hazard of his business, he organized "a company composed of men of honor, family, and fortune," to be ready for any emergency. The Lexington news, four months later, found the best part of Maryland ready to arm. In Baltimore, William Buchanan, lieutenant of the county, collected a body of the older citizens for home defence, while their unmarried sons and others organized themselves into two more companies, donned "an excellent scarlet uniform," and chose Gist for their leader.[1]

Marylanders were appalled by the events occurring in Lexington and Concord. They were only too aware that the time for talking had passed. Thomas Stone, then a member of the Maryland provincial convention and later to be one of the signers of the Declaration of Independence, wrote to his wife on April 28, 1775.

> We have this day received a confirmation of the unhappy contest between the king's troops and the people of New England; and I am afraid it is too true. This will reduce both England and America to a state to which no friend of either ever wished to see; how it will terminate, God only knows. My heart is with you, and I wish it was in my power to see you, but many gentlemen insist that I should stay to assist in deliberation on those important affairs. I wish to do my duty, and shall be obliged to stay here longer than I expected, but I hope to see you on Sunday, if nothing new occurs.
>
> We have accounts that numbers of people are killed on both sides; which I am apprehensive will preclude all hopes of a reconciliation between this and the mother-country; a situation of affairs which all thinking men must shudder at. People here seem to feel very severely on the present occasion. I have determined to act according to the best of my judgement, rightly; but, in the important and dangerous

crisis to which we are reduced, the best may err. Pray God preserve you and bless our little ones. We are like to see times which will require all our fortitude to bear up against. We must do our best, and leave the rest to Him who rules the affairs of men.[2]

On July 26, 1775, the Association of Freeman of Maryland, comprised of representatives from all of the counties, officially declared Maryland in the rebel cause, stating in part:

> We therefore, inhabitants of the Province of Maryland, firmly persuaded that it is necessary and justifiable to repel force by force, do approve of the opposition by arms to the British Troops employed to enforce obedience to the late acts and statutes of the British Parliament, for raising a revenue in America, and altering and changing the charter and constitution of the Massachusetts Bay, and for destroying the essential securities for the lives, liberties and properties of the subjects in the United Colonies. And we do unite and associate, as one band and firmly and solemnly engage and pledge ourselves to each other and to America that we will, to the utmost of our power, promote and support the present opposition, carrying on as well by arms, as by the continental association restraining our commerce.[3]

All freemen within the state were required to subscribe to the proclamation within ten days of receipt. The names of those who did not subscribe were to be reported. Failure to sign resulted in fines and/or confiscation of property.

The proclamation called for the enrollment of forty companies of minutemen across the state. Every able-bodied freeman between the ages of sixteen and fifty was required to enroll in a company of militia no later than March 1776. With the exception of pistols, the firearms of those who refused to enroll or delayed in doing so were seized and redistributed to the militia companies.

Maryland had now officially declared herself at war, although she had in fact been so for quite some time.

With over 400 miles of shoreline, Maryland was vulnerable to invasion and depredations by the enemy, particularly in southern Maryland and along the Eastern Shore, both areas being surrounded by water. While Baltimore and Annapolis were heavily fortified, the people outside of these cities were left largely to fend for themselves.

As a result, Maryland had already been defending her shores long before the official declaration of war, particularly against the incursions of the fleet of the deposed royal governor Lord Dunmore of Virginia who was marauding along the Virginia, shorelines, including the Potomac River, which separates the two states. Plantations along the Potomac were looted and burned. Lord Dunmore even went so far as to plan to abduct Martha Washington from Mount Vernon. In a letter dated August 20, 1775, George Washington, then in Cambridge, Massachusetts, wrote to Lund Washington:

I can hardly think that Lord Dunmore can act so low, and unmanly a part, as to think of siezing Mrs. Washington by way of revenge upon me; howev'r, as I suppose she is, before this time gone over to Mr. Calvert's, and will soon after retng., go down to New Kent, she will be out of his reach for 2 or 3 months to come, in which time matters may, and probably will, take such a turn as to render her removal either absolutely necessary, or quite useless. I am nevertheless exceedingly thankful to the Gentlemen of Alexandria for their friendly attention to this point and desire you will if there is any sort of reason to suspect a thing of this kind provide a Kitchen for her in Alexandria, or some other place of safety elsewhere for her and my Papers.[4]

Now, with the call to war, additional militia companies were being formed all over the state. Contracts were being issued for muskets, ammunition, uniforms, tents, and other materials needed by the troops. Companies were being formed and the men were being trained and drilled.

Most of the militia companies had no equipment, but drills went on. "That January and February, actual battle was well beyond the ken of most of those who drilled outside of Annapolis. Drummer John Meek and fifer Edward George kept the men in step as they marched with their broomstick guns. The Council of Safety was still collecting muskets and ammunition for them."[5]

Smallwood's battalion was created on January 2, 1776. Staff included Colonel William Smallwood, Lieutenant Colonel Francis Ware, First Major Thomas Price, and Second Major Mordecai Gist. The battalion consisted of nine companies, each of which had four officers, four sergeants, four corporals, one drummer, one fifer, and 60 privates for a total of 74 men. At that time, the overall strength of Smallwood's battalion was about 680 men. The Ninth Company, then under the command of George Stricker, was armed with rifles instead of the usual muskets and they had four more privates, for a total of 80 men.[6]

Maryland made several crucial decisions that would affect the quality of her army. Among these were the requirements that her soldiers be trained, well equipped, well fed, and paid.

The Maryland Line displayed soldierly conduct that rivaled or exceeded the best in the Continental Army. The performance and conduct of the troop was a product of their time spent drilling before joining the ranks of the Continental Army — training that differentiated the Maryland Line from other state's troops. While other states responded to Congress's call for recruits with untrained militia, on 18 January 1776, the Maryland Provincial Convention working under the assumption that paid soldiers furnished with rations and suits of clothes would be better soldiers, established the Maryland Line as a regiment of uniformed regulars. The Convention's assumption proved correct as the Line exemplified a cohesive, disciplined unit, especially in comparison to the throngs of untrained militia that formed the bulk of the Continental Army [MSA: 12, 147].

Although the Declaration of Independence was officially adopted on July 4, 1776, it was not signed by the delegates to the Continental Congress until August 2. Maryland's representatives were Samuel Chase, William Paca, Thomas Stone, and Charles Carroll of Carrollton.

> It is stated that, as the signing was progressing, John Hancock, the President of Congress, asked Mr. Carroll, who had not the happiness of voting for the Declaration, if he would sign it. "Most willingly," he replied; and taking a pen, he signed his name, as was his habit, Charles Carroll. A bystander remarked aloud as Mr. Carroll was signing his name, "There go several millions," alluding to the great wealth endangered by his adherence to the cause of independence. "Nay," said another; "there are several Charles Carrolls — he cannot be identified." Mr. Carroll, hearing the conversation, immediately added to his signature the words "of Carrollton," the name of the estate on which he resided, remarking as he did so, "They cannot mistake me now."[7]

Soon it would become apparent that the first clash would occur in New York. The British considered the occupation of New York and control of the Hudson River essential to quell the rebellion. Washington agreed on the strategic significance of this colony and would do everything in his power to keep this from happening.

Thousands of troops began to converge on Annapolis, the point of debarkation and embarkation for all Maryland soldiers. On July 6, 1776, Colonel William Smallwood was ordered to "immediately proceed with your battalion to the city of Philadelphia, and put yourself under the continental officer commanding there, and be subject to the further orders of the congress" (MSA: 178, 203).

Meanwhile, some of the troops ordered to march had to be recalled. The St. Mary's County men began their march to the north but they were brought back as Lord Dunmore and his fleet were again threatening inhabitants along the shores of southern Maryland. The first battle of the Revolution fought on Maryland soil occurred at St. George's Island in St. Mary's County on July 16, 1776, when the British landed to forage for food and water and to unload the bodies of those who had died aboard their ships from smallpox. The dead included slaves the British had taken from Virginia plantations who were promised that if they would fight for the British, they would later be given their freedom. Let us not forget that these slaves and thousands more would later be abandoned by the British in large numbers at the Battle of Yorktown.

As the colonials began sending their soldiers to New York, the British began their buildup as well. Over the summer, the British sent a fleet, the largest amassed in the world since the Spanish Armada. An estimated 427 ships, with 1,200 cannons and vast quantities of munitions, arrived in New York harbor. Residents stated that the "masts appeared as thick as trees in a forest." Also aboard these ships were over 34,000 professional soldiers and seamen, roughly the population of Philadelphia at that time.[8]

The Marylanders March

In making their way north, the Marylanders were generally transported by barge to the Head of the Elk (now known as Elkton, Maryland). From there, they were required to report to the Continental Congress at Philadelphia, a distance of approximately 50 miles. This part of the trip would be made on foot.

When Smallwood's battalion arrived in Philadelphia, they must have made quite an impression on the local residents. An unidentified source said: "Colonel Smallwood's battalion was one of the finest in the army, in dress, equipment, and discipline. Their scarlet and buff uniforms and well-burnished arms contrasted strongly with those of the New England troops, and were distinguished at this time, says Graydon, by the most fashionable cut coat, the most macaroni cocked hat, and hottest blood in the Union."[1]

Major John Adlum of the Pennsylvania Line was present the day Smallwood's regiment arrived in Philadelphia. In 1833 he recollected, from his diaries and papers of the time, the following:

> Smallwood's regiment arrived in Philadelphia about the middle of July, 1776, the day after the York, Pennsylvania, militia got there. I happened to be on Market street when the regiment was marching down it. They turned up Front street, 'till they reached the Quaker meeting-house, called the Bank meeting, where they halted for some time, which I presumed was owing to a delicacy on the part of the officers, seeing they were about to be quartered in a place of worship. After a time they moved forward to the door, where the officers halted, and their platoons came up and stood with their hats off, while the soldiers with recovered arms marched into the meeting-house. The officers then retired, and sought quarters elsewhere.
>
> The regiment was then said to be eleven hundred strong; and never did a finer, more dignified, and braver body of men face an enemy. They were composed of the flower of Maryland, being young gentlemen, the sons of opulent planters, farmers and mechanics. From the colonel to the private, all were attired in hunting-shirts. I afterwards saw this fine corps on their march to join General Washington.
>
> In the battle of Long Island, Smallwood's regiment, when engaged with an enemy of overwhelmingly superior force, displayed a courage and discipline that sheds upon its memory an undying lustre, while it was so cut to pieces that in October following, when I again saw the regiment, its remains did not exceed a hundred men.

Captain Edward De Courcy, Captain Herbert, a captain , and a Doctor Stuart, of Smallwood's were among the prisoners taken at Long Island, with whom I became acquainted, while I was a prisoner in New York.

The wreck of the once superb regiment of Smallwood fought in the battles of the White Plains, and the subsequent actions in the Jerseys, and in the memorable campaign of 1776, terminating with the battle of Princeton, January 1777, where the remains of the regiment, reduced to a little more than a company, were commanded by Captain, afterward Governor Stone, of Maryland.[2]

It is interesting to note that Major John Adlum had two daughters, both of whom married Maryland men. His second daughter, Ann Maria Adlum, married Henry Hatch Dent, the grandson of Ensign Hatch Dent, Jr., one of The Maryland 400.

On July 30, 1776, Smallwood's battalion arrived in New York. Some of the soldiers were undoubtedly shocked by the reception they received there after the warmth given them in Philadelphia. New York was populated overwhelmingly by loyalist Tories, who referred to them as "macaroni," a derisive term from the song "Yankee Doodle."

Departure of Smallwood's Command from Annapolis to Join General Washington, July 10, 1776 by Wordsworth Thompson. This beautiful painting gives us a glimpse of what it may have been like as the men began their long journey to New York (courtesy, Maryland Museum of Military History, Maryland National Guard).

Almost a hundred years later, John Williamson Palmer, a Baltimore native, wrote a poem in honor of these men called "The Maryland Battalion." The first verse of this poem, below, speaks of the arrival of the men in New York and the nickname conferred on them by the Tories.

> Spruce Macaronis, and pretty to see,
> Tidy and dapper and gallant were we;
> Blooded, fine gentlemen, proper and tall,
> Bold in a fox-hunt and gay at a ball;
> Prancing soldados so martial and bluff,
> Billets for bullets, in scarlet and buff—
> But our cockades were clasped with a mother's low prayer,
> And the sweethearts that braided the sword-knots were fair.[3]

Upon their arrival in New York, the Marylanders made camp among their counterparts from all over the colonies. As their ranks multiplied, unfortunately, those of the British did as well, and the colonials found themselves vastly outnumbered.

On August 13, 1776, Thomas Stone advised the Maryland Council: "The enemy's strength at Staten Island is 15,000 men. The Hessians are daily expected — by the last accounts they were shipping their men and making all necessary preparations for an attack. Gen. Washington is not so strong as he could wish. Upon these movements of the enemy he ordered a reinforcement of 2,000 from Jersey to York, the Maryland Battalion was immediately sent to him, but I believe the Camps in Jersey were too weak to spare any more" (MSA: 12, 199–200).

Three days later, on August 16, the Maryland Council wrote to their representatives at the Continental Congress in Philadelphia that: "We have given orders to all the Independent Companies, four in number, to march. We shall have near four thousand men with you in a short time — this exceeds our proportion for the Flying Camp, but we are sending all we have that can be armed and equipped, and the people of New York, for whom we have great affection, can have no more than our all" (MSA: 12, 212).

Sergeant William Sands of the Seventh Company wrote:

> New York August 14th 1776. Honoured Father and Mother, I Send to inform you that I am well and Quite herty as I hope this will find you and all the Family Our Maryland Battalion Is Encamped on a hill about one Mile out of Newyork where we Lay in a Very Secure Place there is about 200 Sail of the King's Ships Lay Close by us.... Yesterday the Enemy had A Reinforcement of that Damn'd Rascal Dummon's Fleet as we Expect. There was About 40 Sail. We are advised to hold our Selves in Readyness we Expect an Attack hourly we have Lost a great many of our Troops Thay have deserted from us at Philadelphia and Elizabeth Town and a Great Many Sick in the Ospitals There is Rations Given out at New York for 6000 Men dayley. John Anderson is in a Company of RifleMen Stationed Close by us I should be Glad if You will Rite to me the first Opportunity and Let me know the News If

there is Any in that part of the Country. We Expect Please God to Winter in Annapolis those that Live of us.

Written in another hand at the bottom of this letter is the note: "Killed on Long Island August 27th 1776."[4]

The British forces increased as every day passed. A few days before the battle it was said that "the tents and camp fires of twenty-seven thousand troops, eleven thousand of whom were Hessians and Waldeckians — hired at thirty-four dollars and fifty cents for every man killed, three wounded to count as one dead man — glistened and gleamed on the shores of Staten Island."[5]

The Americans had to scramble to assemble an adequate force:

> A little more than two weeks before the battle, or on the 8th of August, Washington had at his disposal 17,225 troops of all arms, of whom 3,668 were sick and unfit for duty. With these he was compelled to provide not only for the exigencies of his position in New York, but meet the demands enforced upon him by the invasion of Brooklyn.... And though his force was increased to 27,000 men within the next fortnight by reinforcements of militia, gained through his urgent representations to the Governors of Pennsylvania, Maryland, and the New England States, that he was in reality defending the gate to each of their capitals, 7,000 of this number were either in hospitals or unfitted for service by sickness. Within five days of the great battle, or on the 22nd of August, the entire fighting force defending the Brooklyn lines did not exceed 5,500 troops of all arms.[6]

In those days, a military camp was often more dangerous than going into battle. As more and more soldiers reported for duty, not only did sanitary conditions deteriorate but also the soldiers brought with them illnesses such as smallpox, dysentery, and typhoid fever, infecting others. It is generally believed that the British were intentionally spreading smallpox. They had certainly done so during the French and Indian War. The Continental Congress called for all soldiers to be vaccinated against this dreaded disease. Unfortunately, they were unaware that the men would be contagious for up to two weeks following inoculation. The men often became ill, exhibiting symptoms of the disease itself.

The Marylanders were hit heavily by sickness. It was recorded that "The flower of these troops was Smallwood's Battalion of about 680 men. They were composed of young men from all of the best Maryland families. These brave soldiers were later reduced by camp diseases to about 450 men."[7] "Many were 'emaciated' by what was called 'camp distemper' from drinking foul water from New York's public pumps. Those who had money learned to buy water from vendors."[8]

Nevertheless, Colonel Smallwood was known to be a strict disciplinarian and the men, unless confined by illness, would have spent their days keeping the camp sites clean, marching, and drilling. Time must have weighed heavily upon them after

The Hunting Shirt. The British and Hessians cringed at the sight of the soldiers wearing the hunting shirt based on their previous experience with the excellent marksmen of Captain Daniel Morgan's Company at Quebec in 1775. Captain Morgan said that the Hessians would scamper at the very sight of his riflemen, the soldiers from Germany shouting "Rebel in de bush, Rebel in de bush" (photograph courtesy the Smallwood Foundation).

the days and weeks began to pass. Certainly all eyes were trained on the continuous arrival of British ships, laden with soldiers and weaponry.

On August 22, General Washington was advised that the British were preparing to begin an assault on the Americans camped in Brooklyn. An estimated 20,000 British regulars, German mercenaries, and Highlanders were landed and about 88 frigates were moved to within shooting range. The local residents, who at that time were estimated to be no more than several hundred, fled.

Lapse of Leadership

The American army from top to bottom was unprepared for this battle. Only about 3,000 Americans were sufficiently trained for combat. As to the officers, Colonel Smallwood, despite his protestations, was ordered to remain in New York City to command a court-martial then underway. Smallwood's battalion was left under the command of Mordecai Gist, who, along with the men, had no battlefield experience whatsoever. The men of Maryland, Pennsylvania, and Delaware were combined into one force reporting to General William Alexander (also known as Lord Stirling).

General Nathanael Greene, Washington's friend and one of his best officers, was ill and his troops were left under the command of General John Sullivan who was described as being "wholly unacquainted with the ground or country."[1] General Israel Putnam, initially placed in command of all of the troops, had his own set of problems and concern was expressed as to his ability to command at all. "Some movements being made which the General [Washington] did not approve entirely, and finding a great force going to Long-Island, he sent over Putnam, who had been over occasionally; this gave some disgust, so that Putnam was directed to soothe and soften as much as possible."[2]

These concerns were very real and unfortunately proved to be correct. Although expressly directed by General Washington to adequately guard the Jamaica Road, General Putnam did not do so, leaving the door wide open for the advancing British troops to surround the American army:

> Putnam had utterly neglected to place a competent guard at the latter pass [Jamaica Road], as Washington had ordered him to do; and when he was told of the movement of the British in that direction, instead of informing the commander-in-chief of the imminent danger, or directing Stirling to retreat from almost certain destruction, he allowed Sullivan to go out with a few troops, and take command of New Jersey and other forces on Mount Prospect.
>
> When, at eight o'clock in the morning, the British had reached the Bedford and Jamaica passes, not more than four thousand Americans were out of the lines at Brooklyn — a handful to oppose five times that number, then stretched along a line more than five miles in extent. The Americans on the left did not perceive their danger until the British had gained their flank and began the attack. The incapacity of Putnam for such important service had allowed a surprise.[3]

But that wasn't all. Not only did Putnam allow the British an open door through which to overwhelm the American troops, but he unwittingly shut the back door as well, ordering his men to burn the bridge over the Gowanus Swamp, cutting off the only remaining avenue of retreat.

General Washington's decision to split command of the American troops between generals Sullivan and Putnam just three days before the battle also factored into their difficulties. This last-minute decision created much unneeded confusion, which may have contributed to the American defeat.

The Battle

Washington knew battle was imminent and the day before he addressed the troops of the American advance saying, "Remember, officers and soldiers, you are freemen; that slavery will be your portion and that of your posterity, if you do not quit yourselves like men. Remember how your courage and spirit have been despised and traduced by your cruel invaders, though they have found by dear experience at Boston, Charleston, and other places what a few brave men, contending in their own land and in the best of causes can do against base hirelings and mercenaries."[1]

At about 11 P.M. on August 26, an American scouting party encountered several British soldiers raiding a watermelon patch. The Americans fired on them and they hastily retreated. A couple of hours later, 200 to 300 British soldiers returned, intent on capturing the Americans. The fighting began to escalate and at about 4 A.M. the beating of arms began. By 8 A.M., the British had fully implemented their previously developed plan to surround the Americans, aided by the failure of General Putnam to adequately guard the Jamaica Road. The British could not believe their good fortune and the ease with which they had moved their soldiers into position.

The British began attacking from all sides. The Americans never really had a chance. Contingents of American soldiers were being methodically cut off from the main forces by overwhelming numbers of British, Highlander, and Hessian soldiers. The British were fully defending the escape routes, again as a consequence of General Putnam's ineptitude as the Gowanus Bridge was now in flames.

> The Hessians burst into the wildest music and with a fierce yell the Yagers, followed closely by the Grenadiers, sprang to the charge. With drums and fifes sounding the charge, colors flying, and lines dressed as if on parade, the Hessians bore down on their prey. Broken up into small handfuls, the hapless Americans, fighting hopelessly but desperately, were tossed to and fro between British and Hessian bayonets. No mercy was shown. The hireling mercenaries vied with one another in bayoneting and massacreing [sic] all who fell in their way, and many of the Americans sold their lives as dearly as possible.[2]

Most of the fighting involved hand-to-hand combat. The Americans did not have time to reload their weapons and were reduced to using their rifles as clubs. In some cases, Americans desperately grabbed rocks, throwing them at the throngs of the enemy marching toward them, bayonets drawn.

> It now became apparent to Stirling that the enemy had turned the American flank, and was pressing upon their rear, as was shown by his left wing recoiling back upon his centre; and all doubt was soon removed when he received intelligence that the rest of the American army had melted away before the fierceness of the British assault, and that in the space of ground included between Washington avenue and Third street, the low ground in the neighborhood of Greene and Fourth avenues, and the heights overlooking Flatbush, lay the bodies of nearly one thousand men, slain in the shock of battle, or by subsequent murder.[3]

An officer recorded that

> The Hessians and our brave Highlanders gave no quarter, and it was a fine sight to see with what alacrity they dispatched the rebels with their bayonets, after we had surrounded them so they could not resist. We took care to tell the Hessians that the rebels had resolved to give no quarter to them in particular; which made them fight desperately, and put all to death who fell into their hands.[4]

The battleground became a killing field:

> All over the field, many who tried to surrender were slaughtered and stragglers were shot down or bayoneted when they could not escape. Hessians with leveled bayonets formed circles around terrified groups of Americans in the woods; methodically these rings would close until all life within them was extinguished.
>
> Though the Hessians and Highlanders accounted for much of this massacre, the British troops from Clinton's column did more than their share of the killing....[5]

General Washington now called for a retreat, hoping to save enough of his army to fight another day. He called on the soldiers under the command of Lord Stirling to cover the retreat as they were the only Americans in the field whose ranks remained unbroken. These troops included the Pennsylvania Line under Colonel Atlee, the Delaware Line under Colonel Haslet, and the Maryland Line under Major Gist.

The British began a fierce attack on Colonel Atlee's troops, but they held on. Two Maryland companies were sent to assist the Pennsylvanians. The British assault was renewed and eventually Colonel Atlee's line began to give. Lord Stirling ordered their retreat to safety.

The Delaware troops were also under attack. With no time to reload their weapons, they began throwing rocks at the advancing British lines. They too were ordered to retreat.

Lord Stirling was well aware that drastic action had to be taken if any of the Americans were to survive: "General Stirling saw that nothing but a diversion of the enemy would save the entire detachment from destruction, and to effect this purpose he hurried to the Maryland battalion as a forlorn hope. The young men composing it answered his appeal with the noblest self devotion and enthusiasm. The enterprise was a voluntary exposure to almost certain death. Less than five hundred young men and boys were about to assault a position supported by the whole British army."[6]

In order to reach safety, the fleeing Americans had to pass by an old stone house, then in the possession of the British. Surrounded by British forces, with cannons placed in the upper windows of the house, many soldiers were killed as they tried to get by.

> Cornwallis had taken possession of the Cortelyou house, in the rear of Stirling's line, and the latter saw that if he could not drive him back, or at least hold him where he was, his whole command would suffer death or capture. He resolved upon a costly sacrifice to save his retreating columns, which were now toiling through the salt marshes and across the deep tide-water creek in the rear. Changing his front and taking with him less than 400 of the Maryland regiment under Major Gist, Stirling ordered the rest of his force to retreat across the Gowanus marsh and creek, which the rising tide was making every moment less and less passable. Smallwood's regiment, composed in a large part of the sons of the best families of Maryland, nicknamed "the Macaroni" by the Tories of New York — was now to have its courage, self-devotion and discipline proved. Stirling placed himself at the head of these Marylanders, and the little band, now hardly numbering four hundred men, prepared for an assault upon five times their number of the troops of the invading army, who were inflamed with all the arrogance of successful combat. Forming hurriedly on the ground in the vicinity of Fifth Avenue and Tenth Street, the column advanced with unwavering front along the Gowanus Road into the jaws of battle. Artillery plowed their fast-thinning ranks with the awful bolts of war; infantry poured volleys of musket balls in almost solid sheets of lead, and from the adjacent hills the deadly Hessian Jagers sent swift messengers of death into many a manly form. Still, above the roar of cannon, musketry and rifles, was heard the shout of their brave leaders, "Close up! Close up!" And again the staggering yet unflinching files, grown fearfully thin, drew together and turned their stern young faces to their country's foes.
>
> At the head of this devoted band marched their General, to whom every victory had now become less important than an honorable death, which might purchase of the safe retreat of his army. Amid all the terrible carnage of the hour there was no hurry, no confusion, only a grim despair which their courage and self-devotion dignified into martyrdom. The advance bodies of the enemy were driven back upon the Cortelyou house, now become a formidable redoubt, from the windows of which the leaden hail thinned the patriot ranks as they approached. Cornwallis hurriedly brought two guns into position near one corner of the house and added their canister and grape to the tempest of death. At last the little column halted, powerless to advance in the face of this murderous fire, yet disdaining to retreat with the disgrace of a flight. Again and again these heroes closed their ranks over the bodies of their dead comrades, and still turned their faces to the foe. But the limit of human endurance had for the time been reached and the shattered column was driven back. Their task was not, however, yet fully performed. As Stirling looked across the salt meadows, away to the scene of the last struggle at Bluckie's Barracks, and saw the confused masses of his countrymen crowding the narrow causeway over Freeke's mill pond or struggling through the muddy tide stream, he felt how

precious to their country's liberty were the lives of his retreating soldiers, and he again nerved himself for a combat which he knew could only prove a sacrifice. Once more he called upon the survivors of the previous deadly assault, and again the noble young men gathered around their general. How sadly he must have looked upon them, scarcely more than boys, so young, so brave, and to meet again the pitiless iron hail. The impetus and spirit of this charge carried the battalion over every obstacle quite to their house. The gunners were driven from their battery and Cornwallis seemed about to abandon the position. But the galling fire from the interior of the house and from the adjacent high ground, with the overwhelming numbers of the enemy who were now approaching, again compelled retreat. Three times more the survivors rallied, flinging themselves upon the constantly reinforced ranks of the enemy, but the combat, so long and so unequally sustained, was now hastening to its close. A few minutes more of this destroying fire and 256 of the noble youth of Maryland were either prisoners in the hands of the enemy or lay side by side in the awful mass of the dead and dying. The sacrifice had been accomplished and the flying army had been saved from complete destruction.[7]

Generals Washington, Putnam, and Smallwood, among others, were watching from an observation post on Cobble Hill. An American rifleman wrote: "Most of our generals on a high hill in the lines, viewed us with glasses, as we were retreating, and saw the enemy we had to pass through, thought we could not. Many thought we would surrender in a body without firing. When we began the attack, Gen. Washington wrung his hands and cried out 'Good God! What brave fellows I must this day lose.'"[8]

On August 27, 1846, Walt Whitman, a Brooklyn native and at that time editor of *the Brooklyn Daily Eagle,* penned a stirring tribute:

> Seventy years ago to-day, Washington stood on our Island shores, and wringing his hands, while tears of the bitterest anguish gathered on his cheeks — sighs of agitated anguish which he is said to have never to have given way to, on any other occasion, before or afterward. He found the Maryland regiment, composed of young men — the flower of some of the finest families of the South — cut to atoms in that disastrous slaughter! He found the first battle where he commanded in person, going against him — and at night three thousand of the troops Congress had entrusted to his care, either lifeless on the cold ground on which they lay, or prisoners in the hands of an enemy whose barbarous treatment of them he well knew, would be little preferable to death![9]

Others wrote as well:

> The sacrifice of their lives, so freely made by the generous and noble sons of Maryland, had not been made in vain. An hour, more precious to American liberty than any other in its history, had been gained; and the retreat of many hundreds of their countrymen had been secured across the dreadful creek and marsh, whose treacherous tide and slime now covered so many of their brave comrades. The carnage of the battle could scarcely have been more destructive than the retreat; for, at this time, no vestige of an army-formation existed, and nothing remained but a

mob of flying and despairing men among whose masses officers and privates were borne undistinguished along.[10]

Tench Tilghman, in a letter to his father, dated September 3, 1776, says: "No regular troops ever made a more gallant resistance than Smallwood's regiment. If the others had behaved as well, if General Howe had obtained a victory at all, it would have been dearly bought.... The behavior of the Southern troops in the late action has shamed the Northern people; they confess themselves unequal to them in officers and discipline."[11]

As they observed the carnage, Colonel Smallwood asked General Washington for permission to send in reinforcements to his beleaguered Marylanders. Initially Washington refused but later he relented:

> After some consideration as to the prudence of risking more brave men to their fate, Washington placed him [General Smallwood] in command of a Connecticut regiment and together with Captain John Allen Thomas' company, which had just came over from New York, and two pieces of artillery, he marched to the west bank

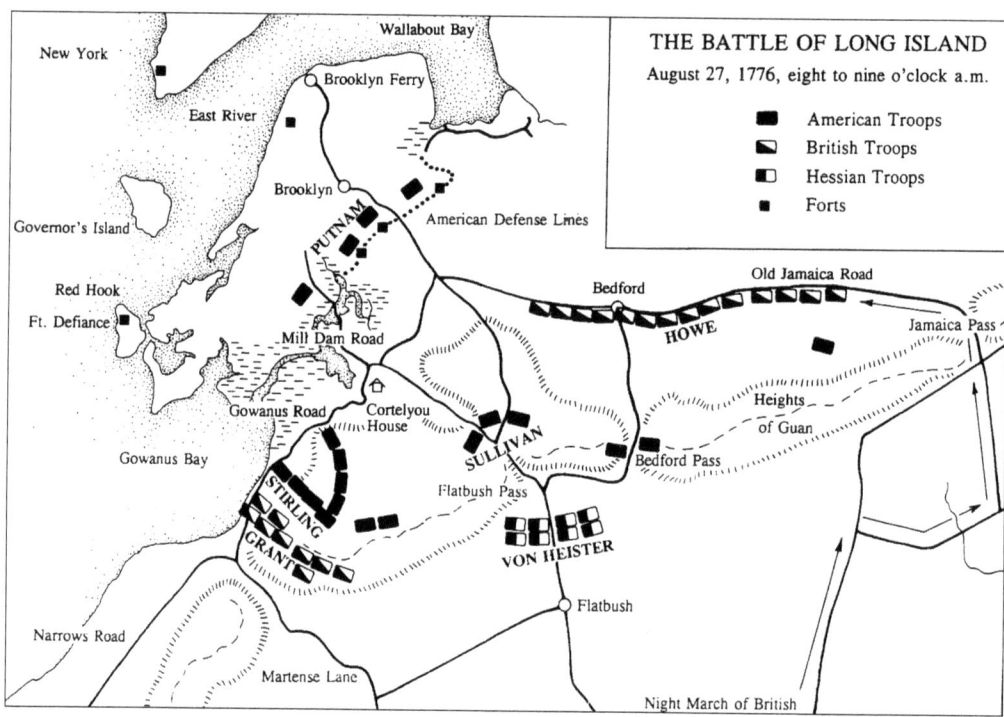

Map of the Battle of Long Island, August 27, 1776. As can be clearly seen on this map, the British had almost completely surrounded the American army and the men under Lord Stirling were being pushed toward the Cortelyou House (now known as the Old Stone House). Reprinted from "Battle of Long Island Rededication Booklet, 1991" (courtesy Maryland Military Monuments Commission).

of Gowanus Creek in time to send a few volleys into the enemy's columns, and to aid the last survivors of Stirling's corps in struggling across its slime.[12]

Douglass' Connecticut levies, just coming up from the ferry, were sent to the extreme right opposite the mouth of the Gowanus creek, where with Capt. Thomas' Maryland Independent Company and two pieces of artillery, they stood ready to prevent the pursuit of the retreating party by the enemy.[13]

He had two field pieces which silenced the six pieces of the enemy, which were firing upon the fugitives, all but 12 of whom waded or swam to safety, helped especially by Thomas's men. Maryland's losses: 256 killed, wounded, or captured.[14]

The conduct of the Connecticut regiment was not such as to inspire the soldiers with that high courage which the exigencies of the battle-field demanded. The only considerable service they did, was the assistance they gave in dragging out upon the firm ground such of Stirling's soldiers as escaped massacre and drowning.[15]

Private Joseph Plumb Martin, a young soldier of the Connecticut regiment, would later write: "There was in this action a regiment of Maryland troops (volunteers), all young gentlemen. When they came out of the water and mud to us, looking like water rats, it was truly a pitiful sight. Many of them were killed in the pond and more were drowned. Some of us went into the water after the fall of the tide, and took a number of corpses and a great many arms that were sunk in the pond and creek."[16]

Other writers recorded:

Each attack was met with the withering counterfire as the British masses swelled against this fanatically determined American rearguard. As Stirling launched his last assault, with a remaining handful of men, even more British reinforcements arrived. At last, the remnant of the Marylanders broke into small parties to fight their way to safety. In the last attack Stirling himself was captured by some Hessians who had outrun their unit. Lord Cornwallis later said, General Stirling fought like a wolf.[17]

Stirling's and Marylanders' gallant action allowed the rest of the Americans remaining in the field to escape across the Gowanus Creek and survive. Only seven men crossing the Gowanus were lost through drowning. But the Marylanders had sacrificed themselves for the sake of the army. Out of barely 400 men, 256 lay dead in front of the Old Stone House. Over 100 others were wounded and/or captured. Only Gist and nine others managed to regain the American lines. This sacrifice was to be remembered throughout the war. The Declaration of Independence that was signed in ink in Philadelphia was signed in blood in south Brooklyn.[18]

The fate of the many wounded was more melancholy than that of their comrades who had been instantly killed, for the Hessian and Highland troops, exasperated by their resistance, bayoneted to death most of those who fell into their hands. Beneath the streets and vacant lots near the western border of Prospect Park lie the remains of these brave sons of Maryland. The proprietors of the adjacent farms were compelled to assist in their burial, and tradition has preserved the site of the spot in which many of the dead were interred.[19]

Ensign Bryan Philpot of the 8th Company would tell his young son John about the events of that day and John would never forget. On May 20, 1856, John Philpot deposed: "That during his said father's lifetime he has often heard him speak of having served in the Revolutionary war, and of being in battle. This deponent has heard his father speak of a retreat after a battle, in which he was obliged to swim a creek, and of the difficulty with which he escaped drowning from the struggles of a soldier who was also in retreat. This deponent has heard his said father describe his feelings

Lord Stirling's Last Struggle Around the Old Cortelyou House. By this time, the Marylanders were fighting in hand-to-hand combat with the British using only their bayonets. The Marylanders were known for their expertise in the use of this weapon and were sometimes called "The Bayonets of the Revolution" (reprinted from "The Battle of Long Island" by John W. Chadwick, *Harpers Magazine,* August 1876, page 342).

on first going into an engagement, and has heard him tell of a wounded soldier who was sitting under a tree by his side during a battle when a cannon ball shot away the top of his head."[20]

In its September 5, 1776, edition, the *Maryland Gazette* printed this extract from a soldier's letter from the battlefield:

> As I expected, we had a general attack on Long Island yesterday. The day before, our battalion, with the Delaware battalion, cros'd over. The next morning, before day-light, the alarm guns on Cobble-Hill fort fired; Lord Stirling's brigade (to which we belonged) were under arms, and ordered to march down the island about four miles, to engage a party of the enemy that had landed the night before, and were marching towards our lines. About sun-rise we were formed in line of battle, the enemy doing the same in front of us. They tried to surround us, but a detachment of our men repulsed them with considerable loss. They did not attempt to attack us in front, but their artillery raked us. We stood our ground till about four o'clock, by which item, it seems, it had gone bad without our army in general, by which means we were surrounded, and had to fight our way out or become prisoners. We retreated in good order about half a mile, when we were attacked, but repulsed them, however, their numbers were far superior to ours; Major Gist, with about 100 men, kept the ground, while the rest of the brigade crossed a creek, which we were obliged to do. The major and his party were drove, and I expected never to see them again, but the greatest part got off with the major. We lost some men in the creek, that got stuck in the mud, and were drowned. We lost our general; whether he fell or not I can't say, but I saw him ride toward the major's party, and not return. Captain Veazey is dead. Lieutenants Butler, Steret, Wright, Fernandes, and deCoursey, with about 250 of our battalion are missing. Steret is a prisoner I believe. Our men sustained the fire of the enemy with a fortitude beyond what could have been expected from such raw troops. All our officers behaved extremely well. Capt. Smith and lieut. Steret conducted their companies to a charm. Our colonels were in town and could not get to us. We brought off thirty prisoners, and killed many more of them than they did of us. General Sullivan is missing and many other officers. The vaunting gen. Grant was killed; he was known by the papers that were about him. Our army was drove to the lines. The enemy came within 150 yards of our fort, but were repulsed with great loss. We expected another attack today, but they are preparing, by their movements to give us a cannonade.
>
> Major Gist says he saw Butler fall, but can't tell whether he was mortally wounded or not; he cried out that he was gone.
>
> I have only leave, for a few minutes, to leave the island so can't be more particular now. I hear the thunder of the cannon and the roar of musketry, so I believe the attack is begun.[21]

Scharf in his *History of Maryland* writes:

> The remnant of Smallwood's battalion, and the Pennsylvania battalions of Colonels Shee and Magaw, and Glover's Marblehead (Massachusetts) regiment, soon after daylight on the morning of the 28th of August, were hurried in a heavy rain to the

extreme left of the entrenched lines, on the ground between Wallabout Bay and Fort Putnam. On this low marshy ground, saturated with the heavy rains of the day and the previous night, these distressed and fatigued troops remained unprotected. Nothing occurred during the day and night except occasional and sometimes severe skirmishing between the outposts. The rain was succeeded on the 29th by a fog so dense that objects could not be discerned at a few yards distance. The position of the American army, at Brooklyn, had now become perilous, and in the disorganized condition of his troops Washington resolved to recross the East River and withdraw into the American lines below Fort Washington.

The embarkation took place under the superintendance of General McDougall, with Glover's Marblehead fishermen. To General Mifflin, commanding the Pennsylvania battalions of Shee and Magaw, and the shattered remnants of Smallwood's and Haslett's battalions, was confided the task of covering the retreat. "Torn with the shock of battle, and enfeebled by the terrible and exhausting exertions of its struggle, these brave men still kept the post of peril; and on their courage and devotion the commander-in-chief depended for covering the retreat."

Under pretence of attacking the enemy, these brave men remained under arms all night, marching and counter-marching, while their comrades were being safely conveyed across the river. On their courage and devotion depended the fate of the army, and perhaps of the cause. As daylight dawned the great task was accomplished,

Lord Stirling Orders His Men to Retreat Across the Gowanus Swamp. With the tide rising, the soldiers began making their way to safety. While crossing, a number of them were killed by British marksmen while others who could not swim were drowned. Nevertheless, they managed to take 30 British prisoners with them (reprinted from "The Battle of Long Island" by John W. Chadwick, *Harpers Magazine*, August 1876, page 345).

as the last of Washington's army crossed from the beach, between Fulton and Main streets. The enemy did not discover the retreat of the American army until the last detachment of the Marylanders and Pennsylvanians was half way across East River and out of reach.[22]

The *Brooklyn Daily Eagle* noted: "The services of the Maryland Battalion were not terminated by the dreadful struggle of the 27th. It is exacting much from our belief in human endurance and courage to find it narrated that two days subsequently the survivors, unappalled by the awful perils of that day, closed their thin ranks around their regimental colors, and again took the post of danger in the final retreat from Brooklyn. Yet such was the fact."[23]

While much bravery was shown that day, and despite General Washington's promise he would shoot anyone who he found fleeing, there was cowardice. Some of the soldiers didn't stay around for the first shot: The small contingent from Queens and Kings Counties [New York], assigned to picket duty guarding the Bedford Pass, were 'spooked' by their British counterparts even before the major battle began, running helter-skelter to the safety of the American lines in Brooklyn."[24]

Hessian colonel Heinrich von Heerington later wrote of the surrender of a Suffolk [New York] regiment saying: "The captured flag, which is made of red damask, with the motto 'Liberty,' appeared with 60 men before Rall's regiment. They had all shouldered their guns upside down, and had their hats under their arms. They fell on their knees and begged piteously for their lives."[25]

Aftermath of the Battle

The British were gloating over their victory:

Extract of a letter from an officer in general Frazier's battalion, dated Sept. 3, 1776. Rejoice, my friend, that we have given the rebels a d — d crush. We landed on Long Island the 22nd ult, without opposition. On the 27th we had a very warm action, in which the Scots regiments behaved with the greatest bravery, and carried the day after an obstinate resistance on the rebel side. But we flanked and overpowered them with numbers. The Hessians and our brave Highlanders gave no quarters; and it was a fine sight to see with what alacrity they dispatched the rebels with their bayonets after we had surrounded them, to that they could not resist. Multitudes were drowned and suffocated in morasses, a proper punishment for all rebels. Our battalion out marched all the rest, and was always first up with the rebel fugitives. A fellow they call Lord Stirling, one of their generals, who with two others, is prisoner, and a great many of their officers, men, artillery, and stores. It was a glorious achievement, my friend, and will immortalize us and crush the rebel colonies. Our loss was nothing. We took care to tell the Hessians that the rebels had resolved to give no quarters to them in particular, which made them fight desperately, and put all to death that fell into their hands. You know all strategies are lawful in war, especially against such vile enemies to their king and country. The island is ours and we shall soon take New York, for the rebels dare not look us in the face. I expect the affair will be over this campaign, and we shall all return covered with American laurels, and have the cream of the American lands allotted us for our services. [Lest any of those persons, who effect not to believe anything against the British soldiery, and will pretend to say, that the above letter, which exactly tallies with their conduct, as heretofore represented, is an American forgery; we would inform them that the English paper, from which the above is taken, may be seen in the hands of the printer, W. and T. Bradford].[1]

There is no complete list of the men killed or taken prisoner that day. Official reports contained only the names of a few of the officers. Much information was lost when the Maryland building that housed many of the official war documents burned in 1800. Information that survives exists in numbers and not in names: "Return of prisoners taken during the campaign, 1776. August 27, Long-Island. Commissioned officers, 3 generals, 3 colonels, 4 lieutenant colonels, 3 majors, 13 captains, 43 lieutenants, 12 ensigns. Staff, 1 adjutant, 3 surgeons, 2 volunteers. Privates, 1006 including 9 wounded officers and 56 wounded privates."[2]

General Smallwood complained to the Maryland Council that he was unable to compile information they had requested since the Marylanders, their numbers depleted, were so often called upon to fend for other American soldiers, not only to allow their retreat but to care for their baggage. This letter is quite long, but the most salient parts are quoted below.

> October 17, 1776: Philips Height's, from Col. Smallwood to the Council of Safety.... There are many other charges exclusive of what articles are and will be enumerated in the returns, which the Continent is charged with, particularly medicine necessaries supplied the troops, arms repaired &o for often on our march and since the Commissaries cou'd not supply nor would the public armourers work, at all events, soldiers must be fed and have their arms repaired, or else it cant be expected they will fight, an account of which can't at this time be rendered, for the retreating and flying disposition which has so much prevailed in our army latterly, made it most safe to send my books, papers &c to Philadelphia lest they should be lost, but be assured a true and particular acct shall be rendered, doubt not the province shall not be injured. This precaution was necessary, for hitherto we have been generally drawn from our station and Baggage, to cover the retreat and defend the baggage of others, which has subjected us to much loss, upon the retreat or rather flight from New York. I have scarce an officer (myself included) or soldier who did [not] lose more or less of their baggage, pillaged by the runaways, indeed I believe many of them never had other views, than flight and plunder, both which they are extremely dexterous at.
> General Washington was so kind after he left the common where we were posted, to stop waggons himself and made one of his aid de Camps attend the sending of our baggage, but as I had left but four soldiers as a camp guard, being desirous the Regt upon this occasion shou'd be as full as possible, these cou'd not guard the Waggons and thus we lost part of our baggage, have since stripped from these poltroons several of our soldiers coats and had them severely scourged. Have purchased from the Continental Store Cloaths for such of the Independant Companies as their Captains inform me have received none before and I think upon good terms, accounts of which shall be transmitted. I think Thomas's company were paid for finding themselves, or at least he prefered this one day when I was present at the Council, you'll inform how this matter is, and whether you supplied him with money to purchase cloaths at Philadelphia, his company being as bare as those who have never had....
> ... We want medicine much, none can be had here, our sick have and are now suffering extremely, the number as you'll observe from the list is very considerable, owing in a great measure to the bad provision made for and care taken of them, the men being oftenmoved and have been exposed to lye on the cold ground ever since they came here, after lying without their tents for several nights as is now the case, having been five nights and days without them, being ever since the enemy landed up here. The inconvenience attending frequent removals of troops when there are not a regular supply of waggons for that purpose, which is much wanting here, no person can conceive who has not experienced it, besides when their tents and baggage cant attend them, they must be injured much by lying in the open air at this season and in this place where heavy dews prevail so much, and I may justly say our corps have had a greater proportion of this duty than any in this army, for we have generally acted in Brigade under Northern Brigadiers General, who have

seldom failed to favor their own and put the laboring oar on our Regiment, but it has perhaps made us the better soldiers....

... Our next greatest suffering proceeds from the great neglect of the sick, and his [General Washington's] orders relative to this Department are most salutary were these to be duly attended to but here too there is not only a shameful but even an inhuman neglect daily exhibited. The Directors of the General Hospitals who supply and provide for the sick, are extremely remiss and inattentive to the well being and comfort of these unhappy men, out of this train they cannot be taken. I have withdrawn all mine long ago and had them placed in a comfortable house in the country, and supplied with only the common rations, even this is preferable to the fare of a general hospital. Two of these regimental Hospitals after I have had them put in order, one has been taken away by the Directors for a General Hospital and my people turned out of doors, and the other would have been taken in the same manner, had I not have applied to Gen[l] Washington who told me to keep it.

... Mr D. Jenifer mate to the Independents has applied to resign and have permitted him. We have now four mates and no head Surgeon which are very sufficient as we have little medicine [MSA: 12, 357–363].

Many of the wounded Americans taken prisoner would receive no medical attention whatsoever: "Extract of a letter from Dr. Silas Holmes. The wounded prisoners taken at the battle of Brooklyn were put in the churches of Flatbush and New Utrecht, but being neglected and unattended were wallowing in their own filth, and breathed an infected and impure air. Ten days after the battle Dr. Richard Bailey was appointed to superintend the sick. He was humane, and dressed the wounded daily; got a sack bed, sheet, and blanket for each prisoner; and distributed the prisoners into the adjacent barns. When Mrs. Woodhull offered to pay Dr. Bailey for his care and attention to her husband, he said he had done no more than his duty, and if there was anything due it was to me.[3]

Those soldiers taken prisoner would now face, at minimum, psychological torture:

Robert Troup, a young lieutenant in Colonel Lasher's battalion, testified that he and Lieut. Edward Dunscomb, Adjutant Hoogland, and two volunteers were made prisoners by a detachment of British troops at three o'clock A.M. on the 27th of August, 1776. They were carried before the generals and interrogated, with threats of hanging. Thence they were led to a house near Flatbush. At 9 A.M. they were led, in the rear of the army, to Bedford. Eighteen officers captured that morning were confined in a small soldier's tent for two nights and nearly three days. It was raining nearly all the time. Sixty privates, also, had but one tent, while at Bedford the provost marshal, Cunningham, brought with him a negro with a halter, telling them the negro had already hung several, and he imagined he would hang some more. The negro and Cunningham also heaped abuse upon the prisoners, showing them the halter, and calling them rebels, scoundrels, robbers, murderers, etc.

From Bedford they were led to Flatbush, and confined a week in a house belonging to a Mr. Leffert, on short allowance of biscuit and salt pork. Several Hessians took pity on them and gave them apples, and once some fresh beef.

From Flatbush after a week, he, with seventy or eighty other officers, were put on board a snow, lying between Gravesend and the Hook, without bedding or blankets; afflicted with vermin; soap and fresh water for washing purposes being denied them. They drank and cooked with filthy water brought from England. The captain charged a very large commission for purchasing necessaries for them with the money they procured from their friends.

After six weeks spent on the snow they were taken on the 17th of October to New York and confined in a house near Bridewell. At first they were not allowed any fuel, and afterwards only a little coal for three days in the week. Provisions were dealt out very negligently, were scanty, and of bad quality. Many were ill and most of them would have died had their wants not been supplied by poor people and loose women of the town, who took pity on them.[4]

Later, many of the prisoners would be shipped as far away as Nova Scotia, England, and the West Indies. As badly as some of the officers were treated, it would be the enlisted man who would bear the brunt of the British fury:

Nearly half the prisoners taken on Long Island died. The privates were treated with great inhumanity, without fuel, or the common necessaries of life, and were obliged to obey the calls of nature in places of their confinement....

It is said that the British did not hang any of the prisoners taken in August on Long Island, but "played the fool by making them ride with a rope around their necks, seated on coffins, to the gallows. Major Otho Williams was so treated.[5]

The greatest suffering in the cause of American liberty was endured in the prison ships in Wallabout Bay. Estimates of the dead from the prison ships exceed 11,000 — nearly triple the 4,400 Americans who died in all the battles of the Revolution.[6]

While we would like to believe that those on both sides of any conflict would conduct themselves with honor, this was certainly not the case. The British were incensed with the rebels and would stop at nothing to put an end to the rebellion. Although never put in writing, it was obvious that the British had a policy of killing as many of the rebels as possible by whatever means necessary.

It is estimated that approximately 4,300 Americans were killed in actual combat during the war, while over 13,000 died while being held in British hands. Those captured were given the choice of renouncing their allegiance to America and serving in the British forces. Only a handful did so.[7]

American prisoners were held in jails, abandoned ships, warehouses, sugar factories, and churches. They were fed only minimal amounts and the food was not fit for human consumption. Many froze to death in the winter from a lack of heat or blankets. Water was dispersed sporadically and often carried diseases. Without the necessities to sustain their bodies the men became weaker as time went on and many died from contagious diseases such as dysentery, smallpox, and typhoid fever.

General Washington wrote innumerable letters to the British High Command demanding better treatment for his men, but was ignored. It was certainly no mistake that Commissioner Joshua Loring, who sold his wife to General Howe in exchange for his appointment, and William Cunningham, known to have a deep and abiding hatred of Americans, were placed in charge of the American prisoners. They acted with no conscience and no mercy. While the men lay dying from starvation, Loring stole two-thirds of the money allotted for food for his own use. Cunningham ordered hangings for his own amusement.[8]

Too few survived, but enough to tell the tale. Even dead men have tales to tell. As they died, the men were buried in shallow graves along the coastline. For well over a hundred years after the war, the bones of these poor souls could still be found.

Neither Loring nor Cunningham would ever face judgment for their various acts of murder and barbarism. William Cunningham, however, was found guilty and hanged for forgery in 1791. Perhaps in an effort to save his own soul, he made a written confession just prior to his hanging.[9]

> When the war commenced, I was appointed provost marshal to the royal army, which placed me in a situation to wreak my vengeance on the Americans. I shudder to think of the murders I have been accessory to, both with and without orders from government, especially while in New York, during which time there were more than two thousand prisoners starved in the different churches by stopping the rations, which I sold. There were also two hundred and seventy-five American prisoners and obnoxious persons executed, out of all which number there were only about one dozen public executions, which chiefly consisted of British and Hessian deserters. The mode for private executions was thus conducted — A guard was dispatched from the provost, about half after 12 at night, to the Barrack street, and the neighborhood of the upper barracks, to order the people to shut their window shutters and put out their lights, forbidding them at the same time to presume to look out of their windows and doors, on pain of death; after which, the unfortunate prisoners were conducted, gagged, just behind the upper barracks, and hung without ceremony, and there buried by the black pioneer of the provost.[10]

The sick and wounded weren't faring much better, even in American hands. The death rate might not have been so high if the sick and wounded had not been housed together, but they were. Captain John Allen Thomas of the Fifth Independent Company stepped outside the chain of command in a desperate move to obtain medical assistance for his men:

> September 4, 1776: J. A. Thomas to Council. Harlem, 4th Sept. 1776. May it please your Honours. The unhappy situation of the Maryland Troops now here, makes it absolutely necessary that you should be acquainted with it, and also you might have received information from others, yet I think it my duty also (tho' low in office) to make you acquainted with it and I have not the least doubt but you will immediately apply a remedy. We have now and have had for some time a number of our men sick, a number very ill. I have had from fifteen to twenty of my men extremely ill and have not yet been able to procure them the least assistance. The Province have but two surgeons here, one of them very ill, and none can be procured here. From the best authority I can assure you we have at this time near two hundred men unfit for duty and

most of them without any assistance from the doctor. The neglect of the troops when sick discourages them more than any other circumstance, and I am convinced if it was generally known, would have the worst of consequences both as to recruiting for the troops already raised or in raising new levies [MSA: 12, 256–257].

Captain Thomas's letter received a response, but no help was forthcoming anytime soon: "September 20, 1776. Philadelphia. We have a letter of the 15th Instant from Capt Thomas from whence it appears our sick have not such care taken of them as they ought, we wish if it is in your power to send a skillful and attentive person who should have the immediate care of the Independent companies, you would do so. We have requested Dr. Bond to recommend such a one that we may propose him to congress for this purpose, but from the Doctor's answer we almost despair of finding a suitable person here" (MSA: 12, 292).

It wasn't just the Marylanders who were suffering from the lack of medical attention. Many of the seriously wounded probably died in the series of moves necessitated by the British advance. Further, as noted below, the sick far outnumbered the wounded:

> As General Washington's army retreated south through New Jersey before the British in the fall of 1776, the sick and wounded, often numbering one-fourth to one-third of the total, were sent ahead and placed in temporary hospitals at Amboy, Elizabeth, Brunswick, Trenton, Fort Lee, Newark, and Morristown. On 1 November, Shippen submitted an optimistic report to Congress on the hospitals in five of these towns, saying that his two units at Amboy contained 90 sick and 7 wounded, that at Brunswick 10 sick, and that at Trenton 56 sick. At Elizabeth he recorded 54 sick, 3 wounded, and 25 "sick from Canada" and at Fort Lee, 75 sick, 9 wounded, and 19 "distressed New England Troops." It should be noted that even at a time of action, the sick outnumbered the wounded sixteen to one. Shippen predicted that four-fifths of his patients would recover but noted that 2,000 more patients who were not yet under his control were scattered in barns around the countryside. By late November, in spite of Shippen's optimism, patients from the flying camp, unattended by physicians, were pouring into Philadelphia, arriving in wagons and threatening to spread putrid or camp fever among the citizens of the city.[11]

Colonel William Smallwood

Colonel Smallwood was born 1732 in Charles County, Maryland, the son of Pryor Smallwood and his wife, Priscilla Heaberd. He was part of a very wealthy and prominent family.

In 1761, at the age of 29, he was elected to the lower house — the House of Delegates — of the Maryland General Assembly. This would be the first of many public offices held by Colonel Smallwood that would culminate with his election to the governorship of Maryland from 1785 to 1788 and finally to the Maryland State Senate in 1791, when he also served as president of that body.

Colonel Smallwood and those around him were firmly in the rebel cause. He would ultimately achieve the rank of major general and was the highest ranking officer from Maryland during the Revolutionary War. His brother-in-law, Colonel William Grayson, was appointed as one of Washington's aids-de-camp on August 24, 1776, and was also at the Battle of Long Island. After the war, Colonel Grayson and Richard Henry Lee were elected the first U.S. senators from Virginia. Colonel Grayson's mother was Susanna Monroe, the aunt of future president James Monroe.

Colonel Smallwood's brother, Captain Heaberd Smallwood, served as captain of the Regiment of Foot from Virginia during the war under the command of Colonel William Grayson. Heaberd Smallwood died in 1780. His nephew, William Truman Stoddert, served on Colonel Smallwood's staff.

One can only imagine the anguish suffered by Colonel Smallwood as he watched his battalion being ripped to pieces that day. He knew that he would have to face his friends, relatives, and neighbors in Charles County in whose grief he would share. He would see, first hand, what the losses meant to them.

Colonel Smallwood was known as a man who did not mince words. While he should have responded more promptly to a request for information about the battle, he openly and candidly reported the activities of his men from the time they left Annapolis until the date of his letter below.

Camp of the Maryland Regulars Head Quarters October 12th, 1776.
Sir:
    Through your Hands I must beg leave to address The Hon[ble] Convention of

Maryland, and must confess not without an Apprehension that I have incurred their Displeasure for having omitted writing when on our March from Maryland for New York, and since our Arrival here, nor shall I in a pointed Manner urge anything in my Defence, but leave them at large to condemn or excuse me, upon a presumption, that should they condemn, they will at least pardon, and judge me perhaps less culpable, when they reflect in the first Instance, on the Exertions necessary to procure Baggage Waggons, Provisions and House Room for 750 Men march'd the whole Distance in a Body, generally from 15 to 20 Miles per Day, as the several Stages made it necessary,— and in the Latter I trust they will give some Indulgence for this Neglect, for since our Arrival at New York it has been the Fate of this Corps to be generally stationed at Advanced Posts, and to act as a covering Party, which must unavoidably expose Troops to extraordinary Duty and Hazard, not to mention the extraordinary Vigilance and Attention in the Commandant of such a party in disposing in the best Manner, and having it regularly supplied,—for here the Commanders of Regiments exclusive of their military Duty, are often obliged to exert themselves in the Departments of Commissary and Quarter Master Genl and even Directors of their Regimental Hospitals.

General William Smallwood. General Smallwood was a very wealthy landowner and could have simply made a financial contribution to the cause without having to lift a finger, but he chose instead to fight. He fought throughout the war and was known for his bravery and excellence as an officer (courtesy Smallwood Foundation).

Perhaps it may not be improper to give a short Detail of Occurrences upon our March to Long Island and since that Period—The Enemy from the 21st to the 27th of August were landing their Troops on the Lower part of Long Island, where they pitched a large Encampment, and ours and their advanced Parties were daily skirmishing at Long Shot, in which neither Party suffered much, on the 26th the Maryland and Delaware Troops which composed part of Lord Sterling's Brigade were ordered over, Col Haslet and his Lt Col: Bedford, of the Delaware Batt^n with Lt Col Ware and myself were detained on the Tryal of Lt Col Zedwitz, and tho' I waited on General Washington and urged the Necessity of attending our Troops, yet he refused to discharge us alledging there was a Necessity for the Tryal's coming on, and that no other Field officers could be then had. After our dismission from the Court Martial it was too late to get over, but pushing over early next Morning, found our Regiments engaged, Lord Sterling having marched them off before Day, to take Possession of the Woods and difficult Passes between our Lines and the Enemy's Encampment—but the Enemy the Overnight had stole a March on our Generals having got through those passes, met and surrounded our troops on the plain Grounds within two Miles of our Lines.

Lord Sterling drew up his Brigade on an advantageous rising Ground, where he was attacked by Two Brigades in Front, headed by the Generals Cornwallis, and Grant, and in his Rear the Enemy's Main Body stood ready drawn up to support their own Parties and intercept the Retreat of ours, this excellent Disposition, and their superior Numbers ought to have taught our Generals, there was no Time to be lost in securing their Retreat, which might at first have been effected, had the Troops formed into a heavy Column and Pushed their Retreat, but the longer this was delayed it became the more dangerous as they were then landing more Troops in Front from the Ships.

Our Brigade kept their Ground for several Hours, and in general behaved well having received some heavy Fires from the Artillery and Musquetry of the Enemy whom they repulsed several Times, but their Attacks were neither so lasting or vigorous as was expected owing as it was imagined to their being certain of mak^z the whole Brigade Prisoners of War, for by this Time they had so secured the Passes on the Road to our Lines (seeing our Parties were not supported from thence; which indeed our Numbers would not admit of) that there was no possibility of retreating that Way.

Between the place of Action and our Lines there lay a large Marsh and Deep Creek not above 80 yds across at the Mouth. The Place of Action upon a direct Line did not much exceed a Mile from a part of our Lines towards the Head of which Creek there was a Mill and Bridge across which a certain Col. Ward from New England, who is charged with having acted a Bashful part that Day, pass'd over with his Regiment and then burnt them Down, tho' under cover of our Cannon, which would have check'd the Enemy's Pursuit at any Time, otherways this Bridge might have afforded a secure Retreat, there then remained no other Prospect but to surrender or attempt to retreat over this Marsh and Creek at the Mouth, where no Person had ever been known to Cross, in the Interim I applied to Genl Washington for some Regiments to march out to support and cover their Retreat, which he urged would be attended with too great Risk to the Party and the Lines; he immediately afterwards sent for and ordered me to march down a New England Regiment, and Cap^n Thomas's Comp^y which had just come over from York, to the Mouth of the Creek opposite where the Brigade was drawn up, and ordered two Field Pieces down, to support and cover their Retreat, should they make a push that Way.

Soon after our march, they began to retreat, and for a small Time the Fire was very heavy on both sides, till our Troops came to the Marsh, where they were obliged to break their order, and escape as quick as they could to the Edge of the Creek, under a brisk Fire, notwithstanding which they brought off 28 Prisoners—The Enemy taking advantage of a Commanding Ground kept up a continual Fire from Four Field Pieces, which were well served & directed, and an Heavy Column advancing on the Marsh must have cut our People off, their Guns being wet and muddy not one of them would have fired, but having drawn up the Musquetry and disposed of some Rifle Men conveniently, with orders to fire on them when they came within Shot, however the Latter began their Fire rather too soon being at 200 yards Distance, which notwithstanding had the desired Effect, for the Enemy immediately retreated to the Fast Land, where they continued parading within 800 yards till our Troops were brought over, most of those who swam over, and others who attempted to cross before the Covering Party got down, lost their Arms and Accoutrements in the Mud & Creek, and some Poor Fellows their Lives, particularly two of the Maryland, two of the Delaware one of Attleys Pensylvania and two Hessian Prisoners were drowned.

Thomas's Men contributed much in bringing over this Party — have enclosed a List of the Kill'd & Missing amounting to 256 officers inclusive, it has been said the Enemy during the Action, also attacked our Lines, but this was a Mistake, not knowing the Ground one of their Columns advanced within Long Shot, without knowing they were so near and upon our Artillery & part of the Musquetry's Firing on them, they immediately fled — The 28th during a very hard Rain there was an Alarm that the Enemy had advanced to attack our Lines, which alarm'd the Troops much, but was without Foundation.

The 29th it was found by a Council of War that our Fortifications were not tenable, and it was therefore judged expedient that the Army should retreat from the Island that Night, to effect which notwithstanding the Maryland Troops had had but one Days respite, and many other Troops had been many Days clear of any Detail of Duty, they were ordered on the Advanced Post at Fort Putnam, within 250 yds of the Enemy's Approaches and join'd with two Pensylvania Reg^{ts} on the Left, were to remain and cover the Retreat of the Army, which was happily compleated under cover of a thick Fog & a South West Wind, both which favored our Retreat, otherwise the Fear, Disorder, and Confusion of some of the Eastern Troops must have retarded & discovered our Retreat and subjected Numbers to be cut off.

After remaining two Days in New York, our next Station was at Harlaem, 9 Miles above at an Advanced Post opposite Montresore's and Bohana's Islands, which in a few Days the Enemy got Possession of without opposition, from the former of which we daily discoursed with them, being within two Hundred yards and only a small Creek between — It being judged expedient to abandon New York and Retreat to our Lines below Fort Washington, the military Stores &c. had been removing some Days, when on the 15th Sepr the Enemy effected a Landing on several parts of the Island below, (and it is cutting to say without the least opposition) I have often read and heard of Instances of Cowardice, but hitherto have had but a faint Idea of it, 'till now I never could have thought Human Nature subject to such Baseness — I could wish the Transactions of this Day blotted out of the Annals of America, — nothing appeared but Flight Disgrace and Confusion, let it suffice to say that 60 Light Infantry upon the First Fire put to flight two Brigades of the Connecticut Troops — Wretches, who, however strange it may appear, from the Brigadier General down to the Private Sentinal, were caned and whip'd by the Generals Washington Putnam & Miflin, but e'ven this Indignity had no Weight they could not be brought to stand one Shot.

Genl Washington expressly sent and drew our Regiment from its Brigade, to march down towards New York, to cover the Retreat and to defend the Baggage, with direction to take Possession of an Advantageous Eminence near the Enemy upon the Main Road, where we remained under Arms the best part of the Day, till Sergant's Brigade came in with their Baggage, who were the last Troops coming in, upon which the Enemy divided their Main Body into two Columns, one filing off on the North River endeavored to Flank and surround us, the other advancing in good order slowly up the Main Road upon us, we had orders to retreat, in good order which was done, our Corps getting within the Lines a little after Dusk.

The next Day about 1000 of them made an Attempt upon our Lines, and were first attacked by the brave Col. Knolton of New England who lost his Life in the Action, and the 3ᵈ Virginia Regiment, who were immediately joined by Three Independant Compˢ under Major Price & some part of the Maryland Flying Camp who drove them back to their Lines, it is supposed with the Loss of 400 Men kill'd and wounded — Our Party had about 100 Kill'd and Wounded, of the former only 15. Since which we have been viewing each other at a Distance and strongly intrenching till the 9th October, when three of their Men of War, pass'd up the North River above Kings bridge, under a very heavy Cannonade from our Batteries which has effectually cut off our Communication, by Water, with Albany — I must now break off Abruptly being ordered to march up above Kings bridge, the Enemy having Landed 6000 Men from the Sound on Frog's Point. 50 Ships are got up there, landing more Troops, there is nothing left but to Fight them, an engagement is generally expected and soon, have enclosed a Copy of a General Return of the Battalion & Veazy's Company being all the Troops I march'd from Maryland with the Accoutrements & Camp Equipage taken in Philadelphia to to be rendered the Congress together with our Weekly Genˡ Return.

The Independants are now about their Returns of Arms Accoutrements & Camp Equipage brought by them from Maryland, but not having Time to finish, they must hereafter be return'd to Council of Safety, we have upwards of Three Hundred Officers & Soldiers of the Maryland Regulars very sick which you will observe by the Return and I am sorry to say, it's shocking to Humanity [to have no more Care taken of them —] this must hurt the Service upon the New Enlistments — Majors Price & Gist & Capⁿ Stone are in the Jerseys very Sick, and Col: Ware and myself are very unfit for Duty tho' we attend it — many more Officers are very unwell — I am very respectfully

Your obedient & very hble Servant, W. Smallwood [MSA: 12, 338–343].

Colonel Smallwood died on December 12, 1792, unmarried, and in debt like so many others who had given not only of themselves but also of their estates for their belief in the patriot cause. "Died on the 12th instant at The Woodyard on his journey from Annapolis to his place of residence, William Smallwood, Esq., formerly a general officer in the Army of the United States and late Governor of the State of Maryland. A gentleman much respected by a numerous acquaintance."[1]

While everyone is certain that Colonel Smallwood was buried at his home plantation, no one is certain exactly where. One unlikely theory is that his body lies marked by a chestnut tree that grew from a nut placed in his grave. The newspaper article that follows was probably all too true.

Gen. William Smallwood, of the Md. Line: his Revolutionary services, the neglected state of his remains. I call on the proprietor of the land in Charles Co., Md. in which Gen. Smallwood was buried, that he is lying in a sort of commons infested by hogs, many of whom make their beds upon this patriot soldier's grave. South Carolina beheld Gen. S's valor at the disastrous battle of Camden, where, after the flight of most of Gen. Gates' army, this intrepid officer three times charged a superior foe and where, after the death of the brave De Kalb, the commander of the

Home of General Smallwood. Now known as "Smallwood's Retreat," the home of General Smallwood was reconstructed from ruins by the Smallwood Foundation in 1958 and donated to the State of Maryland. The remains of General Smallwood lie buried on these grounds, but the exact site is unknown (photograph courtesy the Smallwood Foundation).

> only fighting portion of the defeated army devolved upon him. Three times he returned to the charge with desperate valor, until Dixon's Regt of South Carolinians, who, for a time, seemed resolved to wipe away the stain from their flying countrymen, at last followed their example, and compelled the Marylanders to quit the unequal contest.[2]

Colonel Smallwood's home, built about 1760, still stands and is now the site of Smallwood State Park in Charles County, Maryland.

Although he was not present at the battle, Colonel Smallwood still deserves special mention here, for he was the one responsible for the recruitment, training, and deportment of the men under his command.

Lord Stirling

William Alexander was born in New York City in 1726 and was the son of James Alexander who immigrated to America from Scotland in 1715. James Alexander lived the American dream and became extremely wealthy. He was recognized as one of the leading attorneys in New York and New Jersey, and he was one of the founders of King's College (now known as Columbia University).

In 1756, while in London, William Alexander, with questionable evidence, attempted to claim the vacant title of Earl of Stirling. He would unsuccessfully spend the rest of his life and most of his fortune attempting to prove his right to the title. Although never formally acknowledged, he insisted on being addressed as Lord Stirling from 1761 until his death. Had his title ever been proven he would have been able to claim ownership of all of New Brunswick and Nova Scotia, much of Maine, a large portion of Long Island, Nantucket, Martha's Vineyard, and large tracts of land on both sides of the St. Lawrence River and the Great Lakes.

When the Revolutionary War began, Lord Stirling was commissioned as a colonel in the New Jersey militia, outfitting the militia with his own funds. The Continental Congress appointed him brigadier general in March 1776. He was not generally recognized as a particularly brilliant leader, but he was a team player and willing to serve wherever General Washington thought his talents could best be used.

His actions in leading The Maryland 400, however, were praised not only by General Washington but the British as well. Lord Cornwallis later said, "General Lord Stirling fought like a wolf."[1]

On August 29, while being held prisoner, Lord Stirling wrote to General Washington about the battle saying, in part,

> ... We continued the attack a considerable time, the men having been rallied and the attack renewed five or six several times, and were on the point of driving Lord Cornwallis from his station, but large succours arriving rendered it impossible to do more than to provide for safety. I endeavoured to get in between that house and Fort Box, but on attempting it, I found a considerable body of troops in my front, and several in pursuit of me. I immediately turned the point of a hill which covered me from their fire, and I was soon out of the reach of my pursuers. I soon found it would be in vain to attempt to make my escape, and therefore went to

surrender myself to General De Heister, commander-in-chief of the Hessians.[2]

Three weeks later Lord Stirling was exchanged for the loyalist governors of Florida and the Bahamas. Upon his release he was promoted to major general and would serve successfully until his death on January 15, 1783, just a few months before the official end of the war.

> Albany [New York], January 20. On Tuesday morning last at 6 o'clock died in the fifty-seventh year of his age, the Right Honorable William Alexander, Earl of Stirling, Viscount of Canada, Major-General in the service of the United States, and Commander in Chief of the American forces in the Northern Department. On the Thursday following his remains, attended by the troops in town, with a numerous and respectable concourse of inhabitants, were interred, with honors of war, in the Low Dutch Church of this city.
>
> While the immediate relations and friends of his Lordship are discharging their tribute of grief on this occasion, the decided and unshaken part he has invariably acted in the cause of his country must render his memory sacred to all who feel themselves interested in the welfare of American, or the rights of mankind. His conduct, whether in council or the field, while it reflects honor on his country, has secured to himself the reputation of a brave, discerning and intrepid officer. Those who have found under his banners, need not be reminded with what coolness and gallantry he led them to action; and while their bosoms expand with the sigh of anxiety at the deep wound the service has received by his Lordship's death, they will derive some consolation from the reflection of having had the honor of acting under a General of his distinguished talents and valour.[3]

General William Alexander. Known as Lord Stirling, he was a friend and confidant of George Washington. With the absence of General Smallwood, who was at a court-martial in the city of New York on the morning of August 27, 1776, it would be Lord Stirling who would lead the Marylanders into battle (reprinted from Benson J. Lossing, *The Pictorial Field-book of the Revolution; Or, Illustrations, by Pen and Illustrations, By Pen and Pencil, of the History, Biography, Scenery, Relics, and Traditions of the War for Independence*, vol. 2, New York: Harper and Brothers Publishers, 1852, chapter 23, figure 5).

The Men of The Maryland 400

With few exceptions, as in all the wars fought by Americans, the men who went to battle that day were very young. They ranged in age from seventeen to their early twenties. The officers, of course, tended to be a little older. Only a handful were married.

It should also be remembered that not every man who enlisted actually served. Some would be too young or too old, physically unfit, or have dependent families for whom they were the only support. In enlisting their men, the captains were given these instructions:

1. You are to enlist no man who is not able bodied, healthy, and a good marcher, or such whose attachment to the liberties of America you have any cause to suspect. Young, hearty robust men, who are tied by birth, or family connections or property to this county; and are well practiced in the use of firearms, are by much to be preferred.

2. You are to have great regard to moral character, sobriety in particular.

3. You are not to enlist any servant imported, nor, without the leave of the master, any apprentice.

4. Those who engage in the service shall be enlisted according to the form prescribed by this convention.

   Their rations consisted of one pound of beef, or three quarters of a pound of pork, one pound of flour or bread per man per day, three pints of peas at six shillings per bushel per week, or other vegetables equivalent, one quart of Indian meal per week, a gill of vinegar and a gill of molasses per man per day, a quart of cider, small beer, or a gill of rum, per man per day, three pounds of candles for one hundred men per week, for guards; twenty-four pounds of soft soap, or eight pounds of hard soap for one hundred men per week.[1]

There has been confusion about the actual companies that comprised The Maryland 400. Traditionally, it is said that the 400 came from First, Second, Third, Sixth, and Ninth Companies. My research tallies with this finding, and this author believes they participated because of three factors, namely, illness, age, and lack of experienced officers.

Due to the absence of Colonel Smallwood, Major Mordecai Gist was in command of the Marylanders. It would be likely, however, that Captain John Hoskins Stone of the First Company would have been second in command, albeit unofficially, both because Gist was totally inexperienced and because Smallwood knew and relied on Stone since they were both from Charles County and were friends and neighbors.

Captain Barton Lucas of the Third Company and Captain Peter Adams of the Sixth Company were both ill the day of the battle. Given their absence, the men of those companies would have reported directly to Major Gist.

Benjamin Ford of the Ninth Company had been promoted to captain only a few months before and was still in his twenties. He too was from Charles County and was well known to Captain Stone, who would likely have taken him under his wing. The same can be said for Captain Patrick Sim of the Second Company as he was from neighboring Prince George's County. He too was still quite young and inexperienced.

The lack of officers would be addressed several months later in a letter from James Hindman to the Maryland Council dated October 12, 1776, in which he said, in part, "I think that melancholy day on Long Island convinced us of the want of Field officers, having none but Major Gist to command us, who behaved as well as a man could do" (MSA: 12, 344–346).

Tradition has always held that 256 of The Maryland 400 were killed that day. This statistic appears to be incorrect. My research confirms that at least 225 of the 400 survived. While it is probably true that the bodies of 256 Marylanders lie beneath the streets of Brooklyn, the author does not believe they were all from that small contingent. The survival of that many is even more phenomenal.

Tradition also tells us they were buried in their scarlet and buff uniforms. That may have been the case of the officers, but the enlisted men would have gone to battle in their hunting shirts. "The hunting-shirt, the emblem of the Revolution, is banished from the national military, but still lingers among the hunters and pioneers of the Far West. This national costume, properly so called, was adopted in the outset of the Revolution, and was recommended by Washington to his army, in the most eventful period of the War for Independence."[65]

The mere sight of hunting shirts struck fear in British and Hessian hearts as they equated them with General Daniel Morgan's sharpshooters:

> When Morgan's riflemen, made prisoners at the assault on Quebec, in 1775 were returning to the South to be exchanged, the British garrisons on the route beheld with wonder these sons of the mountain and the forest. Their hardy looks, their tall athletic forms, their marching always in Indian file, with the light and noiseless step peculiar to their pursuit of woodland game; but above all, to European eyes, their singular and picturesque costume, the hunting shirt, with its fringes, the wampum belts, leggings, and moccasins, richly worked with the Indian ornaments of beads and porcupine quills of brilliant and varied dyes, the tomahawk and knife; these, with the well known death-dealing aim of those matchless marksmen,

created in the European military a degree of awe and respect for the hunting-shirt which lasted with the War of the Revolution.[3]

General Morgan frequently observed, "The very sight of my riflemen was always enough for a Hessian piquet. They would scamper into their lines as if the d — l drove them, shouting in all the English they knew, 'Rebel in de bush! Rebel in de bush!'"[4]

General Smallwood was also adamant that his men have spatterdashes as a part of their uniforms. Spatterdashes were the forerunner of today's spats and were coverings for the legs to protect the soldier from water and mud.

> Letter from General Smallwood to the Maryland Council. Annapolis 27 January 1776. Gentlemen. I observe the Gentlemen of the convention have allowed the soldiers as a uniform hunting shirts, but no spatter dashes, which renders the regimentals incompleat, this they certainly have not adverted to, otherways am persuaded they must have seen the impropriety of allowing one & not the other, for you must be sensible that clean spatterdashes as well as hunting shirts must cover a multitude of blemishes in the dress & appearance of the regiment, which I would most earnestly wish to appear as respectable, & to become as formidable as might be, under our present disadvantageous situation respecting military matters; this therefore I hope you'll take under consideration, flatter myself as the expence will be trifling, you will be induced to purchase as much oznabgs or whats much better (if to be had) Russia sheeting as will answer this purpose. I know the Public business is very pressing & that you will be much engaged, yet I must entreat you to purchase what cloths are to be had in Baltimore suitable for soldiers cloathing (also sail duck for Tents) the men inlisted must be very bare, as the Capts are continually pressing me to know how they are to be furnished with cloaths, urging that they cannot march them to their station till clad. Intrenching tools &c imagine may be made here at any time, I think you must judge it essentially necessary to request Mr Johnson or some other of our Congress members, to write Genl Washington to send us a good adjutant or two, for the use of the Province in general, who as an incouragemt might be allowed more than the common wages. I am with much defference Gentn Yr very obedt Hble Sert W. Smallwood [MSA: 11, 110–111].
>
> Letter from General Smallwood to Thomas Johnson, Esq. Annapolis 25th May 1776. Sir. Being conscious that you & the Honble convention at this time are much engaged in Public business of much consequence, it is with reluctance that I am obliged to address you on Business of less importance, but am persuaded as it will trespass not much on your time, & that it will appear necessary, hope this will in some measure excuse the application at this busy period. I find leather breeches & stockings are with much difficulty procured, & those in all probability not to be had in such quantities as will be wanting by the fall, when they will be absolutely necessary, this perhaps might be remedied by allowing the soldiers breeches & spatterdashes in one piece made of oznabgs which would not only be uniform with the hunting shirts, but a good substitute for leather breeches & stockings, & would enable those who have been furnished, to lay them up for the winter, the soldiery would willingly purchase one, if the convention would allow another pair, which would enable them to be clean & comfortable; I am with much Regard Sir. Yr very obedt Humb Servt W. Smallwood [MSA: 11, 445–446].

Lastly, the role played by the Fifth Independent Company from St. Mary's County is never included in the story of The Maryland 400. While they were not a part of The Maryland 400, they did assist in their escape. Hopefully this acknowledgment will make up for a lapse of over 230 years.

Mordecai Gist

Prior to his departure for New York City, Colonel Smallwood placed Major Mordecai Gist in temporary command of the Maryland battalion. Mordecai Gist was born in 1743 in Baltimore County, Maryland. He was the son of Thomas Gist, a training officer during the Revolutionary War, and his wife, Susannah Cockey. He was the nephew of Christopher Gist, who during the French and Indian War had saved the life of young George Washington not once but twice during the winter of 1753–1754.

Christopher Gist was one of the most distinguished Indian scouts and surveyors of his time. While Daniel Boone is generally given credit for opening Kentucky to white settlement, Gist preceded him by more than fifteen years. Nathaniel Gist, son of Christopher, and first cousin of Mordecai Gist, married an Indian girl named Wurteh, sister of the great Indian chiefs Old Tassel and Doublehead. Nathaniel Gist and his wife, Wurteh, were the parents of Sequoyah, who invented the Cherokee alphabet.

Prior to the Revolutionary War, Mordecai Gist was a wealthy sea captain and merchant. In December 1774 he was commissioned a captain in the Baltimore Independent Company (later to become the Ninth Company). On January 14, 1776, he was commissioned as a second major in Colonel Smallwood's battalion.

On the day of the battle, Major Gist assumed command of the Maryland troops in the absence of Colonel Smallwood. This was to be his first actual battle experience. He provided an account of the battle saying:

> I have just time to give you a short account of our late engagement at Long Island. On Tuesday we received intelligence that the enemy had landed their troops about five miles below our lines. In consequence of which General Stirling was ordered to march to the right to take possession of some rising grounds. We began our march to the right at three o'clock in the morning, with about 1,300 men, and about sunrise, on our near approach to the ground, discovered the enemy making up to it, and in a few minutes our advanced parties began the attack. We immediately advanced and took possession of the ground and formed line of battle. In the meantime, they began a warm fire with their artillery and light infantry, from their left, while the main body was forming in columns to attack us in the front. Our men

behaved well, and maintained their ground until ten o'clock, when the enemy retreated about 200 yards and halted, and the firing on each side ceased.

We soon heard the fire continue round on our left, and in a short time discovered part of the enemy in our rear, going on to our lines, in order to cut off the communication between us. Being thus surrounded, and no probability of reinforcement, his Lordship ordered me to retreat with the remaining part of our men, and force our way through to our camp. We soon fell in with a party of the enemy, who clubbed their firelocks and waved their hats to us, as if they meant to surrender as prisoners; but on our advancing within 60 yards, they presented their pieces and fired, which we returned with so much warmth that they soon quitted their post and retired to a large body that was lying in ambuscade.

During this interval the main part of our force retreated from the left through a marsh. We were then left with only five companies of our battalion when the enemy returned, and after a warm and close engagement for near ten minutes, our little line became so disordered we were under the necessity of retreating to a piece of woods on our right, where we formed and made a second attack, but being overpowered with numbers, and surrounded on all sides by at least 20,000 men, we were drove with much precipitation and confusion. [General Stirling's] brave example had encouraged and animated our young soldiers with almost invincible resolution.

Major Mordecai Gist. In December 1774, sensing the impending conflict, Mordecai Gist organized a company of Marylanders to be composed of "men of honor, family, and fortune to be ready for any emergency." After the war, he moved to South Carolina and had two sons, one of whom he named Independence and the other States (reprinted from *The Masonic Correspondence of George Washington* Julius F. Sachse, comp., Press of the New Era, 1915, 57).

The impracticability of forcing through such a formidable body of troops, rendered it the height of rashness and imprudence to risk the lives of our remaining party in a third attempt, and it became necessary for us to endeavour to effect our escape in the best manner we could. A party immediately retreated to the right through the woods, and Captain Ford and myself, with 20 others, to the left, through a marsh; nine only of whom got safe in.

The killed, wounded, and missing amount to 259. The above is as circumstantial an account as the hurry and want of time will admit of.[1]

After the Battle of Long Island, Major Gist was promoted to colonel in December 1776 and attained the rank of brigadier general on January 9, 1779. He would play a prominent role in the Battle of Camden (South Carolina) and was recognized for his bravery.

Major Gist's dedication to the cause was single-minded. To that end, he named his first son Independence and his second, States. After the war, he settled in Charleston, South Carolina, where he died on August 2, 1792. A newspaper account reported his death:

> Died. In Charleston, in the prime of life, General Mordecai Gist, a man who was always greatly esteemed for his honor and bravery in our last war, in which he took an active part in defence of invaded liberty. He has left behind him, to lament his loss, an amiable wife and family. The death of this truly good man ought not with justice to be passed over in silence, but his name should be handed down to posterity amongst the list of brave patriots.[2]

First Company

The men of the First Company, under the command of Col. John Hoskins Stone, were primarily from Charles County, Maryland. This county would contribute many leaders to the revolutionary cause, including John Hanson, first president of the Continental Congress, Thomas Stone, one of the signers of the Declaration of Independence, and Dr. Daniel of St. Thomas Jenifer who, as one of Maryland's representatives to the Continental Congress, fought for a strong and permanent union of the states.

Long before war was officially declared, the people of Charles County had suffered from the depredations of Lord Dunmore and his marauding fleet, who had landed on their shores multiple times, burning and looting their way up and down the Potomac River. There likely would have been no problem raising the troops needed to form the First Company and there was probably some level of comfort among the enlistees and their families knowing that Colonel William Smallwood, a fellow Charles Countian, would be in charge of all Maryland troops. George Washington would have been known to most of them as well since Mt. Vernon is but a short boat ride across the Potomac River. Washington was a frequent visitor to Charles County and had many friends there. Two of the three physicians in attendance at the time of his death in 1799 were Dr. Richard Gustavus Brown and Dr. James Craik, both residents of Charles County.

Captain John Hoskins Stone was born about 1745 in Charles County. He was the son of David Stone and Elizabeth Jenifer. His brother was Thomas Stone, one of the signers of the Declaration of Independence and his great-great-grandfather was William Stone, Maryland's first Protestant governor. Captain Stone was also the nephew of Daniel of St. Thomas Jenifer (president of the Maryland Council of Safety, 1775–1777; president of Maryland's first State Senate, 1777–1780, and member of the Continental Congress, 1778–1782).

In 1776 Captain Stone was promoted to lieutenant colonel of the First Maryland Regiment of the Continental Army. Early in 1777 he was made colonel and commander of the First Regiment and led his men in the battles of Princeton, Brandywine, and Germantown. He was shot through the ankle at Germantown on October 4, 1777, and was lame for the rest of his life.

I have just seen Capt Cox, who acted as Brigade Major to Col^o Stone, he informs me, that Col^o Stone is wounded in the Ankle and is now at one John Rialy who lives at 32 Mile Stone from Philad^a in Limerick Township, where he is attended by Dr Craigg, Cochran & Wallace, his Brother is with him, and several Gentlemen from Philad^a have offered him their Houses, but he is in too much pain to bear Removal at this Time. Major forrest had his Thigh broke by a Musquet Ball. Captn Brookes received a Ball through his Mouth which split his Tongue & went out at the back of his Jaw-Bone. Capt Bowie was wounded slightly in the shoulder. Capt Lawrence was also slightly wounded. Col^o Halls Horse ran away with & flung him, but he is not much hurt. Major Cox of Baltimore Town is killed, and Col^o Marbury is missing, a few subs: weare killed and several others wounded. Capt Cox further adds that our Loss is between 6 & 700 killed wounded and missing, that our army marched from their Camp last Wednesday.[1]

On March 21, 1778, while in Annapolis, Stone submitted his resignation to General Washington.

May it please your Excellency, From my present situation I cannot flatter myself that I shall ever be able to take the field as an officer, as yet I cannot walk without my crutches nor shall ever be able to walk well, my command will be so very small that it will not entitle me to ride, and as my Regiment must suffer much for the want of a field officer, I shall, if ever, not be able to take the field 'til after the ensuing campaign and by holding my commission I may prevent the promotion of some good officer — for these and other reasons I must beg your Excellency's permission to retire from the army whenever my health and situation will permit. I shall always think it the greatest honor and it is the utmost of my wishes to serve my Country where your Excellency commands.[2]

General Washington, now at Valley Forge, responded on April 4, 1778 saying,

Dear Sir, I am sorry to find your own account of the state of your wound contradicts the favorable one which I have rec'd from others. Your desire to quit the service because you cannot be longer useful is certainly laudable, but perhaps you judge your case desperate before you have given it sufficient tryal. Good and moderate weather, in which you can take exercise may have an effect beyond your hopes and I would therefore advise you to defer your Resignation at least a month or six weeks longer. If at the expiration of that time you still find yourself unlikely to recover you can put your present resolution into practice. If you are obliged to do it, I shall regret that the service has lost so good an officer.[3]

Captain Stone stayed on until he was wounded in the hand and head at the Battle of Stony Point on July 14, 1779. It was at this battle that Lieutenant James Fernandis, also wounded, carried Captain Stone on his back to safety. The wounds sustained by both men were severe enough that they both resigned their commissions within a few days. In 1790 Captain Stone was "put on the half pay establishment by a law of this State" (MSA: 18, 627–628).

On February 15, 1781, at Annapolis, Captain Stone married Mary Coudon, a native of Scotland. She died on March 4, 1792. John Hoskins Stone served as a member of Maryland's Executive Council from 1779 until 1785. The people of Charles County elected him to the Maryland House of Delegates for the term 1785–1787 and again in 1790. In 1794 he was elected as the eighth governor of Maryland, serving from 1794–1797. He died on October 5, 1804. The *Maryland Gazette* recorded:

> The Knell. On Friday last, about four o'clock in the morning, passed out of this life, in the fifty-fourth year of his age, General John Hoskins Stone, after a long and painful illness, which he bore with the resignation and fortitude of a christian soldier.
>
> For year after year, the grave bids from our view some of the remaining patriots who shed their blood in support of American Independence, and soon they will be seen no more.
>
> Among these, Maryland can boast few more distinguished than General Stone. Early in life, and at an early period of the American Revolution, he appeared in the great theatre of action that then opened, as a captain in the celebrated regiment of Smallwood. He highly distinguished himself at the battles of Long Island, White Plains and Prince-town, and in those decisive actions which decided the fate of our country, until the battle of German-town, where he received a wound that deprived him of bodily activity for the remainder of life.
>
> In this situation the powers of his mind did not remain inactive, they were steadily and diligently exercised in the same cause for which he had fought and bled and as representative of his native county of Charles, and as a member of the executive council he continued to serve his country until he was promoted to the highest station reserved by our constitution for a citizen of Maryland. In 1794 he was elected Governor of Maryland, and during the term of three successive years, to which the constitution limits the continuance of an individual in that station, he was re-elected with unanimity, and discharged the duties of the office with applause.
>
> After this period, it is probable that the hardships contracted in the American revolution, and the decreptitude arising from his wounds, contributed to bringing on a premature decline, and rendered the evening of life more uncomfortable than a soldier and public servant of his rank and merit had a right to expect, and finally he sunk into the grave, leaving that behind him of which no circumstance can now deprive him, the character of an honest and honourable man, an intrepid soldier, a firm patriot, and a liberal, hospitable and friendly citizen.
>
> The uniformed corps of Annapolis having determined to attend the funeral of this distinguished citizen with military honours, On Saturday the 5th, Captain Muir's company of artillery and Captain Duvall's company of infantry paraded at 10 o'clock in front of Mr. Caton's tavern, and received the corpse, which had been brought thither from the country, and thence, with solemn music and under the discharge of artillery, proceeded to the following order to the grave-yard:
>
> In front a detachment of artillery, headed by Captain Muir.
>
> The physicians and attendants of the deceased.
>
> The hearse with the corpse.
>
> On the right and on the left a detachment of infantry, in single file, headed by Captain Duvall.
>
> The relations of the deceased.

Officers of the revolutionary army and Members of the Cincinnati, two and two.
A detachment of infantry, with arms reversed.
Citizens, two and two.
And at the grave those melancholy duties closed, by the customary religious ceremonies and appropriate military honors.[4]

While his obituary was quite thorough, it does not tell us where Captain Stone was buried. However, he and his wife are probably buried in that part of the cemetery of St. Anne's Episcopal Church in Annapolis that was donated by Elizabeth Bordley in 1790. If stones marked the site, they no longer remain.

A letter written to George Washington Parke Custis by an unidentified gentleman from Washington, D.C., dated February 24, 1841, contains many details about the service of Colonel John Hoskins Stone:

> Dear Sir: I was much gratified at the publication in the Intelligencer, on the 22d instant, of your reminiscences of the battle of Germantown, but regret that your information was not sufficient to embrace Colonel John H. Stone, of the Maryland brigade. This patriotic and gallant soldier was conspicuous in the battles of Long Island, White Plains, Trenton, Princeton, and Brandywine, in all of which his conduct commanded the high admiration and warm approbation of his commander-in-chief, General Washington. In the latter battle the duty assigned him was, with his men, to cover and protect the American artillery, which he did — the corps, however, under his command suffering immensely, as was expected. When the order for retreat was given, in wheeling, his horse was killed and he was slightly wounded, but in the confusion, dropped behind a bush exhausted with fatigue; he was discovered by one of his men, whom he begged to pass on and make his escape, as he (Stone) was exhausted, wounded, and must inevitably be taken prisoner; he was prepared to meet his fate, whatever it might be; the soldier, however, could not be persuaded to leave him; he raised him from the ground, took off his boots, threw out the sand and pebbles, and finally they succeeded in making their escape under cover of the wood.
>
> At the battle of Germantown he was again found at the head of his men, and in the midst of that disastrous action had his leg shattered by a musket-ball, when his brother-officers implored him to allow himself to be taken from the field; his reply was 'No, never while I can wield a sword, will I desert my corps and colors in the face of an enemy.' He soon, however, became faint from the loss of blood and anguish of the wound (the bone being shattered in a thousand pieces), when, to all appearance in a dying state, three of his faithful soldiers bore him off the field. He was taken five or six miles and placed in a farm-house. When General Washington heard of it, he despatched Doctor Craik, his family surgeon, and Doctor Rush, the physician-general to the army, bidding them to be kind and attentive, and leave nothing undone which was in the power of man, or skill of physicians, to save his life. They immediately advised amputation, but he refused, and was on the next day returned as mortally wounded. After lingering some time in great torture, and suffering from a severe attack of tetanus, he recovered so far as to be able to be taken on a litter to Annapolis, where he lingered out some fifteen or twenty years a suffering cripple, and at length fell victim to the irritation of his wounded condition. After death several buckshot were taken from his groin.[5]

Private John Adams enlisted January 24, 1776. By December 10, 1776, when he reenlisted, he had been promoted to corporal; reduced January 1, 1778; and discharged March 6, 1778. It was noted that he had deserted (MSA: 18, 78).

Private Francis Green Baggett enlisted January 24, 1776 (MSA: 18, 6). His surname was spelled Baggott. Private Baggett was the son of John and Henrietta (Hamilton) Baggett of Charles County, Maryland.

Private John Boone enlisted January 24, 1776, "sick, in hospl" (MSA: 18, 6). His surname was spelled Boen. By May 26, 1777, he had attained the rank of corporal. He was listed as sergeant on July 1, 1779, and a resignation date given of March 26, 1780. He had actually reentered the service on March 14, 1780, with the rank of ensign. He is then shown as lieutenant, but with no date. His surname was spelled Boon (MSA: 18, 81). "John Boone Lieut. 3rd Reg., commissioned 12th April, 1781, under Peter Adams, Lieut. Col. commanding; wounded at Eutaw Springs, 8th September, 1781; served till April, 1783."[6]

This soldier not only fought at the Battle of Long Island but he also served throughout the war. On September 8, 1781, he was injured at the Battle of Eutaw Springs, but the wound was not serious enough to keep him from the Battle of Yorktown just one month later.

Family lore says that "Among the officers of the Continental Army represented in the 'Surrender of Cornwallis,' one of the four pictures in the Rotunda of the Capitol at Washington, is the portrait of John Boone, Lieutenant 3rd Regiment, Maryland Line, taken from life."[7]

On January 12, 1782, John Boone married Ann Hardy, daughter of Henry Hardy, Jr. and Mary Boone.

> On January 7, 1812 the Maryland Legislature passed a resolution in favor of John Boone. "RESOLVED, That the treasurer of the western shore be, and he is hereby authorised and required to pay to John Boone, of Charles county, a lieutenant in the late revolutionary army, the sum of one hundred and twenty-five dollars annually, in quarterly payments, out of any unappropriated money in the treasury [MSA: 192, 2961].

John Boone was the son of Henry Boone and Jane Spalding of Charles County, Maryland. He was the great-grandson of John Boone of the Cliffs who immigrated to Maryland in the 1670s and died at his plantation called Rockhold in Calvert County, Maryland, about 1689.

On May 15, 1828, John Boone, a resident of Charles County, applied for a pension stating "I was an officer in the Continental Line of the Army of the Revolution and served as such at which period I was Lieutenant in the Third regiment of the Maryland line."

Mary Jane Boone, daughter of John Boone, made an affidavit in Charles County on November 8, 1853, "for the purpose of obtaining the increase & Balance of said pension under said Act of Congress both as Lt.& Capt." She further stated that she was John Boone's only living child, no widow survived, and that he died on the 31st day of ____.

The Charles County court then began taking depositions to confirm the date of death of John Boone. On November 28, 1853, Underwood Liser and John D. Wilkinson deposed that they were personally acquainted with John Boone and that he died on the 31st day of January 1834.

On the same date Zadock Robinson made oath that "he did make the coffin on the first day of February 1837 for Lt. John Boone, A Revolutionary pensioner and was present and saw him dead." The court affirmed the date of death of John Boone based on Mr. Robinson's statement. This was confirmed by his obituary: "Died on the 31st ult. At his residence in Charles County, Maryland, in his 78th year, Capt. John Boone, an officer of the Revolution."[8]

Lieutenant Daniel Bowie was commissioned January 3, 1776 (MSA: 18, 5). He was born in Prince George's County in 1754 and was the son of Thomas Bowie and Hannah Lee, both of very wealthy and prominent families. He probably served in the Charles County company because of a lack of officers.

Lieutenant Bowie was wounded and taken prisoner the day of the battle. He died while in captivity. Perhaps fearing he might die or having a premonition that he would, he made out his will the night before the battle.

> Bowie, Daniel, Prince George's Co. 26 Aug. 1776; 3 May 1777. To bro. Philip Sprigg, classical books, mathematical instruments and wearing apparel. To Walter Bowie, Ex., remainder of books at my plantation and at Baltimore. To Mother and sisters, Elizabeth Belt, Barbara Hall, Littie Sprigg, each a mourning ring. To aunt Eleanor Skinner and Miss Miliant Tyler, each a mourning ring. To Mrs. Eleanor Cowan, in Harford County, a mourning ring. To Negro lad Basil, his freedom. To Capt. Patrick Sim, all my wearing apparel in camp. To Joseph Butler, military accoutrements, and a mourning ring to him and one each to Lieut's Butler and Beans. Residue to Walter Bowie (and a mourning ring) and Aunt Eleanor Skinner. If Walter Bowie refuses Executorship to friend James Mullican. Wit: William Sterett, Boran Philpott, Henry C. Gaither.[9]

Lieutenant Bowie was the great-grandson of Colonel Richard Lee, the immigrant ancestor and progenitor of the Lee family of Virginia and Maryland. Colonel Richard Lee, Esquire, came from Stratford, Langton, County of Essex, England, and was in Virginia by 1642. He served as attorney general, justice, burgess, councilor and as secretary of state from 1649 to 1652.[10]

Private Patrick Brady enlisted January 14, 1776. On December 10, 1776, Sergeant Patrick Brady reenlisted in the First Regiment. He was discharged on October 12, 1778 (MSA: 18, 6, 81).

Private Dennis Broderick, Fifer enlisted April 17, 1776. Musicians were at a premium and not every county had one. As a result, musicians were paid more than enlisted men. Private Broderick reenlisted in the First Regiment as a Fife Major on December 10, 1776, and served until April 1, 1777. He was then shown as a part of the Seventh Regiment from February 6, 1777, to August 16, 1780; as a prisoner on August 22, 1777; missing July 1778; and then returned (for a while he was said to have deserted, but that was probably not the case) (MSA: 18, 5, 81, 188, 308).

Private Thomas Burrows enlisted January 24, 1776. He reenlisted on December 10, 1776, and was discharged April 4, 1777. On October 15, 1792, it was ordered that the auditor issue a "Certificate for the Depreciation of pay to Thomas Burrows late a soldier in the 1st Maryland Regiment and deliver the same to the Treasurer of the western shore who is ordered to pay it to Capt. Thomas A. Dyson in virtue of a Power of Attorney from Joshua Burrows, father and administrator of the said Thomas" (MSA: 18, 6, 81) (MSA: 72, 293).

Private Joseph Chatham enlisted January 24, 1776 (MSA: 18, 6). His enlistment record shows his surname as Cheatham, but it is believed that it should be Chatham. No further records have been found for this soldier.

Private Jonathan Chunn was born in Trinity Parish, Charles County, Maryland, on November 7, 1754. He was the eldest child of Lancelot Chunn and his wife, Judith Cartwright. Private Chunn enlisted on January 24, 1776, and was then "sick and on furlough." He reenlisted in the First Regiment on December 10, 1776. The official records show him as being discharged on March 6, 1777, when he was reported to be dead (MSA: 18, 6, 91).

Private William Clark enlisted February 4, 1776. He reenlisted in the First Regiment on December 10, 1776 and was discharged in July 1777. It was noted that he had deserted (MSA: 18, 7, 91).

Private Thomas Way Connell enlisted January 24, 1776 (MSA: 18, 6). No further records have been found for this soldier.

Lieutenant William Courts enlisted January 14, 1776, as a cadet. On July 9 of the same year he was appointed as ensign (MSA: 12, 15). Wounded and taken prisoner at the battle, he was exchanged on December 9 and the very next day was appointed as a second lieutenant of the First Regiment. He resigned his commission on April 25, 1777.

After the war, Lieutenant Courts married Betsy Thomas of St. Mary's County. They had two daughters, one of whom named Elizabeth married her cousin, Dr. James Thomas, the 26th governor of Maryland. Lieutenant Courts died sometime prior to December 5, 1792, when his estate was admitted to probate in Charles County.

Private Edmund Cox was the son of William Cox and his wife, Mary Burn of Charles County, Maryland. He enlisted on January 24, 1776. At the time of his reenlistment on December 10, 1776, he was listed as Sergeant Cox. He appears to have been a bit of a maverick as he was reduced in rank several times, but each time reinstated. By July 19, 1777, he was quartermaster. He was dismissed from the service on October 3, 1778.

Sergeant Cox reentered the service on March 15, 1779. By January 1, 1780, he was Private Cox but was shown as Sergeant Cox again by April 1, 1780. He was again reduced in rank on September 1, 1780, and discharged on November 1, 1780 (MSA: 18, 6, 91, 94).

Private Ignatius Douglass enlisted January 24, 1776. His surname is erroneously shown as Doyglass (MSA: 18, 5). Sergeant Ignatius Douglass of the First Regiment enlisted from February 20, 1777, and was discharged on December 25, 1779 (MSA: 18, 100).

Private Nathaniel Downing enlisted January 27, 1776. He reenlisted in the First Regiment on December 10, 1776, and was discharged on December 27, 1779 (MSA: 18, 6, 100). On February 7, 1818, the Maryland General Assembly passed legislation directing the treasurer of the Western Shore to "pay annually to Nathaniel Downing, or his order, of Prince George's county, an old revolutionary soldier, a sum of money equal to the half pay of a private solder, as a further remuneration to the said Nathaniel Downing for the services rendered his country in that war" (MSA: 192, 2997).

Private Edward Edelen, Jr. enlisted on January 24, 1776 (MSA: 18, 6). On December 10, 1776, Private Edward Eadlin (*sic*) reenlisted. He was discharged on December 27, 1779 (MSA: 18, 106). Edward Edelen was born in Charles County in 1752 and was the son of Edward Edelen and Susanna Wathen. He married Eleanor Boarman on February 12, 1782. This soldier died in Charles County in 1834.

Cadet James Fernandis was just 21 when he enlisted January 30, 1776 (MSA: 18, 5). Within a few months of enlistment, July 19, 1776, he was commissioned ensign (MSA: 12, 16). This soldier was taken prisoner at the battle and held in captivity until March 24, 1777: "A list of the killed and missing in the Maryland Battalion: Capt. Veazey, killed; Lt. Butler, said to be killed; Ensign Fernandes, Lt. Dent, Capt. Bowie, missing; Lt. Sterret, Coursey, and Wright, Ensign Ridge [should be Ridgely], 13 Sergeants, and 259 privates."[11] "Ensign James Fernandez, 1st Md. Regt., exchanged March 24, 1777" (MSA:18, 616).

Initially, Fernandis, like William Sterrett, was erroneously reported as having been killed. "Extract of a letter from New-York, dated August 31, 1776. Captain Veazy, Ensign Fernandez, Sgt. Sands killed. Capt. Bowie, Lts. Butler, Sterret, Ridgely,

Dent, and Ensign Coats missing. Mr. Coursey taken prisoner. Adjutant Brice was taken prisoner by two officers of Light-Horse and was delivered to a private who told him he was his prisoner, which Brice denied, and immediately shot him and got clear."[12]

While being held prisoner, he was commissioned second lieutenant December 10, 1776 (MSA: 18, 108) and on April 17, 1777, shortly after his release, was made first lieutenant. On March 1, 1778, he was commissioned captain lieutenant and held that rank until his resignation on July 15, 1779.[13]

Lieutenant Fernandis is said to have "bore his wounded commander, Col. John H. Stone on his back to a place of safety after he himself had been wounded." Although many contend this occurred at the Battle of Long Island, it was actually at the Battle of Stony Point on July 14, 1779. The next day, Lieutenant Fernandis resigned his commission and shortly thereafter so did Colonel Stone, undoubtedly because of the severity of their wounds.

> 7/27/1780. James Fernandes, Capt. Commissions issued to the following Officers appointed to Command the Regim^t Extra raised in Virtue of "An Act entitled a Supplement to the Act to procure Recruits to complete the Battalions of this State in the service of the United States and to raise an Additional Reg^t if necessary, and an Act to expedite the raising an Additional Battalion of Regulars." [MSA: 43, 234–235].
>
> 9/1/1780. Charles Smith instead of James Fernandes resigned. Commissions issued to fill up the vacancies in the Regiment Extra [MSA:.43, 272–273].
>
> A petition from James Fernandes, setting forth, that he served as a soldier in the first Maryland regiment, and was made prisoner at the battle of Long-Island, during which he sustained and despised every cruelty and temptation, and praying to be allowed the depreciation of his pay while in service, was preferred and read. May 10, 1782.[14]

James Fernandis was married twice. His first wife was Elizabeth Wallace, daughter of Wheedon Wallace and Elizabeth Mankin. They had four children before Elizabeth's death about 1788. His second wife was Chloe McPherson, sister of his fellow soldier, Samuel McPherson.

James Fernandis died in Charles County in 1790 at the very young age of 35 leaving, in addition to his widow, four young children all under the age of ten.

Peter Fernandis, the immigrant ancestor and great-grandfather of James Fernandes, was born in Spain in 1652. He was transported to Maryland in 1668 by Captain James Neale who claimed 350 acres for transporting "Pedroe Farnandise and 6 others." In April 1669 Capt. James Neale presented three servants to the Charles County Court to judge their ages, one of which was Pedro Faarnandez who was judged to be about 17 years old.[15]

Private Gilbert Garland enlisted February 7, 1776 (MSA: 18, 7). No further records have been found for this soldier.

Private Matthew Garner enlisted January 25, 1776. He reenlisted in the First Regiment as Sergeant Matthew Garner on December 10, 1776. By the time of his resignation on March 5, 1778, he was Ensign Matthew Garner (MSA: 18, 6, 112). He was living in Port Tobacco Parish in Charles County at the time of the 1800 census.

Private Samuel Granger enlisted January 24, 1776 (MSA: 18, 6). No further records have been found for this soldier.

Private Benjamin Gray enlisted February 1, 1776 (MSA: 18, 7). He is shown to have reenlisted in the First Regiment December 10, 1776. He was discharged on December 27, 1779, whereupon he immediately reenlisted again for the duration of the war, but was discharged on November 1, 1780 (MSA 18, 111).

On January 23, 1780, the commissary of stores was ordered to deliver to Benjamin Gray a recruit in the First Regiment, one shirt, one pair of shoes, and one pair of stockings (MSA 43, 65).

Private Charles Green enlisted January 24, 1776 (MSA: 18, 6). No further records have been found for this soldier.

Private Edward Green enlisted January 24, 1776 (MSA: 18, 6). No further records have been found for this soldier.

Private Charles Griffin enlisted January 24, 1776 (MSA: 18, 6). No further records have been found for this soldier.

Private Samuel Hamilton enlisted January 24, 1776 (MSA: 18, 6). By the time he reenlisted in the First Regiment on December 10, 1776, he had been promoted to sergeant. He was discharged July 11, 1778 (MSA: 18, 117).

On July 27, 1780, this soldier briefly reentered the service and his name was included in a list of "Commissions issued to the following Officers appointed to Command the Regim^t Extra raised in Virtue of 'An Act entitled a Supplement to the Act to procure Recruits to complete the Battalions of this State in the service of the United States and to raise an Additional Reg^t if necessary, and an Act to expedite the raising an Additional Battalion of Regulars'" (MSA: 43, 234–35). "Samuel Hanson in the room of S. Hamilton resigned. Commissions issued to fill up the vacancies in the Regiment Extra. September 1, 1780" (MSA: 43, 272–73).

Samuel Hamilton was the son of Patrick Hamilton and his wife, Ann Green of Charles County. On February 9, 1773, he married Christina (nee Smith), widow of Henry Clements. By 1787 Hamilton had moved his family to Montgomery County, Maryland, where he was a tavern keeper. He died in Washington, D.C., on March 4, 1807. An account of his death states: "Died, the 4th instant, at Washington City, Mr. Samuel Hamilton. A few minutes before his death, he was engaged in writing, and in enjoyment of his usual health. He rose and complained to Mrs. H. that he felt himself suddenly seized with very unusual and unpleasant sensations. A physician, who was then in the house, was called for, but before he could reach Mr. H., he was a corpse."[16] Confirmation that this was the same Samuel Hamilton was obtained when Christina Hamilton posted a notice in the April 27, 1807, edition of the *National Intelligencer* stating that letters of administration had been granted to her by the Orphan's Court of the District of Columbia.

Corporal Samuel Hanson enlisted January 24, 1776 (MSA 18, 6). "*Ensn Samuel. Hanson*" is shown reenlisting December 10, 1776. He resigned December 7, 1777 (MSA: 18, 117). He is believed to be Samuel Hanson of Walter who was commissioned lieutenant in the Extra Regiment on July 27, 1780. Several former soldiers of the First Company were recruited for this new regiment.

"Samuel Hanson of Walter, Lt. July 27, 1780. Commissions issued to the following Officers appointed to Command the Regim.ᵗ Extra raised in Virtue of 'An Act entitled a Supplement to the Act to procure Recruits to complete the Battalions of this State in the service of the United States and to raise an Additional Regᵗ if necessary, and an Act to expedite the raising an Additional Battalion of Regulars'" (MSA: 43, 234–235). "Samuel Hanson in the room of S. Hamilton resigned. Commissions issued to fill up the vacancies in the Regiment Extra. September 1, 1780" (MSA: 43, 272–273).

Corporal Hanson was the son of Walter Hanson and Elizabeth Hoskins. He was the uncle of fellow soldier John Mitchell and nephew of John Hanson, first president of the Continental Congress.

Private Truman Hilton enlisted February 6, 1776. It was noted that he was "sick in barracks" (MSA: 18, 7). Despite extensive searches, no further military records have been found for Private Hilton including reenlistment, discharge, bounty land warrant, and so forth. He died in 1829 in Clark County, Indiana; therefore, he lived long enough to have applied for a pension, but he did not. My belief is that Private Hilton may have been medically discharged for whatever illness he had at the time of his enlistment, but without additional proof, he remains as one of the 400.

Truman Hilton was born in Prince George's County in 1758. He was the son of James Hilton, a native of St. Mary's County, and his wife, Monica Cavenaugh. On October 27, 1780, he married Christena Patrick in Frederick County, Maryland. The family moved to Iredell County, North Carolina, by the time of the 1800 census. Some time after 1810 and before 1820, they settled permanently in Clark County, Indiana.

Private John Hopson enlisted January 24, 1776 (MSA: 18, 6). No further records have been found for this soldier.

Private Joseph Jason Jenkins enlisted January 27, 1776. As Corporal Jason Jenkins, First Regiment, he is shown as having enlisted again on March 11, 1779, and discharged, with the rank of sergeant on December 27, 1779 (MSA: 18, 6, 125).

Lt. John Kidd was not originally from Charles County, but was assigned as an officer to the First Company. On October 8, 1776, he was convicted by court-martial for "taking fatigue men from their duty." His conviction was upheld and approved by General Washington. He was immediately dismissed from the service.[17] At the court-martial, Lt. Kidd pled guilty but said that he was not acquainted with the orders. Testimony was given by a Lt. Cole, who stated that: "As soon as Lt. Kidd had marched his men to the fort, he drew an order for the rum, and paraded them down to march home. I then ordered him to go to work with his men, and told him 'twas contrary to general orders to go home to breakfast, and if he did not go home he would report him. He informs that he (Lt. Cole) had occasion to be absent about 15 minutes, and when he returned, Lt. Kidd had his party paraded and marched them off, and did not return till after 11 o'clock, and before 12 he marched off to return his tools."

Additional testimony was provided by Capt. Thomas Woolford who said: "That he was that day on fatigue, and saw Lt. Kidd marching off to return his tools; that he immediately went and ordered him back; he answered that it rained and his men should not work. The Captain then says that he informed him that rain was very trifling; and, as he was under his command, he should return; with which he complied. That at 1:00, the Capt. dismissed the party for dinner, and Lt. Kidd did not return in the afternoon. Lt. Kidd pleads that he was sick, and unable to go in the afternoon." "The Court, being cleared, are of the opinion that the prisoner ought to be dismissed from the service for his offence. Francis Ware, President."[18]

Private Samuel Kurk enlisted January 24, 1776, (MSA: 18, 6). No further records have been found for this soldier.

Private Andrew Ross Lindsay enlisted January 24, 1776 and was shown on detachment duty (MSA: 18, 5). No further records have been found for this soldier.

Private Francis Ware Luckett enlisted January 24, 1776 (MSA:18, 6)."Corporal F. Ware Luckett, 1st Regt., enlisted December 10, 1776; discharged April 16, 1778. Died" (MSA: 18, 132).

Francis Ware Luckett was the son of William Luckett and his wife, Susanna Ware. He was named for his maternal grandfather, Francis Ware, a wealthy Charles County merchant and landowner.

Private Samuel Luckett was born June 12, 1756, in Port Tobacco Parish, Charles County, Maryland. Just 20 years old and newly married, he enlisted on January 24, 1776. On December 10, 1776, he reenlisted in the First Regiment for three years. In 1779 he enlisted for a third time, serving as ensign and then first lieutenant in the company of Captain Francis Mastin of the Maryland militia. "7/27/1780. Samuel Luckett, Ensign. Commissions issued to the following Officers appointed to Command the

Regim^t Extra raised in Virtue of 'An Act entitled a Supplement to the Act to procure Recruits to complete the Battalions of this State in the service of the United States and to raise an Additional Reg^t if necessary, and an Act to expedite the raising an Additional Battalion of Regulars'" (MSA: 43, 234–235). "9/1/1780. Samuel Luckett in the room of S. McLane [Lt.] promoted. Commissions issued to fill up the vacancies in the Regiment Extra" (MSA: 43, 272–273).

Samuel Luckett was born June 12, 1756, in Port Tobacco Parish, Charles County, Maryland. He was the son of Ignatius Luckett, Jr. and Margaret McLean. About 1775, he married Monica Kennedy, daughter of Clement Kennedy and Mary Ratcliff. On October 20, 1806, Samuel Luckett conveyed property in Charles County to Ignatius Luckett for $250 for "Frog Nest," "Slipe," and "Aspinal." This is perhaps the approximate date of his leaving Maryland for Kentucky.

In May 1818, Samuel Luckett, a resident of Barren County, Kentucky, applied for a pension stating that he was crippled in the left shoulder, foot, and right hip from injuries sustained during the war at Kemble's Farm in the Jerseys when he was constructing huts for the soldiers. The soldier said he had been unable to work for the previous three years and was dependent upon the labor of his children. He died in Barren County in 1828.[19]

Private John McPherson enlisted January 24, 1776 (MSA: 18, 6). No further records have been found for this soldier.

Private Mark McPherson enlisted March 6, 1776, at the age of 22. He is shown reenlisting in the First Regiment as a sergeant on December 10, 1776. He would ultimately rise to the rank of lieutenant and served throughout the war. He was discharged in 1783 (MSA: 18, 6, 137).

> January 26, 1780: [Council to Hon'ble The Board of War]. Gentlemen Brigadier General Smallwood some time past, wrote us.... "I have enclosed you a List of such Sergeants and others of the first Brigade, who have been recommended for Commissions, by their Field Officers and Captains. I believe their Services and Merit entitle them to such Reward, where it can be granted consistent with the Views of the State. Perhaps it might be well to avoid fixing their relative Rank, as that might be determined by a Board of the Field Officers, agreeable to their Merit and Pretensions "Here follows the List William Noyes Serg^t Major, Francis Shepherd, Mark McPherson, Richard Coe, of the first: John Trueman, Henry Clements, Robert Halkerston, Walter Dyer, of the 3rd William Reason, John Cheers of the 5th David Green, Serg^t Major, Robert Green, Thomas Jenkins, Benjamin Fickle, Robert Yeates of the 7th James Thompson and William Smoot of the first and John Smith of the 3^d Regiment. We appoint them to Ensigncies in the first Brigade and desire Commissions may issue, leaving the Rank to be setled hereafter" [MSA: 43, 71].

After the war, he moved to Lincoln County, Kentucky, where he married Mary Middleton on November 25, 1795.[20]

On January 23, 1816, the Maryland General Assembly ordered the treasurer of the Western Shore to "pay to Mark McPherson, or to his order annually, in quarterly payments, during his life, a sum of money equal to the half pay of a lieutenant" (MSA: 192, 2978).

On August 17, 1820, Mark McPherson, aged 67, and a resident of Lincoln County, Kentucky, applied for a pension based on his war service. He deposed that he was born in Charles County on February 15, 1754. This soldier died in Kentucky on February 8, 1847.[21]

Ensign Samuel McPherson enlisted January 14, 1776 (MSA: 18, 5). He reenlisted in the First Regiment on December 10, 1776, and remained in the service for the duration of the war, eventually achieving the rank of captain.

On October 14, 1780, it was ordered "that the said Treasurer pay to Capt. Saml McPherson of the 1st Reg^t Thirty Dollars of the new Emission due him for Stores to be Accounted for" (MSA: 43, 326). "McPherson, Samuel (Md). Ensign 1st Maryland, 10th December, 1776; 2d Lieutenant, 17th April, 1777; 1st Lieutenant, 27th May, 1778; transferred to 2d Maryland, 1st January, 1781; Captain, 25th April, 1781; retained in Maryland Battalion April, 1783, and served to 15th November, 1783."[22]

His sister, Chloe McPherson, was the second wife of his fellow soldier, James Fernandis.

Private Josias Miller enlisted January 27, 1776 (MSA: 18, 6). On December 10, 1776, Corporal Josiah (*sic*) Miller reenlisted in the First Regiment and was discharged on December 27, 1779 (MSA: 18, 137).

"Ensign Josias Miller. Commissions issued to the following Officers appointed to Command the Regim^t Extra raised in Virtue of 'An Act entitled a Supplement to the Act to procure Recruits to complete the Battalions of this State in the service of the United States and to raise an Addtional Reg^t if necessary, and an Act to expedite the raising an Additional Battalion of Regulars.' July 27, 1780" (MSA: 43, 234–235). "9/1/1780. Josias Miller in the room of Nathaniel Magruder resigned. Commissions issued to fill up the vacancies in the Regiment Extra" (MSA: 43, 272–273).

Miller moved to Franklin County, Ohio, after the war. In 1818 he went to Washington, D.C., and applied for a pension deposing that he had served in the battles of Long Island, White Plains, Monmouth, Germantown, Stony Point, and several smaller skirmishes. Like most of the men who applied for pensions, he had lost his discharge papers and other information. There was some confusion with the dates as he initially indicated he enlisted in 1777 under Captain James Peale.

On June 24, 1820, Franklin Co., Ohio, Josias Miller, age 63 the 8th day of April 1820, deposed that he enlisted on the 13th of January 1776 in Capt. John Hoskins Stone's Company, the First Maryland Battalion commanded by Colonel William Smallwood and continued in service until about the 16th of April 1778.[23]

Cadet John Mitchell enlisted January 24, 1776 (MSA: 18, 5). As Lieutenant John Mitchell he is shown reenlisting in the First Regiment on December 10, 1776, with a notation that he was commissioned captain on July 15, 1777 (MSA:18, 136).

"Mitchell, John (Md). 2d Lieutenant 1st Maryland, 10th December, 1776; 1st Lieutenant, 10th June, 1777; Regimental Adjutant, 1st May, 1779; Captain, 15th July, 1779; transferred to 4th Maryland, 1st January, 1781, and served to April, 1783."[24]

John Mitchell was born about 1760 in Charles County, Maryland. He was the only son of Hugh Mitchell, a merchant and native of Glasgow, Scotland. His mother was Ann Hanson, niece of John Hanson, first president of the Continental Congress. It is recorded that "John Mitchell was a young man at the outbreak of the Revolutionary War and spent most of his fortune in helping equip a company of militia from Charles County. He was an officer in the company and became a captain in the Revolutionary Army before the end of the war. He was later known as General Mitchell, having been in charge of the State Militia."[25]

His obituary reads:

> Died on Sunday, the 11th day of October at his farm in Charles County, Gen. John Mitchell. He was born at that period in the history of America when heroism and love of country were common virtues; moved by the same noble impulse which raised to arms each gallant freeman of Charles, he early entered on a career of glory. His heart beat high with liberty, and he bred his breast in her defense. Proud to serve his country, her good was all he fought — to purchase it, health, friends, life, were but a paltry consideration. Like most of the wreck of this gallant band who survived the storms of war, he was rich in fame but poor in worldly circumstances. Unfortunately, he attached himself to the dominant faction, whom he found alien to gratitude. His applications for compensation for his services met with no encouragement. In vain it was pleaded that he was a remnant of that heroic band who, under the command of the gallant Smallwood, rushed to battle, resolved to conquer or die, protected by a kind providence, he escaped the reiterated shocks of war. He lived to feel the ingratitude of his country and to witness her disgrace. But he has now found a refuge in the silence of the tomb and we trust his patriotism will now be rewarded. Light lie the sod that covers the breast of a soldier. Honored be his memory.[26]

Pvt. Barnard Nash enlisted on January 24, 1776 (MSA: 18, 6). He was discharged on March 17, 1777, "dead" (MSA: 18, 146).

Pvt. John Neale was just 19 when he enlisted on January 24, 1776 (MSA: 18, 6). He reenlisted on December 10, 1776, was promoted to sergeant in 1778 and discharged on December 27, 1779 (MSA: 18, 146).

John Neale probably met his future wife while serving in and around New Jersey. After his marriage, he served in the New Jersey Militia several times through the end of the war. He would eventually move his family to New York.

On May 18, 1818, in Seneca County, New York, John Neal, aged 61 years deposed that he enlisted in the spring of 1776 at Port Tobacco in the state of Maryland in the company commanded by Captain John Stone in Colonel Smallwood's regiment and served until December 1779 when he was discharged at Morris Town, New Jersey. He deposed that he was in the battles of Long Island, White Plains, German Town, Brandywine, and Monmouth. He reapplied on October 4, 1820, reciting the same service but stating additionally that he was a cooper by trade but because of his health he was "unable to pursue his occupation any more than one fourth part of the time."[27]

On November 4, 1847, in Tompkins County, New York, Margaret Smith, age 81, deposed that she was previously married to John Neal, a former pensioner. She stated that he was in the first part of the Revolution from the state of Maryland, but during the war settled in New Jersey. After their marriage, he served several times in the militia of New Jersey until the close of the war and he was probably a sergeant, at least some part of the time. They were married on February 27, 1780, at Bound Brook, Somerset County, New Jersey. John Neal died on July 22, 1825. Afterward, she married John Baryann Smith who died on the 9th day of October 1847.[28]

On November 8, 1847, in Seneca County, New York, Benjamin Neill, "a highly respectable person," deposed that Margaret Smith, the widow of John Neal, is his mother and that John Neal was his father. He reiterated that his father died on July 22, 1825.[29]

John Neale was the son of Bennet Neale and Elizabeth Sprigg of Charles County, Maryland. He was the great-great-grandson of Captain James Neale and his wife, Ann Gill of Wollaston Manor. Concerning Neale's family heritage, it is reported that

> Continuing down the (Potomac) river, we pass Swan Point and just beyond Neale Sound on which was located the lands of "Wolleston Manor." They comprised 2,000 ac., the peninsula between the Potomac and the Wicomico on the west side of the estuary and were granted in 1641–42 to Capt. James Neale. Neale came to the Potomac about 1636 from London. Wilstach in "Potomac Landings" states: "His authority was at once recognized by the Government, for whom he performed many commissions in addition to his definite public services as a member of the Assembly, as one of the Governor's Council and as Commissioner of his Lordship's Treasury. He married Ann Gill and with her returned to Europe. Capt. Neale returned to "Wolleston Manor" in 1660 and brought with him 5 children, three of which were attractive daughters, Henrietta Maria, James, Dorothy, Anthony, and Jane, all born abroad, for whom the Captain petitioned and received naturalization.[30]
>
> Capt. James Neale was the ancestor of: 5 governors of Maryland (Gen. Edward Lloyd II; Edward Lloyd V; Henry Lloyd; Lloyd Lowndes; and Charles Goldsborough); two of Maryland's Confederate Generals (Lloyd Tilghman and Charles Sidney Winder); U.S. Senators Edward Lloyd V; Gen. James Lloyd; and William Duhurst Merric; Roger Brooke Taney, Attorney General and Chief Justice of the U.S.; Leonard Neale, second Archbishop of Baltimore; Charles Carroll, the Barrister (author of the Maryland Declaration of Rights) and the wives of William Paca, Francis Scott Key, Admiral Franklin Buchanan, and Sen. Stephen Arnold Douglas.[31]

Private John Neary enlisted February 1, 1776 (MSA: 18, 7). "Sergeant John Nayry, 1st Regt., enlisted June 10 (no year); discharged November 1, 1780. Time out, January 1, 1780; reenlisted March 11, 1780" (MSA: 18, 146).

Private John Norris enlisted January 27, 1776 (MSA: 18, 6). No further records have been found for this soldier.

Private Thomas Norris enlisted January 24, 1776 (MSA: 18, 5). No further records have been found for this soldier.

Private John Plant enlisted January 24, 1776 (MSA: 18, 5). His pension papers show that he was appointed corporal in the First Regiment on December 10, 1776, and discharged on July 6, 1778, with a notation "appd. a Sergt." This record should probably read that this soldier was appointed a sergeant on July 6, 1778, as he continued in service beyond this date) (MSA: 18, 149).

On March 24, 1780, it was ordered that the treasurer of the Western Shore "pay to Serj. John Plant of the 1st Regimt. lately Discharged Twenty Pounds the All° made to the non Commissioned Officers & Privates by the Gen¹ Assembly, he having not received the same as appears by a Cert from Capt. John Mitchell of the first Maryland Regiment" (MSA: 43, 118).

"July 27, 1780. John Plant was commissioned Ensign of the Extra Regiment on July 27, 1780 (Commissions issued to the following Officers appointed to Command the Regimᵗ Extra raised in Virtue of 'An Act entitled a Supplement to the Act to procure Recruits to complete the Battalions of this State in the service of the United States and to raise an Additional Regᵗ if necessary, and an Act to expedite the raising an Additional Battalion of Regulars'" (MSA: 43, 234–235). "John Plant in the room of Charles Magruder promoted [to Lieutenant] in the Extra Regiment" on September 1, 1780" (MSA: 43, 272–273).

Plant was in the service as late as January 28, 1782, when it was ordered "that the said Treasurer pay to William Whetcroft, one hundred and ninety one pounds, thirteen shillings and seven pence of the same Emission due him for a Certificate of John Plant Lieut in the late Extra Regiment as settled by the Aud. Gen¹—" (MSA: 48, 58).

On September 17, 1838, Mary Ann Plant, age 68, a resident of Washington, D.C., deposed that she was the widow of John Plant "who was a Sergeant in the Maryland line of the Revolutionary War." Her maiden name was Mary Ann Davis and she stated that they were married in Charles County, Maryland, on June 17, 1788, and that John Plant had died on November 13 or November 14, 1808.[32]

Private John Shaw enlisted January 27, 1776 (MSA: 18, 6). He reenlisted in the First Regiment on December 10, 1776, and was discharged on February 1, 1780 (MSA: 18, 160). Just prior to his discharge on January 22, 1780, John Shaw, among others, was provided with "1 p^r Shoes, 1 p^r Stockings & 1 Shirt, in part of the Cloathing due them from the Continent—" (MSA: 43, 65).

John Shaw was living in Delaware County, Ohio, when he applied for a pension on May 15, 1818. He deposed that:

> ... he was in the service of the United States in the revolutionary war, that he enlisted under Capt. afterwards Col. Stone in the Maryland line about the last of January in the year 1776 as he believes [and] that after one years service in said Company he was put under Capt. James Fernandez belonging to the Regiment of said Col. Stone—also that he served as a recruiting Sergeant and was in the immediate service of General Smallwood for some time—That he was regularly discharged from the service of the United States about the first of the year 1781—said discharge this Deponent saith he hath lost by accident—that he served the whole of the above time—that he is never been allowed any pension or remuneration whatever—that by reason of his reduced circumstances he stands in need of assistance from this country for support—and further this deponent saith not.

This soldier was awarded an annual pension of $8 per month.[33]

Pvt. Luke Matthews Sheirburn enlisted January 24, 1776 (MSA 18, 6). This soldier died while in the service.

On July 25, 1778, the final account of the estate of his father, Nicholas Sheirburn, was filed in Charles County. This account listed the widow and children of Nicholas Sheirburn, specifically stating that the son, Luke Matthews Sheirburn, had died since his father. Nicholas Sheirburn died prior to July 19, 1777, when letters of administration were granted on his estate.[34]

Luke would not be the only son lost to this family during the Revolution. On December 17, 1796, Mary Sheirburn of Charles County petitioned the General Assembly saying that she had two sons in the service of the United States during the late war and praying for the depreciation of their pay. The other son was Charles Sheirburn who "mustered dead on the 29th day of September 1778."[35]

Private Francis Shepard, erroneously listed as Francis Sherrard, enlisted January 24, 1776. Sergeant Francis Shepard, First Regiment, reenlisted December 10, 1776, and was discharged on December 27, 1779 (MSA: 18, 18, 160).

> January 26, 1780: [Council to Hon'ble The Board of War]. Gentlemen Brigadier General Smallwood some time past, wrote us.... "I have enclosed you a List of such Sergeants and others of the first Brigade, who have been recommended for Commissions, by their Field Officers and Captains." Here follows the List ... Francis Shepherd, ... of the first (see page 63 for the complete record) [MSA: 43, 71].

"7/27/1780. Francis Shepard, Lt. July 27, 1780. Commissions issued to the following Officers appointed to Command the Regim^t Extra raised in Virtue of 'An Act entitled a Supplement to the Act to procure Recruits to comple'te the Battalions of this

State in the service of the United States and to raise an Additional Reg^t if necessary, and an Act to expedite the raising an Additional Battalion of Regulars'" (MSA: 43, 234–235). "Francis Shepard in the room of V. Burgess promoted. Commissions issued to fill up the vacancies in the Regiment Extra. September 1, 1780" (MSA: 43, 272–273).

"Ordered that the said Treasurer pay to Capt. Francis Shepard Two Pounds, nineteen shillings of the new Emission in lieu of one hundred and Eighteen Pounds due p Acc^t passed by the Dep^y Aud. October 19, 1780" (MSA: 43, 333).

"Ordered that the western shore Treasurer pay Captain Francis Shepard and Lieut Charles Magruder of the Extra Regiment, each, Sixty pounds in lieu of Twenty pounds Specie in part of their Accounts passed by the Aud. General. April 26, 1781" (MSA: 45, 415).

Deed from "Francis Sheppard, commonly called Capt. Francis Sheppard, son and heir at law to John Sheppard dec'd of Charles County, planter to Colonel John Hoskins Stone of Charles County for 500 lbs. all that tract of land in Durham Parish in Charles County called Middle Green Enlarged originally on May 2, 1774 granted to John Sheppard, being a resurvey of Middle Green containing 155 ac. Wit: Dan Jenifer and George Dent. Mary Ann Sheppard, the wife and relict of the late John Sheppard dec'd relinquished her right of dower to the within land, she being left by the devise of her sd. late husband in consideration thereof, to hold and enjoy during her natural life, the two tracts called Linn and Linnshin which was exchanged for the sd. land called "Middle Green Enlarged." Recorded July 17, 1790.[36]

Private Andrew Green Simms enlisted January 24, 1776 (MSA: 18, 6). No further records have been found for this soldier.

Private James Simms, Jr. enlisted January 24, 1776 (MSA: 18, 6). No further records have been found for this soldier.

Corporal James Simms, Sr. enlisted January 24, 1776. He was shown absent, on furlough on May 23, 1776 (MSA: 18, 5).

Ensign James Simms, First Regiment, reenlisted December 10, 1776, and rose to the rank of first lieutenant by May 27, 1778. On September 16, 1778, he was taken prisoner at the Battle of Philips Heights and was held until January 1780. He did not rejoin his regiment.[37]

On January 2, 1813, the treasurer of the Western Shore was ordered to "pay to James Semmes, of Charles county, late a second lieutenant in the revolutionary war, or to his order annually in quarterly payments, during his life, a sum of money equal to the half pay of a second lieutenant" (MSA: 618, 249).

It should not be construed that James Simms, Jr. and James Simms, Sr. were father and son. These terms were used to denote who of the two men was younger and who was older to keep their identities separate.

Private Thomas Simpson enlisted January 24, 1776. He enlisted in the First Regiment on May 28, 1777, was promoted to corporal on August 1, 1777, and was discharged on January 5, 1780 (MSA: 18, 5, 160).

On January 2, 1813, the treasurer of the Western Shore was directed "to pay to Thomas Simpson, late a corporal in the revolutionary war, or to his order, a sum of money annually in quarterly payments, equal to the half pay of a corporal, as a further remuneration for those services rendered his country in her struggle for liberty and independence" (MSA: 618, 249).

Private John Skipper enlisted January 24, 1776. He reenlisted in the First Regiment on December 10, 1776. He was discharged in August 1777 and it was noted that he had died (MSA: 18, 6, 160).

Private Alban Smith enlisted January 24, 1776. This is undoubtedly the same man as Private Alvin Smith who is shown to have enlisted on December 10, 1776 and discharged on March 5, 1777, with the notation that he had died. Private Smith is presumed to have been taken prisoner at the battle (MSA: 18, 6, 159).

Cadet Charles Smith enlisted January 24, 1776 (MSA: 18, 5). "Smith, Charles (Md). 2d Lieutenant 1st Maryland, 10th December, 1776; 1st Lieutenant, 20th February, 1778; Captain-Lieutenant, 1st August, 1779; resigned 18th February, 1780 (Died 1822). Widow applied for pension."[38]

"July 27, 1780. Charles Smith, Capt. Commissions issued to the following Officers appointed to Command the Regim^t Extra raised in Virtue of 'An Act entitled a Supplement to the Act to procure Recruits to complete the Battalions of this State in the service of the United States and to raise an Additional Reg^t if necessary, and an Act to expedite the raising an Additional Battalion of Regulars'" (MSA: 43, 234–235).

"Passed March 8, 1833. Resolution in favor of Mary Smith, of the District of Columbia. Resolved by the General Assembly of Maryland, That the Treasurer of the Western Shore, be, and he is hereby authorised and required to pay to Mary Smith, (widow of Captain Charles Smith,) of the District of Columbia, or to her order during life, in quarter yearly payments, a sum of money equal to the half pay of a Captain, in consideration of the services rendered by her husband during the revolutionary war" (MSA:210, 348).

Charles Smith married Mary Bowling on January 19, 1782, in Charles County. Their only child, Mary Smith, married Raphael H. Boarman, had four children, and predeceased her mother, dying in 1836. On September 17, 1847, Horatio Dyer, who had married Mary Rose Boarman, the Smith's granddaughter, applied "to recover the balance of the pension due Mrs. Smith, being the difference between that of a Lieutenant and a Captain's pay."[39] "I hereby certify that on the nineteenth day of

October in the year one thousand eight-hundred and forty three I buried Mary Smith for whose funeral escpences [sic] I was paid by Ninian Beall. November 7th 1850. Signed by Wm King."[40]

Private Edward Smith enlisted January 27, 1776 (MSA: 18, 6). No further records have been found for this soldier.

Private John Smith enlisted January 24, 1776 (MSA:18, 7). He reenlisted in the First Regiment on December 10, 1776, and was discharged on December 14, 1782. Another discharge date of December 27, 1779, is also shown (MSA: 18, 160).

On February 19, 1819, the treasurer of the Western Shore was directed "to pay unto John Smith, of Charles county, late a revolutionary soldier, or to his order, annually, in quarterly payments, during life, a sum of money equal to the half pay of a private" (MSA: 637, 149).

Private Richard Smith enlisted February 2, 1776 (MSA: 18, 7). He reenlisted in the First Regiment on December 10, 1776, and was discharged on December 27, 1779 (MSA: 18, 159).

Richard Smith, then a resident of Rowan County, North Carolina, applied for a pension on May 20, 1833. He deposed that he was born in Charles County, Maryland in 1755 and that he was living there at the time of enlistment. He deposed that he was in the battles of Long Island, Princeton, Germantown, and Stony Point. He gave his wife's name as Elizabeth and said they had been married in January 1785 in Prince George's County, Maryland, and that they had moved to North Carolina 21 years before. This soldier died on June 13, 1840. His pension file includes certification by John B. Brooke that a marriage license was issued in Prince George's County on January 12, 1786, to Richard Smith and Elizabeth Church.[41]

Elizabeth Smith, widow of Richard Smith, applied for a pension on January 2, 1844. She was then 79 years of age and was still living in Rowan County, North Carolina.

Private Thomas Smith enlisted January 24, 1776 (MSA: 18, 6). No further records have been found for this soldier.

Private John Smoot enlisted February 3, 1776 (MSA: 18, 7). No further records have been found for this soldier.

Private William Smoot enlisted January 24, 1776 (MSA: 18, 5). He had been promoted to sergeant by the time of his reenlistment in the First Regiment on December 10, 1776. He was discharged on December 27, 1779 (MSA: 18, 159).

> January 26, 1780: [Council to Hon'ble The Board of War]. Gentlemen Brigadier General Smallwood some time past, wrote us.... "I have enclosed you a List of such Sergeants and others of the first Brigade, who have been recommended for

Commissions, by their Field Officers and Captains." Here follows the List ... William Smoot of the first... (see page 63 for the complete record) [MSA: 43, 71].

Private Richard Speake was a bit older than most of his fellow enlisted men. He had been married at least 10 years prior to the war. He enlisted on January 24, 1776 (MSA: 18, 6).

Less than three weeks after the battle, Richard Speake was home in Charles County, where he executed his will on September 14, 1776. Although it will probably never be known for sure, the assumption is that he was severely wounded at the battle and never fully recovered. Private Speake died in Charles County in November 1779. In previous listings of the soldiers of The Maryland 400, this soldier's surname had been erroneously given as Sheake.

Private George Thomas enlisted January 24, 1776. He reenlisted on December 10, 1776, and was discharged on March 7, 1777, when it was noted that he died (MSA: 18, 6, 168).

Private James Thompson enlisted January 24, 1776. As Sergeant James Thompson, he reenlisted in the First Regiment on December 10, 1776, and was discharged on December 27, 1779 (MSA: 18, 6, 168).

> January 26, 1780: [Council to Hon'ble The Board of War]. Gentlemen Brigadier General Smallwood some time past, wrote us.... "I have enclosed you a List of such Sergeants and others of the first Brigade, who have been recommended for Commissions, by their Field Officers and Captains." Here follows the List ... James Thompson ... of the first ... (see page 63 for the complete record) [MSA: 43, 71].

Private Samuel Thompson enlisted January 24, 1776. He reenlisted on December 10, 1776, and was discharged on April 10, 1777. It was noted that he had died April 10, 1777 (MSA: 18, 6, 168).

On September 2, 1777 letters of administration on the estate of Samuel Thompson were granted to his brother, George Thompson. Private Thompson was the son of John Thompson (died 1756) and his wife, Ann, of Charles County, Maryland.

Private Samuel Vermillion enlisted February 6, 1776 (MSA: 18, 7). He reenlisted in the First Regiment on December 10, 1776, and is shown to have "deserted, joined" on March 12, 1777. His first name was given erroneously as Saul (MSA: 18,172). He is shown having served from August 1, 1780, to November 15, 1783 (MSA: 18, 559).

This soldier applied for a pension on April 11, 1833, while a resident of Macon County, North Carolina. He deposed that he was born on April 6, 1755, in Charles County, Maryland.

Private Vermillion stated that he was in the Battle of Long Island "from said battle, [we] were marched across King's Bridge to the battle at White Plains." In November 1776 he was taken sick and was in hospitals in Morristown, Bethlehem, Philadelphia, and finally Annapolis where he was furloughed by General Smallwood to go home and to stay home "'til the time be made known by the public paper to go to headquarters."

The soldier related that he was then taken with smallpox and, after getting well, he started toward headquarters in Philadelphia, but found himself weak and not able to travel by land so he went onboard a naval trading vessel as a passenger. While enroute, the vessel was accosted by a British warship and Private Vermillion was taken prisoner. For 18 months, he was confined on a naval vessel. In April 1779 he managed to escape while the ship was enroute from Savannah, Georgia, to Petersburg.

In 1781 he joined the company under the command of Captain John Moulton and Colonel Kinion in Duplin County, North Carolina. He served with the North Carolina troops for eight months. At Bacon's Bridge, South Carolina, he joined the Maryland Regiment commanded by Colonel Stewart, under Captain Winchester and served until peace was declared in 1783. He died on February 8, 1837.[42]

Private Henry Walworth, Drummer enlisted March 6, 1776, and was noted to be "sick in barracks" (MSA: 18, 5). No further records have been found for this soldier.

Private John Ward enlisted January 24, 1776 (MSA: 18, 6). No further records have been found for this soldier.

Private Samuel Wheatley enlisted January 24, 1776. As Corporal Samuel Wheatley of the First Regiment, he reenlisted on December 10, 1776, and was discharged on August 11, 1777 "prisr. war" (MSA: 18, 6, 173).

Private William Wheatley enlisted January 24, 1776. As Corporal William Wheatley of the First Regiment, he reenlisted on December 10, 1776, and was discharged on June 28, 1778, "killed" (MSA: 18, 6, 173). "William Wheatley, Cpl., 1 MD, killed June 28, 1778."[43]

The names of four soldiers, who were originally listed, have been removed from the roster of the First Company. They are:

Private Clement Edelen is shown as having enlisted January 24, 1776 (MSA: 18, 6). Edelen, however, deposed twice in 1818 and 1823 that he did not enter the service until 1777, therefore, he was not one of The Maryland 400.

Private James Hogg enlisted January 27, 1776. His surname was erroneously spelled Hoge (MSA: 18, 6). By May 29, 1776, Private James Hogg had been transferred to the Fifth Company, under the command of Capt. Nathaniel Ramsey. While this soldier fought at the Battle of Long Island, he did so as a member of the Fifth Company and therefore was not one of The Maryland 400.

Cadet Samuel Jones originally enlisted in the First Company, but on July 29, 1776, he was commissioned as a second lieutenant in the company commanded by Captain Thomas Hanson (MSA: 18, 31). He was, therefore, not one of The Maryland 400.

Cadet Henry Ridgely, originally listed as a member of the First Company, was commissioned a first lieutenant and transferred by July 26, 1776, to a company based in Anne Arundel County (MSA: 18, 39). He was, therefore, not one of The Maryland 400.

Summary

Seventy-five soldiers were originally shown as enlisted in the First Company. Of those, 71 are presumed to have gone into battle (excluding the four men listed above). Forty-nine of these men are known to have survived (including Bowie) and 21 are unaccounted for (excluding Daniel Bowie who was taken prisoner on the day of the battle and died at a later date while in captivity). William Courts and James Fernandis were also taken prisoner, but they survived.

Second Company

Most of the men of this company were from Prince George's County, home of many revolutionary patriots, including John Rogers, a member of the Continental Congress, and Daniel Carroll, one of the signers of the Declaration of Independence.

Prince George's County was established by the Maryland General Assembly in 1695 from parts of Calvert and Charles Counties. It originally included all or part of the current area of Frederick and Montgomery Counties and the District of Columbia. It was named for Prince George of Denmark, husband of England's Queen Anne.

Captain Patrick Sim was commissioned captain of the Second Company, Smallwood's regiment on January 20, 1776. In January 1777 he was promoted to major in the First Regiment, then commanded by Colonel John Hoskins Stone. In March 1777 he was promoted to lieutenant colonel.

Captain Sim was the son of Colonel Joseph Sim and his first wife, Catherine Murdock. He was the grandson of Dr. Patrick Sim of Kilcairn, Scotland, who is said to have fled to Maryland from Scotland where he was implicated in the Scottish rebellion of 1715.[1]

Patrick Sim married Mary Carroll on July 11, 1777, in Prince George's County. Mary died in 1784. On August 28, 1787, Patrick Sim married Arianna Henderson.

In 1800 Patrick Sim posted several notices in the *National Intelligencer* stating that he had applied to the General Assembly of Maryland for an Act of Insolvency. This may have led to the breakup of his marriage. In 1807 Patrick and Arianna Sim applied to Maryland's General Assembly asking that their marriage be annulled. The marriage was officially annulled on January 18, 1808.

On April 9, 1818 Patrick Sim, a resident of Prince George's County, applied for a pension, deposing:

> ... that he was appointed a Captain in the fall of the year 1775 in the regiment commanded by Colonel Smallwood of Regulars, was on the recruiting service till February then joined said regiment in Annapolis, was ordered to New York in July, arrived at Headquarters near said place in August, was in Battles of Long Island, Morrisania Heights, White Plains, Mamaroneck, Brunswick, and Trenton and many other small affairs. In January 1777 returned to Annapolis to recruit, was then

"Bellefield." This was the boyhood home of Captain Patrick Sim. The house was built about 1720 by his grandfather, Dr. Patrick Sim, who fled Scotland after the 1715 rebellion (photograph and information courtesy the Maryland Historical Trust).

promoted to a Major in the same Regiment then commanded by Colonel Stone, in March promoted to Lieutenant Colonel in the same regiment, in May marched to join the Army at Buttermilk Falls in Jersey, in July ordered to return to Maryland by Col. Stone to superintend the recruiting service for said regiment, in August resigned. This deponent further states in the several Battles above stated he received no other injury than a violent bruise from a soldier falling against him.[2]

In a letter dated July 29, 1915, from G. M. Saltzgater, commissioner of the Revolutionary War section, to Mrs. Florence M. Thompson, the commissioner recited the service performed by Patrick Sim, adding that he had received "no other injury than a violent bruise from a soldier (whose head was shot off by a cannon ball at the battle of Long Island) falling against him."

His request for a pension was approved, but Patrick Sim would only live another few months, dying on January 7, 1819. Colonel Patrick Sim is believed to be buried at Sim's Delight in Prince George's County, Maryland.[3]

Private James Adams enlisted April 6, 1776 (MSA: 18, 7). "Cpl. James Adams, 1st Regt., enlisted December 10, 1776; discharged September 13, 1777. Missing" (MSA: 18, 78).

Private Michael Barnitt enlisted February 5, 1776 (MSA: 18, 8). No further records have been found for this soldier.

Lt. John Hancock Beanes was commissioned as second lieutenant on January 3, 1776 (MSA: 18, 7). On July 9, 1776, he was appointed first lieutenant (MSA: 12, 16).

As Captain J. H. Beanes, he reenlisted in the First Regiment on December 10, 1776 and resigned on December 2, 1777 (MSA: 18, 81).

After the war, Captain Beanes was married twice. His first wife was Henrietta Dent, widow of John Dyer, whom he married in 1785. In 1796 he married Harriett Sothoron of St. Mary's County, widow of William Clagett.

Captain Beanes died sometime prior to March 20, 1811, when letters of administration on his personal estate were granted to his widow, Harriett Beanes.

Dr. William Beanes, brother of Lt. John Hancock Beanes, also served during the Revolutionary War as a physician in the American hospital in Philadelphia. Dr. Beanes would make a place for himself in history, not during this war, but in the War of 1812. To protect official Maryland records from burning by British forces, Maryland officials carefully packed and shipped them to Upper Marlboro, where they were to remain under the care of Dr. Beanes. As it so happened, Annapolis was never invaded by British forces, but Upper Marlboro was on three different occasions. The last time was immediately after the British burned Washington, D.C., on August 13, 1814.

Just prior to the departure of the British forces from Upper Marlboro, Dr. Beanes arrested two drunken British soldiers and threw them in jail. One of the men escaped and reported the incident to his superiors. A detachment of British soldiers returned, freed the other soldier, and then arrested Dr. Beanes, who was placed onboard one of the British warships.

The people of Upper Marlboro enlisted the help of Francis Scott Key, then a well-known Washington lawyer, to secure the release of Dr. Beanes from the British. Key traveled to Baltimore and was able to obtain Dr. Beanes's release; however, both men were detained on ship overnight as the British shelled Ft. McHenry. It was this event that inspired Key to write "The Star Spangled Banner."[4]

John Hancock Beanes and William Beanes were the sons of William Beanes (1726–1801) and his wife, Mary Bowie (1726–1792) of Prince George's County, Maryland. They were the great-grandsons of Christopher Beanes, a native of Scotland, who arrived in Maryland in 1671 and his wife, Ann Brooke (daughter of Robert Brooke and Mary Mainwaring of Delabrooke Manor, St. Mary's County, Maryland). They also had Scottish blood by way of their mother, Mary Bowie whose father was John Bowie, born in 1688 in Scotland. The Beanes brothers were first cousins to Lieutenant Daniel Bowie of the First Company.

Private Edward Blacklock enlisted February 10, 1776 (MSA: 18, 8). No further military records have been found for this soldier. He was the son of Thomas Blacklock (1716–1790) and his wife, Charity Lanham (1718–1781) of Prince George's County, Maryland.

Private Christopher Brumbargher enlisted April 9, 1776. His name was given as Christr. Brumbargher (MSA: 18, p. 7). No further records have been found for this soldier.

Private Vachel Burgess enlisted February 29, 1776 (MSA: 18, 8). He was born in All Hallow's Parish, Anne Arundel County, Maryland, on May 9, 1756 and was one of the six sons of Captain Joseph Burgess and Elizabeth Dorsey who served during the Revolutionary War along with their father. In the past his name has been given erroneously both as Veach Burgess and as Basil Burgess.

Corporal Vachel Burgess, First Regiment, was shown as ensign on April 17, 1777 (MSA:18, 81). He was commissioned as a second lieutenant on February 20, 1778, and resigned on August 22, 1779.[5]

Vachel Burgess reentered the service on July 27, 1780, with the rank of captain. "Vachel Burgess. Commissions issued to the following Officers appointed to Command the Regim^t Extra raised in Virtue of 'An Act entitled a Supplement to the Act to procure Recruits to complete the Battalions of this State in the service of the United States and to raise an Additional Reg^t if necessary, and an Act to expedite the raising an Additional Battalion of Regulars'" (MSA: 43, 234–235).

Captain Burgess married Rebecca Dorsey, daughter of Thomas Dorsey and Mary Warfield, on October 1, 1782 at All Hallow's Parish, Anne Arundel County, Maryland.

On November 18, 1808, the following report of the General Assembly was recorded in response to a petition filed by Vachel Burgess:

> The committee to whom was referred the petition of Vachel Burgess, of Anne-Arundel county, report, that they find, from documents herewith exhibited, the said petitioner entered into the service of his country at an early period of the revolutionary war, that he was appointed an ensign in the second regiment of the Maryland line on the 17th of April, 1777, and that he was afterwards promoted to a lieutenancy, which commission he resigned on the 22d of August. 1779, from the circumstance alleged by him, and which your committee fully believe, of an officer of inferior rank having received a commission of a date prior to his. Your committee further report, that it also appears from the documents, the said Vachel Burgess was appointed a captain in the extra regiment raised in the year 1780, in which capacity he served until the said regiment was deranged, and that during the whole of his service he behaved in a manner highly honourable to himself, advantageous to his country, and truly characteristic of the American patriot; that the said petitioner is now far advanced in life, with a wife and nine children dependent on him for support, borne down with infirmities consequent on the labour and fatigue he

sustained at an early period of his life, while fighting the battles of his country, and in possession of pecuniary resources too narrow to afford a comfortable maintenance to himself, and those most dear to him; they therefore recommend the following resolution: Resolved that the treasurer of the western shore be and he is hereby directed and required to pay unto Vachel Burgess, of the county of Anne-Arundel, late a lieutenant in the Maryland line during the revolutionary war, a sum of money equal to half pay as a lieutenant, annually, in quarterly payments, during his life, as a further reward to those invaluable services which he rendered his country in securing her liberty and independence [MSA: 556, 15–16].

In November 1810, Vachel Burgess again petitioned the Maryland Legislature asking for commutation in lieu of half pay for life. "Resolved that the Treasurer of the Western Shore pay to the said Vachel Burgess four years full pay as a Captain free from interest as to full compensation for his services during the late Revolutionary War" (MSA: 599, 100).

Captain Burgess died on March 30, 1824. His obituary appeared in the April 12, 1824, issue of the *Baltimore Patriot*.

> Another Revolutionary Hero gone. Died at his residence in Anne Arundel county, on the 30th ult. Captain Vachel Burgis, in the 68th year of his age, a gallant soldier of the revolutionary army, attached for seven years to the Maryland line; he evinced a bold and heroic spirit, in the several actions in which the corps was engaged — he particularly distinguished himself, and obtained the eulogies of his commanding officers at Gilford Court House, Eutaw Springs, and in the unfortunate battle of Camden, under Baron de Kalb. His heroism as a soldier, in achieving the independence and liberty he so long lived to enjoy, found an accompanying luster in his virtues, as a citizen and a man. He was upright in his dealings, hospitable, cheerful, and kind hearted, intelligent in conversation, pious in his life, and deeply lamented in his death by a numerous family, and a large circle of friends.

Private Benjamin Burroughs enlisted March 10, 1776 (MSA: 18, 8). No further records have been found for this soldier.

Private Charles Burroughs enlisted March 11, 1776 (MSA: 18, 8). No further records have been found for this soldier.

Private James Byzch enlisted February 6, 1776 (MSA: 18, 8). No further records have been found for this soldier.

Private Edmund Carroll enlisted March 6, 1776, "sick." His name was given as Edmd. Carroll (MSA: 18, 9). No further records have been found for this soldier.

Sergeant Peter Clarke enlisted March 7, 1776 (MSA: 18, 7). On February 20, 1777, he was commissioned a second lieutenant in the Third Maryland Regiment and, on July 13, 1779, he resigned.[6]

In 1778 and 1779, he was assigned to recruit soldiers. On February 24, 1778, the treasurer was ordered to "pay to Peter Clark of the Third Regiment of Continental Troops one hundred and twenty Dollars to be expended in the recruiting service and charged to that Regiment" (MSA: 16, 519).

By the time of his resignation, Peter Clarke had served over three years in the army but in 1780 he was drafted to serve yet again. He objected, saying he was in poor health. Maryland's only relief was to allow him to hire a substitute.

In apparent desperation, he wrote a letter to Governor Lee on July 26, 1780 saying:

> Sir The bearer is an Invalid who had a Furlow from Colonel Nicola some time before the Troops came down here & has been very ill ever since he got his Furlow lengthen'd by Genl Mordecai Gist which he has lost it was lengthened for four months on Acct of his inability to march to Philadelphia he is blind of his right Eye & has got a very bad leg occasion'd by the bite of a Dog there has been People here to take him up as a Diserter as the furlow he had from the Invalid Colonel is out and the one he had from Genl Gist is lost which wou'd not be out for some time He is not able to walk five miles at this time if you wou'd be so good as to give him a furlow for some time I'll be answerable for him as I am sure he wou'd be willing to march any time he was able your Excellency will confer a particuar obligation on me if you will let me know if an Officer who has served 3 years in the Continental Service and resign'd on Acc^t of losing his health is obliged to contribute in a Class of Militia to find a Substitute [MSA: 45, 29].

The Council of Maryland responded on July 27, 1780, in saying, "By the late Acts of Assembly to procure Troops, your Case is not considered and, though there may be a Hardship in your being compelled to contribute your Quota, to procure a Substitute; yet we cannot see how it is to be avoided, as you are neither expressly nor impliedly exempted by the Laws" (MSA: 43, 235).

Private Milburn Coe enlisted February 3, 1776. His surname at the time of enlistment was shown erroneously as Cox (MSA: 18, 7). Corporal Milburn Coe was discharged on December 27, 1779 (MSA: 18, 91).

Milburn Coe was born in Prince George's County, Maryland, and was the son of John Coe and Mary Milburn. He married Mary Tongue on January 8, 1783. By 1807 Milburn Coe had moved his family to Adams County, Ohio, where his name appeared on the tax lists in 1807 and 1808.

While some of his descendants claim that Milburn Coe died in Prince George's County in 1812, it appears that he actually died in Brown County, Ohio, and was buried in an "old cemetery near [a] farm, Eagle Creek, Brown Co., Ohio."[7]

Sergeant Alexius Conner enlisted March 3, 1776, "sick in barracks" (MSA: 18, 7). No further records have been found for this soldier.

Private Thomas Connor enlisted March 6, 1776 (MSA: 18, 8). He reenlisted in the First Regiment on December 10, 1776, and was discharged on March 27, 1779 (MSA: 18, 91).

Cadet Walter Brooke Cox is shown as enlisted, but no date provided. It was noted that he was on furlough, May 25, 1776 (MSA: 18, 7).

He was commissioned as an ensign on July 9, 1776, and at this time, his name was given as Walter Brook Cox (MSA: 18, 16). By April 17, 1777, he had been commissioned as a first lieutenant and is shown to have also resigned by that date (MSA: 16, 216).

Walter Brooke Cox was the son of John Cox and Sarah Brooke (daughter of Walter Brooke and Mary Ashcom Greenfield). He married Ann Hollyday in Prince George's County on November 19, 1778. Their only child was Sarah Ann Cox, who married Lt. Richard Harwood of the U.S. Navy on October 28, 1799. Sarah died in November 1800 just a little over a year after her marriage. He was a direct descendant of Robert Brooke (1602–1665). "Robert Brooke, Esquire, arrived out of England on the 29th day of June, 1650, in the forty-eighth year of his age with his wife and ten children. He was the first that did seat on the Patuxent [River], about twenty miles up the river, at De La Brooke. Besides his own family, he brought at his own cost and charge, twenty-eight other persons. De La Brooke, containing two thousand acres, which formed the chief seat of the Brooke colony, was erected into a manor, with the right of Court Baron and Court Leet, and his oldest son, Baker Brooke, made Lord of the Manor"[8]

Walter Brooke Cox appears to have fallen on hard times as in 1799 a chancery court case was filed involving "the insolvent estate of Walter B. Cox of Prince George's County."[9] He died prior to April 14, 1801, when administration of his estate was granted to Thomas Contee.[10]

Private Thomas Daws enlisted May 10, 1776 (MSA: 18, 9). No further records have been found for this soldier.

Private John Edelen enlisted March 6, 1776. His surname was spelled Edelin (MSA: 18, 6). He reenlisted in the First Regiment on December 10, 1776, and was discharged on December 27, 1779. His surname was spelled Eadlin (MSA: 18, 106).

Corporal John Elson enlisted January 29, 1776 (MSA: 18, 7). No further records have been found for this soldier.

Private William Evans enlisted February 23, 1776 (MSA: 18, 8). He reenlisted in the First Regiment on December 10, 1776 and was discharged on November 27, 1777, with the notation that he had deserted (MSA: 18, 106).

On April 4, 1782, the Western Shore treasurer was ordered to pay to "Capt Robert Denny fifteen pounds of the Bills emitted under the Act for the Emission of Bills of Credit &ca to be delivered over to John Vansant, James Smith and William Evans soldiers in the Maryland Line, lately returned from Charles Town, each, five pounds" (MSA: 48, 120).

Private William Evans was invalided November 15, 1783, and it was noted that he served from August 1, 1780, to November 13, 1783 (MSA: 18, 533).

William Evans, Private, Revolutionary Army, an invalid pensioner, was placed on the rolls beginning March 4, 1789, at the rate of $40 per annum. "He was the only William Evans in Maryland (under any spelling of that surname) found on the Revolutionary War records of this Bureau. His papers were destroyed either when the War Office burned in November 1800 or when the British burned the City of Washington in 1814."[11]

Private Elisha Everett enlisted March 11, 1776. His surname was erroneously spelled as Everit (MSA: 18, 8). He reenlisted in the First Regiment on March 12, 1778, and was discharged on April 18, 1779 (MSA: 18, 106).

The reenlistment of Private Everett was not entirely voluntary. On March 7, 1778, the council sent a letter addressed to the attorney general of Maryland or the prosecutor of the Montgomery County court in which they stated: "Sir, Information being received that one Elisha Everitt who was inlisted in the Service of this State in the Regiment commanded by Smallwood is a prisoner in Montgomery Jail charged with Horse stealing, you are desired and Authorised to stay any Criminal prosecution against the said Elisha Everitt of or for the said Offence and accordingly enter a Noli prosequi in his favor on his enlisting into the first Maryland Continental Regiment now Commanded by Col Stone" (MSA: 16, 529).

Ensign Henry Gaither received his commission on January 3, 1776 (MSA: 18, 7). By the time of the battle, he had achieved the rank of first lieutenant.

Henry Gaither, son of Henry Gaither and Martha Ridgely, was born in 1751. He is said to have served in every major battle of the Revolutionary War with the exception of Monmouth. By the end of the war, he was a brevet major. In 1791, Henry Gaither was commissioned as major in the "levies of 1791," serving under General St. Clair against the Miami Indians.[12]

Most people believe that hostilities ended with the official end of the Revolutionary War in 1783; however, the British and their Indian allies continued to raid and illegally hold military posts in American territory. It would not be until 1794 when General Anthony Wayne and the Legion of the United States defeated British and Indian forces at the British garrison of Fort Miamis that all British forces were finally withdrawn from U.S. territory.

The Legion of the United States was abolished and disbanded in 1796 when the Army of the United States was officially created. At this time, Major Henry Gaither was shown as having served in the Maryland Third Sub-Legion.[13] In 1793 Gaither was appointed lieutenant colonel of the Third Infantry, serving until June 1, 1802. In the interval he was placed in command of Fort Adams (Mississippi), which at that time was a port of entry to the United States.[14] In 1802, Henry Gaither was honorably discharged from the army and returned to private life. Little is known about him after that date except that he was called as a witness for the defense in the treason trial of Aaron Burr in 1807.[15]

Colonel Gaither died on June 22, 1811.

> Died on the 22nd inst. Col. Henry Gaither, in the 61st year of his age. This valuable man was among the few remaining officers of the revolutionary army. His services in the cause of his country were unusually severe, having been in every battle (Monmouth excepted) which was fought by the American army. His zeal for the honor of his country did not cease upon the accomplishment of our independence. His tried patriotism and bravery induced the government to solicit his usefulness against the Indians upon our frontier — he obeyed, and was always the American Gaither! He next was required to command on the southern frontier and here his discipline, his integrity and his virtues were not less conspicuous.
>
> Worn down by a series of hardships, his bad health obliged him to retire from the service of his country and seek a respite in the bosom of his friends. Here it was his virtues were conspicuous in every thing which adorns a private citizen. He threw off the discipline of the camp and adopted the soft and endearing offices of brother, neighbor and friend. He was interred with the honors of war, and with the respect which was indeed justly his due. — Spirit of '76.[16]

Private Peter Gallworth enlisted January 31, 1776 (MSA 18: 8). No further records have been found for this soldier.

Private John Grant enlisted February 8, 1776 (MSA: 18, 8). No further records have been found for this soldier.

Private Amos Green enlisted April 8, 1776 (MSA: 18, 7). He reenlisted in the First Regiment on December 10, 1776. No date of discharge was given (MSA: 18, 112). He was in the service from August 1, 1780, through July 10, 1784 (MSA: 18, 535).

Private Paul Hagarty enlisted February 13, 1776 (MSA: 18, 8). He reenlisted in the First Regiment on December 10, 1776 (record shows December 10, 1777, but it is believed to be an error) and he was discharged December 17__ (no year given, but it was probably 1777). His surname was given as Hagarthy (MSA:18, 117).

Private Hagarty was disabled at the Battle of Brandywine on September 11, 1777 (MSA: 18, 630). "The General Assembly in 1778 passed an act for the relief of the maimed officers, soldiers, and seamen from Maryland engaged in the Revolutionary cause. Under its provisions those in necessitous circumstances were entitled to half-pay, and the children of those deceased to certain annuities. The records of the Orphans' Court show that the children and wives of the following soldiers from Western Maryland availed themselves of this act: ... Paul Haggerty, disabled."[17] "Pvt. Paul Hagarty, 1st Regt., disabled at Brandywine; invalid pension commenced on December 27, 1783 and ceased November 1, 1789."[18]

Private Hagerty was born in St. John's Parish, Prince George's County, Maryland, on February 23, 1751–1752. He was the son of John Hagerty, a native of Cork County, Ireland.

Paul Hagerty married Eleanor Magruder on May 2, 1784, in Frederick County, Maryland. Shortly thereafter, they moved to Hardy County, Virginia (now West Virginia), where he died in 1805.

Private William Heyder enlisted February 14, 1776. His name was given as Willm. Heyder (MSA: 18, 8). No further records have been found for this soldier.

Private Jacob Holland enlisted February 29, 1776 (MSA: 18, 8). No further record appears for Private Holland until February 19, 1819, when the treasurer of the Western Shore was directed to "...pay unto Jacob Holland, late a revolutionary, now a commissioned officer, or to his order, annually, in quarterly payments, during life, a sum of money equal to the half pay of a corporal of dragoons" (MSA: 192, 3016).

On July 27, 1832, while a resident of Monongalia County, Virginia, Jacob Holland, aged 79 years, deposed that he was enlisted for and during the dispute between Great Britain and America about the 1st of March 1776 at a place now called Unity in Montgomery County, Maryland by Ensign Henry Gaither of Patrick Sim's company in the First Maryland Regiment commanded by Colonel William Smallwood. In a second deposition dated November 29, 1834, Jacob Holland deposed that he was born in March 1754 and said that he had joined the First Regiment, then at Annapolis, where he remained until the British came to New York:

> My regiment marched to New York and found the main army at headquarters; remained there for weeks and then marched to Long Island and joined General Stirling. The day after we arrived, a battle was fought in which the American army was defeated; *it was nearly cut to pieces*. Remained at Long Island several days throwing up breast works, finally after spikeing the cannons, we retreated after night on into New York. We were pursued by the British but not one taken. We marched towards Ft. Washington and on the way at Harlem Heights we were again attacked by the British. We retreated across King Bridge to Stony Point where we had another skirmish.
>
> From the last mentioned place we marched to the White Plains at which place another engagement took place in which were again unsuccessful. We then crossed the North River on into Jersey and retreated before the British army to Trenton, then crossed the Delaware in Pennsylvania and lay up and down the river until Christmas 1776.
>
> We crossed the Delaware at a place called Farley's Ferry and marched down the river to Trenton and captured the Hessians. I was not in this latter engagement. I had left the army on furlough having been in this company 10 months in which I was a private. At this time I was anxious to join the Cavalry and applied to General Smallwood for permission. He agreed that I might by furnishing a man in my place. I did so.
>
> In May 1777 I enlisted under Capt. V. A. Stinson [should be Vachel Denton

Howard] of Maryland of the 6th troops for three years. I enlisted as a corporal. The first campaign in war was at the head of the Bay in 1777 and 1778. We wintered in Trenton. In the spring we then scattered along the shore watching the movements of the enemy. In this service, we were under Capt. Manifold. We remained in this vicinity and in the winter quarters at Lancaster. In the spring we returned to Jersey and in the course of the summer were in New York and Connecticut. In the following spring my term of service expired and I was discharged.

Jacob Holland was the son of Jacob Holland, Sr. and his wife, Elizabeth. He married Mary Smith circa 1786 in Montgomery County, Maryland.

He died on September 17, 1838, while on a visit to a son in Harrison County, Virginia. The Holland family Bible says that at the time of his death he was 84 years, six months, and 12 days old.[131]

Private Thomas Horson, Fifer enlisted February 3, 1776 (MSA: 18, 87). He reenlisted in the First Regiment as a drummer on December 10, 1776, and was discharged on December 27, 1779 (MSA: 18, 116).

Private Philip Jenkins enlisted January 3, 1776. His surname was erroneously spelled as Jinkins (MSA: 18, 8). As "Private Phil. Jenkins, 1st Regt." he reenlisted on December 10, 1776, and was discharged on September 16, 1778. The record is somewhat confusing as there is not another enlistment shown, but he was discharged again on December 27, 1779, at which time he was shown as a prisoner (MSA: 18, 125). He was back in the service by November 29, 1781, when Philip Jenkins of Montgomery County, among others, "to serve 'till the 10th December next are hereby Discharged" (MSA: 48, 7).

On February 13, 1836, the Maryland General Assembly passed the following: "Resolution in favor of Sarah Jenkins. Resolved by the General Assembly of Maryland, That the Treasurer of the Western Shore, be, and he is hereby authorised to pay Sarah Jenkins, widow of Philip Jenkins, or order, out of any unappropriated money in the Treasury, the half pay of a private during her life, as a further remuneration for his services during the revolution" (MSA: 537, 357).

Private Richard Johnson enlisted March 5, 1776 (MSA: 18, 8). No further records have been found for this soldier.

Private Edward Jones enlisted April 19, 1776 (MSA: 18, 9). He reenlisted in the First Regiment on February 10, 1777, and was discharged on March 13, 1777 with a notation that he had died (MSA: 18, 282).

Private Philip King enlisted February 2, 1776 (MSA: 18, 8). He reenlisted in the First Regiment or December 10, 1776, and was discharged on January 22, 1778. It was noted that he had deserted (MSA: 18, 129).

Private Henry Lanham enlisted February 3, 1776 (MSA: 18, 8). He was born in Prince George's County, Maryland, on July 28, 1761, and died in Braytown, Switzerland County, Indiana, on November 20, 1849. He married Eleanor McKay about 1789.[20]

Private John D. Lanham enlisted February 3, 1776 (MSA: 18, 8). John Downs Lanham was born on August 13, 1758, in Prince George's County. He was the son of Josias Lanham and his wife, Elizabeth. He married Susanna Allen on February 27, 1791. This soldier died in 1801.

On May 3, 1840, Mr. A. D. Hiller of the War Office, in response to a query, wrote the following letter:

> John Lanham served as a private in the First Maryland Regiment and was discharged December 27, 1779 because of total disability. He was placed on the roll of the Virginia Agency on September 4, 1789. In 1826, Mrs. Susanna Lanham stated she was his widow and that he had died 20–22 years before. In 1827 she was living in Annapolis and furnished evidence that she was the administratrix of the estate of John Lanham, late of Charles County, Maryland. In 1827, Henry W. Lanham and Cloe Lanham (relationship not stated) deposed that John Lanham died in the fall of 1801 and that Susanna Lanham took out letters of administration on his estate in 1802. The pension due up to November 21, 1801 (which was assumed to be the date of death of John Lanham) was paid on November 14, 1805 to William Berry for the estate of John Lanham.
>
> In September 1838, William Brown, aged 86 and his wife, Tabitha Brown, age 90 (John Lanham was referred to as a connection in her family) both residents of Washington, D.C., stated that they had lived in Charles County before and during the Revolutionary War and were acquainted with John Lanham. They said that John Lanham had returned to Charles County and about 12 months later, he'd married Susanna (maiden name not shown). They also stated that Susanna had died about four months before the date of their affidavit, leaving two children, John Lanham and Betsy who were then living in Baltimore.
>
> In September, 1838, John Lanham, age 45 and upwards, stated that he was the son of Susanna Lanham, then deceased and he and his sister, Elizabeth (wife of Robert Bier) were the only children of Susanna Lanham. Susanna Lanham died in Baltimore on or about the 15th of May last past.[21]

Private Lanham was a descendant of Josias Lanham, a native of Suffolk, England, who was transported to Maryland as an indentured servant in 1668 at the age of fifteen.

Private Henry Leeke enlisted January 29, 1776 (MSA: 18, 7). At that time his surname was spelled Leek. He reenlisted in the First Regiment on December 10, 1776, and had attained the rank of sergeant by April 17, 1777, when he is shown enlisting yet again. He was discharged on December 10, 1779 (MSA: 18, 131).

On December 5, 1812, Henry Leeke of Montgomery County petitioned the General Assembly "praying that the levy court of said county may be authorized to levy a sum of money for his support" (MSA: 618, 53). His petition was granted on December

14, 1812 when the General Assembly directed that: "...the justices of the levy court of Montgomery county shall be, & they are hereby empowered, at their levy court annually, so long as they shall see cause, to assess and levy on the assessable property of said county, a sum. of money not exceeding forty dollars, for the support and maintenance of the said Henry Leeke, and that the same be collected annually by the collector of Montgomery county, and by him paid to the said Henry Leeke, or his order" (MSA: 618, 52–53).

He died sometime prior to January 9, 1821, when James Brown filed a petition to the General Assembly asking that he be given authority "to receive the pension due to Henry Leeke, deceased, a revolutionary soldier."[22]

The petition of James Brown was granted on February 16, 1821. "RESOLVED, That the treasurer of the western shore be and he is hereby directed, to pay to James Brown, of Montgomery county, or to his order, the sum of ten dollars, which appears to be the balance due Henry Leake, late of Montgomery county, deceased, who was a pensioner of this state" (MSA: 625, 176).

Private Benjamin Lewis, Drummer enlisted January 29, 1776 (MSA: 18, 7). He reenlisted in the First Regiment on December 10, 1776, and was discharged on April 10, 1777 with the notation that he had died (MSA: 18, 131).

Private John Lindsay enlisted February 7, 1776 (MSA: 18, 7). He reenlisted in the First Regiment on December 23, 1776, and was discharged on August 16, 1780, with a notation that he was missing (MSA: 18, 135). He was probably then a prisoner of war as the record shows him as having served from August 1, 1780, to January 1, 1782 (MSA: 18, 544). A little over two weeks later, on January 17, 1782, "Pvt. John Linday paid 5 lbs. as an exchanged prisoner from Charles Town [Charleston, SC]" (MSA: 18, 617). John Lindsay was born in Prince George's County on March 15, 1758, and he died there on May 3, 1840.[23]

Private Richard Lowe enlisted March 22, 1776 (MSA: 18, 8). The record spelled his first name as "Richd." He reenlisted in the First Regiment on December 10, 1776, but a notation was made that he "never joined" (MSA: 18, 132). He was married and had two children, which was unusual among the men who enlisted.

Private Middleton Marlow enlisted February 3, 1776 (MSA: 18, 8). No reenlistment date is shown for him, but he was listed as "Sgt. Middlen." Marlow, First Regiment and was discharged on December 27, 1779 (MSA: 18, 136).

This soldier's full name was Ralph Middleton Marlow and he was born in St. John's Parish, Prince George's County, on September 21, 1746. He was the son of John Marlow and his wife, Lydia Coghill.

Private Moses McNew enlisted February 9, 1776 (MSA: 18, 8). He reenlisted in the First Regiment on December 10, 1776, and was discharged on August 31, 1780.

He enlisted a third time on October 18, 1780, and was discharged less than two weeks later (MSA: 18, 137).

On August 3, 1792, Maryland's auditor was requested to "issue Certificates for Depreciation of pay to Ignatius Martin, and Moses McNew late soldiers in the first Maryland Regiment, and deliver the same to the Treasurer of the western shore who is Ordered to pay them to the following, the one to Michael Martin, Brother and Administrator of Ign's Martin and the other to Ruth Marlow Admin'r of Moses McNew" (MSA: 72, 286).

The estate of Moses McNew (soldier) was probated on July 18, 1792.[24]

Private John Mills enlisted February 3, 1776 (MSA: 18, 8). Corporal John Mills of the First Regiment served from August 1, 1780, until April 14, 1783, when he was discharged (MSA: 18, 546).

On January 1, 1778, Private Mills married Ruth Jacobs in Anne Arundel County. After the war they moved to North Carolina.[25] At the time of the 1810 census, the family was living in Rowan County, North Carolina, where other members of the Jacobs family were also residing.

Private James Mitchell enlisted January 29, 1776 (MSA: 18, 7). He reenlisted in the First Regiment on December 14, 1776, and was discharged on August 16, 1780, with the notation that he was missing (MSA: 18, 136).

Private Robert Nelson enlisted February 8, 1776 (MSA: 18, 8). No further records have been found for this soldier.

Private Patrick Nowlan enlisted February 1, 1776 (MSA: 18, 8). He reenlisted December 10, 1779 in the First Regiment and was discharged on December 27, 1779 (MSA: 18, 146). He enlisted for a third time on August 15, 1780. It was noted that he died on August 19, 1780 (MSA: 18, 147).

On November 9, 1776, Robert Harris wrote to the council in Philadelphia saying: "Honorable Sirs. I arrived here the 2nd Inst, with 76 Privates, a return of my company stores, & the state of our Guns I deliv^d the Board of War, and beg^d that those wanting repairs might be sent to the Smiths for that purpose. My request was not complied with, to have marched to Camp with Guns in such order would have been folly. I therefore applied to Col^o Ramsey for money who procured me 250 Pounds. I have taken the Liberty to Inclose my account, by which you will see there is a Balance due the Company which I beg may be sent, or an order therefore to Col^o Ramsey. I have been obliged to advance money, as the Company was in need, and unwilling to march without being paid. I am Honble Sirs, Your most obed^t H^{le} Servant." Patrick Nowlan's name was included in the list of men and it was noted that he was paid previously on September 21, 1776, for five weeks subsistence (MSA: 12, 435).

Private Francis Osborn enlisted January 29, 1776 (MSA: 18, 8). His surname was spelled Osburne. No other enlistments are shown for this soldier and, by October 28, 1779, questions must have been raised about his fitness for duty. "Francis Osborn who was of Simms's Company of the old Maryl^d Regim^t was brought before the Board and on Examination appearing to be in no sort fit for the Service nor likely to be so. It is ordered that he be not interrupted but permitted to go at Large at his own Will and Pleasure" (MSA: 43, 4).

Private Osborn married Charity Pope on July 19, 1778. They were living in Prince George's County at the time of the 1790 and 1800 censuses.

Private Jacob Penn enlisted February 29, 1776 (MSA: 8, 8). No further records have been found for this soldier.

Private Thomas Perkins enlisted February 3, 1776 (MSA: 18, 8). No further records have been found for this soldier.

Private Elias Perry enlisted February 3, 1776 (MSA: 18, 8). No further records have been found for this soldier.

Private James Perry enlisted January 28, 1776 (MSA: 18, 8). No further records have been found for this soldier.

Private Lawrence Querney enlisted February 7, 1776 (MSA: 18, 7). On December 10, 1776, "Pvt. Lawce. Quarney" of the First Regiment reenlisted. He was discharged on December 27, 1779 (MSA: 18, 154). Lawrence Querny was listed as head of household in the 1800 census of Rowan County, North Carolina.

Private Basil Ridgley enlisted February 3, 1776. At that time his surname was spelled Ridgly (MSA: 18, 8). Bazil Ridgely of the First Regiment "Ensn 17 Apr Corp from to dec 75, resigned 7 dec 77" (MSA: 18, 155).

Private Ridgely was the son of William Ridgely and his wife, Margaret, of Anne Arundel County.[26] On May 5, 1784, he married Actions Gaither in Baltimore County, Maryland.[27]

Private Jonathan Robinson enlisted January 28, 1776, and was shown on detachment duty (MSA: 18, 7). He reenlisted in the First Regiment on December 10, 1776, and was discharged on August 16, 1780, at which time it was noted he had been a prisoner (MSA: 18, 155).

Private John Rodery enlisted February 6, 1776 (MSA: 18, 8). This man may be the same as Sergeant John Radery, who was shot on September 1, 1781. He served from August 1, 1780, to January 1, 1782 (MSA: 18, 554).

Private John Russell enlisted January 26, 1776. His surname was spelled Russel (MSA: 18, 8). This soldier reenlisted in the First Regiment on July 7, 1779, and was discharged on November 1, 1780 (MSA: 18, 159).

Private Robert Sapp enlisted May 12, 1776 (MSA: 18, 9). He reenlisted in the First Regiment on April 16, 1777, and then deserted (MSA: 18, 159). "A List of Deserters taken up and Brought before the Lieutenant of Frederick County who were Committed to the Public Gaol of said County. Robert Sapp, First Regiment, May 7, 1778" (MSA: 18, 327).

Private Thomas Simpkins enlisted March 7, 1776 (MSA: 18, 8). No further records have been found for this soldier.

Private William Skipper enlisted March 5, 1776 (MSA: 18, 8). He reenlisted in the First Regiment on February 22, 1777, and it was noted that he had deserted (MSA: 18, 160).

Private Joseph Steward enlisted February 26, 1776. No further records have been found for this soldier.

Private Coxon Talbott enlisted February 17, 1776 (MSA: 18, 7). He reenlisted in the First Regiment on December 10, 1776, and was discharged on May 23, 1777, with a notation that he had died (MSA: 18, 168).

Private Francis Thompson enlisted January 28, 1776 (MSA: 18, 8). He reenlisted in the First Regiment on December 10, 1776, and was discharged on December 27, 1779. Private Thompson enlisted a third time and was mustered in June 1780 and discharged on November 1, 1780 (MSA: 18, 168). There must have been yet another enlistment as he is shown as having served from January 1, 1782, to April 18, 1783, when he was discharged (MSA: 18, 512, 558).

On May 7, 1783, the treasurer was ordered to pay to "Francis Thompson four pounds, nine shillings and six pence specie agreeable to the Act to adjust the Debts due from this State per Accounts passed" (MSA: 48, 409).

Private Hugh Tomlin enlisted April 6, 1776 (MSA: 18, 7). As Private Hugh Tomling of the First Regiment he is shown as reenlisting on December 10, 1776. He was discharged on December 27, 1779 (MSA: 18, 168). At the time of the 1790 census, Hugh Tomlin was head of household in Frederick County, Maryland.

Private John Veach enlisted March 5, 1776 (MSA: 18, 8). On July 2, 1777, "John Veach who inlisted in Cap.ᵗ Sims Company of Smallwoods Battalion from his Indisposition is adjudged incapable of Service and is therefore discharged" (MSA: 16, 306).

John Veach took the Oath of Allegiance in 1778. His estate was probated on February 14, 1785, in Prince George's County.[28]

Private Benjamin Vermillion enlisted February 3, 1776 (MSA: 18, 8). No further records have been found for this soldier.

Private John Walker enlisted February 3, 1776 (MSA: 18, 8). Private Walker of the First Regiment reenlisted on December 10, 1776, was promoted to corporal on October 1, 1777, and was discharged on December 27, 1779 (MSA: 18, 174).

Private Thomas Walsh enlisted February 7, 1776 (MSA: 18, 8). No further records have been found for this soldier.

Private Michael Waltz enlisted February 20, 1776 (MSA: 18, 8). On April 6, 1818, in Harrisburg, Dauphin County, Pennsylvania, Michael Waltz deposed that he:

> ... enlisted in the Army of the United States raised for the defense of American liberty on the 16th day of February 1776 in the State of Maryland in Captain Sim's Company of Infantry which was attached to Col. Smallwood's regiment; that he served in sd. regiment about 10 months, during which time he fought in the Battle on Long Island, at East Chester, at the White Plains, and was at the capture of the Hessians at Trenton on the 26th of December 1776. That on the 28th of December 1776, he enlisted in the Pennsylvania line, in Captain Miller's Company of Infantry in the 12th regiment of Pennsylvania troops commanded by Col. Cooke. That in June 1777 he was transferred to the service of General Conway with whom he served until the General left the country. That he afterwards enlisted in the Pennsylvania regiment commanded by Col. Craig, that he served in said regiment until the close of the war. He was discharged in August 1783.[29]

On June 28, 1820, Michael Waltz, age 67, then a resident of Dauphin County, Pennsylvania provided a schedule of his property and deposed regarding his service while a member of the Pennsylvania Line. By October 25, 1834, this soldier had moved to Medina County, Ohio. He stated that he had removed first from Harrisburg, Dauphin County, Pennsylvania, then to Chippeway, Wayne County, Ohio, to be close to his relations who had previously moved there from Pennsylvania. He ultimately removed to Medina County. Private Waltz died on March 6, 1839, place not stated.[30]

Corporal Gassaway Watkins enlisted January 29, 1776. His first name was given as Gazaway (MSA: 18, 7). He had actually enlisted two weeks before, on January 14, with the rank of sergeant. By December 10, 1776, he had attained the rank of ensign and had been reassigned to the Third Maryland Regiment. This soldier would serve throughout the war and would ultimately reach the rank of captain on May 13, 1782. He resigned his commission in April 1783.[31]

In 1807, Captain Watkins petitioned the Maryland General Assembly for assistance. The House of Delegates passed a resolution on December 5, 1807, that read:

> THE committee to whom was referred the petition of Gassaway Watkins, of Anne-Arundel county, beg leave to report, that after examining into the matters therein stated, find, that the said Watkins entered into the service of his county as a soldier in the revolutionary war, and continued to serve as such to the end there, of; his conduct during this struggle, placed him high in the opinion of his companions in

war, and acquired him the reputation of a brave and valuable officer. Your committee further find, that his circumstances are much straitened, and having a large family of children to provide for, an annuity from the state would greatly contribute to render easy his declining days, and give to his children and family a decent though frugal support. Your committee, in order to bring the subject before you, beg leave to submit the following resolution: RESOLVED, That the treasurer of the western shore be and he is hereby directed and required to pay unto Gassaway Watkins, of Anne-Arundel county, late a captain in the revolutionary war, a sum of money equal to half pay as a captain, annually, in quarterly payments, during his life, as a reward to those meritorious services which he rendered his country in establishing her liberty and independence [MSA: 555, 47].

Despite the financial and other problems Captain Watkins encountered supporting his large family, he immediately heeded the call of his country again during the War of 1812, serving as a colonel in the Department of Drafted Militia of the State of Maryland and he was also placed in command of the defenses of Annapolis.[32]

On January 28, 1816, the treasurer of the Western Shore was directed to: "...pay unto Gassaway Watkins, late a captain in the revolutionary war, annually in quarterly payments, a sum of money equal to the half pay of a captain, in lieu of the sum already allowed him by a resolution passed at November session eighteen hundred and eleven, as a further remuneration for those services which so essentially contributed to the independence of his country" (MSA: 192, 2984).

On April 23, 1818, Gassaway Watkins, a resident of Anne Arundel County, deposed:

... that he Enlisted in the Company of Captain Patrick Sim in the Regiment from the State of Maryland commanded by Colonel William Smallwood as a Sergeant in January in the year Seventeen Hundred and Seventy Six. That he was appointed and commissioned an Ensign in the Seventh Maryland Regiment in April Seventeen Hundred and Seventy Seven and in May of this same year, a Lieutenant therein. He was afterwards appointed and commissioned a Captain and in those several stations served in the War of the Revolution from the time first mentioned till the conclusion of the war and that he was in the Battles of Long Island, White Plains, German Town, Monmouth, Camden, Cowpens, Guilford, Ninety-Six, and Eutaw.[33]

Colonel Watkins died on July 19, 1840, in Howard County, Maryland, at his home, Walnut Grove. At the time of his death, he was the president of the Society of the Cincinnati of Maryland and he was the last surviving officer of the Maryland Line. He was described as "a man of magnificent physique, six feet two inches in height, well proportioned and developed. His height and size made him conspicuous in battle."[34]

After his death, Colonel Watkins's family found, among his papers, his own handwritten version of his adventures from the beginning of the Revolutionary War through 1781. Though incomplete, it is most interesting and leaves the reader wanting to know more:

I entered the Revolutionary Army with Colonel Smallwood's regiment in January 1776, and was in the battles of Long Island and White Plains as sergeant. Was taken sick in November, and sent to and left at Morristown, Jersey. I put my clothing in the regimental wago, and the driver carried all to the enemy. I traveled from Morristown to Annapolis without money or clothing, and got to Annapolis and January, '77 and lay confined to my room until the last of April. I was then inoculated for the small-pox, and remained in Maryland as lieutenant on duty until September. I joined the army a few days before the battle of Germantown and remained with the army and wintered at Wilmington, in 1778. I was in the battle of Monmouth and was attached to the command of General Scott's light infantry and after the battle, came to Bownbrook. Left camp the 24th of December, on furlough, and joined the army 26 of April, 1779. Continued in camp at West Point and wintered at Heck's farm. I was several times in the vanguard and was on Staten Island, in March, 1780, and was in Elizabethtown a few hours, after Major Egleston and his guard was taken. Was present when Colonel Hazen arrested Colonel Howard, for not keeping his men on the parade until they were frozen. I left camp the last of April for the South, and was in the battle of Camden. Was sent to a house by General Greene for information; was pursued by Tarleton's horse, jumped a fence eleven logs high and was two nights and days without eating and without seeing anyone and slept in the woods. Rejoined General Smallwood, at Elizabethtown. Was sent by General Smallwood, in September, with special dispatches to General Marion. Joined the General at Hillsborough. Left Hillsborough under the command of Colonels Howard and Morgan. Commanded a company in the battle of the Cowpens, 1781. In February, the day General Davidson was killed, I left camp with orders from General Greene and was with the retreating militia, two miles from the battle ground. At twelve o'clock that night, I stopped at a house on the road, cold, wet and hungry, but got nothing to eat. There were at least one hundred persons in the house. My dress was noticed by an old man of the country, who asked to speak in private with me. He told me there were enemies as well as friends in the house and offered his services to me. I started in a few moments after, and told him what I wanted. He was faithful. We rode all night and got to the foard, about ten o'clock next morning. The trees came tumbling down one after the other down the Yadkin. The old man said it was impossible to cross. I was satisfied there was nothing to stop the enemy and the wish of my general to bring his troops to a point near action, so I immediately pulled off my coat and boots, put the dispatches in the crown of my hat, tied it on my head, took leave of my friend, who, with tears in his eyes, wished me well, and with difficulty crossed the river. My guide and friend expressed his joy by throwing up his hat and I returned it with gratitude. About seven o'clock I got to headquarters and was received by Generals Greene and Morgan.[35]

Private John Willey enlisted February 3, 1776 (MSA: 18, 7). No further records have been found for this soldier.

Bozely Wright enlisted February 17, 1776 and it was noted he was "on guard" (MSA: 18, 7). No further records have been found for this soldier.

The names of five soldiers, who were originally listed, have been removed from the roster of the Second Company. They are:

Cadet John Burgess was commissioned a first lieutenant in the Third Maryland Battalion of the Flying Camp by July 1776, therefore he was not one of the 400.[36]

Corporal Michael Burgess was commissioned an ensign in the Third Maryland Battalion of the Flying Camp by July 1776, therefore he was not one of the 400.[37]

Private Richard Coe had originally been listed erroneously as Richard Cox. This soldier applied for a pension on April 10, 1818, and again on July 9, 1832. On neither occasion did he mention the Battle of Long Island or the Battle of Brooklyn, stating that he had served in the battles of White Plains, Brandywine, and Germantown. Private Coe was not one of The Maryland 400.

Lieutenant Benjamin Ford was commissioned captain in May 1776. In July of that year he was transferred to the Ninth Company to replace Captain George Stricker.[38] He remains one of The Maryland 400, but his information is contained under the Ninth Company.

Private Daniel Rankins enlisted February 3, 1776 (MSA: 18, 8). He reenlisted on December 10, 1776, and was discharged on December 27, 1779 (MSA: 18, 154). The pension file of Daniel Rankins contains an undated document, which reads:

> A memorandum of Battles that Daniel Rankins was in in the Revolutionary War at the Battle of long island I herd them afireing and I went over [the] East river and our men was retreating and [I] assisted them over the river. I was in the Battle at White Plains, Battle at Trentown. I was not able to be in the ranks I had a swelling in my limbs at this time but about the same time I pest a waggon & took the Congresses goods to the head of the Elk and delivered them there then I reenlisted for 3 years from the head of Elk we marched to Brandywine and there I was sent of with the generals waggon. I was in the Battle at Germantown and I was in the Battle at Monmouth thence I was in Detached parties sommers about nine months a garding the Comesaries Store thence I went in the detached parties three months in the enemies lines and from this out I was in detached parties and Senumeyes the balance of my time. I think it unessary to mention all of my Perseding as it is tedious to relait.

Based on this document, Daniel Rankins was not one of The Maryland 400.

Summary

Seventy-five soldiers were originally shown as enlisted in the Second Company. Of those, 70 are presumed to have gone into battle (excluding the four men listed above and accounting for the transfer of Benjamin Ford). Forty-six of these men are known to have survived and 24 are unaccounted for.

Third Company

The men of the Third Company were primarily from Prince George's County and Montgomery County (created from Prince George's County in 1776). They served under the command of Captain Barton Lucas, son of Thomas Lucas and Ann Hungerford, who was born in Rock Creek Hundred, Prince George's County, on January 29, 1730. He served as a soldier from Maryland and also from Virginia during the French and Indian War.[1]

Captain Lucas was commissioned Captain of the Third Company in Smallwood's regiment on January 3, 1776 (MSA: 23, 9). He was ill the day of the Battle of Long Island. He would, therefore, not have been one of The Maryland 400. "Major Guest (sic) commanded the Maryland battalion (the col. and lt. col. being both at York). Capts. Adams and Lucas were sick."[2]

Captain Lucas resigned his commission just a few months after the battle, on October 11, 1776, probably as a result of the illness he contracted in New York.[3] Nevertheless, it appears he continued to serve since on April 18, 1779, he was listed as colonel of the Lower Battalion of Prince George's County. Captain Lucas died in Prince George's County in 1784.

Private Alexander Allen enlisted February 8, 1776. His first name was given as Alex (MSA: 18, 10). Private Allen Alexander, First Regiment, was discharged on December 27, 1779 (MSA: 18, 78).

On November 4, 1836, Winifred Allen, widow, age 83, of Washington, D.C., deposed that her husband, Alexander Allen of William, enlisted under Captain Barton Lucas in the First Maryland Regiment and served in Pennsylvania and New York. She stated that he was at the Battle of Long Island where he was wounded and taken prisoner and that when he came home on furlough in October, they were married. He served after that in Marlborough and Frederick in charge of the prisoners. Alexander Allen died on or about March 15, 1815.[4]

> Land Office, Annapolis, May 10th 1830. Mrs. Sarah Kirkwood. Madam, The Clerk of the Executive Council has handed me your letter of the 24th ultimo in which you request to be informed whether your father, Alexander Allen, is entitled to bounty land from this State for Revolutionary services or not. I have to inform you

that I have carefully examined the Records in the office and it does not appear on said Records that he is entitled to any bounty land from this State. By reference to the old muster Rolls, it appears, that Mr. Alexander Allen enlisted for only three years, and was discharged at the expiration of the time, as he did not therefore serve until the close of the Revolutionary war, he of course, I presume was not entitled to any bounty land from the State for Revolutionary services. (In haste,) I am most respectfully Yr. Obed.' Svt., George G. Brewer, Register of the Land Office, State of Maryland.[5]

Private Amos Allen enlisted February 8, 1776 (MSA: 18, 10). No further records have been found for this soldier.

Private John Armstrong enlisted February 17, 1776 (MSA: 18, 10). "Payroll for prisoners taken on Long Island from 27th August to 10th December 1776: Zachariah Gray, corporal; Zachariah Weilling; Philip Wellen; Daniel M. Kay; Joseph Beary; William Backer; Christopher Beall; George Nott; John Armstrong. I hereby certify that the above-named soldiers, belonging to the Company of Maryland Regulars

"Walnut Grove." This home was built by Colonel Gassaway Watkins about 1785 on property he acquired through his marriage to Ruth Dorsey. It is located in Clarkesville, Maryland. There is a small family graveyard located here where Colonel Watkins, his wife, and other family members are buried (photograph and information courtesy the Maryland Historical Trust).

under the command of Capt. Barton Lucas last campaign and taken prisoners in the action on Long Island of the 28th August last, are returned to Maryland. Signed by Peter Brown, Late Ensign of said Company.⁶

Private John Baker enlisted January 22, 1776 (MSA: 18, 9). He reenlisted in the First Regiment on May 3, 1777, and was discharged on August 10, 1780. It was noted that he had deserted (MSA: 18, 81).

Private William Baker enlisted February 25, 1776 (MSA: 18, 10). Private Baker was taken prisoner at the battle. His name, given erroneously as William Backer, was among the names of prisoners returned to Maryland in the entry noted above under Private John Armstrong.⁷

Private Baker reenlisted April 7, 1777, was shown as being present on November 1, 1780, and then "deserted, so says Capt. Belt" (MSA: 18, 88). "Willm. Baker. LIST OF DEFECTIVES FROM THE MARYLAND LINE, FROM JUNE, 1780, TO FEBY., 1782. Residence '81, Baltimore" (MSA: 18, 415).

Private Joseph Barry enlisted February 13, 1776 (MSA: 18, 10). This soldier was taken prisoner at the battle. The payroll return noted under Private John Armstrong shows his surname erroneously as Beary.⁸

Private Christopher Beall enlisted January 20, 1776 (MSA: 18, 9). This soldier was taken prisoner at the battle and was listed among those exchanged. He is noted as returned to Maryland in the payroll entry noted above.⁹

Private Christopher Beall of the First Regiment reenlisted on December 21, 1777, and was discharged on December 27, 1779 (MSA: 18, 81). "In Council Annapolis 22ᵈ June 1778. Sir, We are informed that Christopher Beall, whom you sent hither as a Deserter, John Wilson, Charles Jennings and Robert Orme Drafts from your County, have gone home again. We have sent Mʳ Gordon after them and request you to give him any necessary Assistance. We are &ᶜᵃ Joshua Beall Esqʳ Lᵗ of Prince George's County" (MSA: 21, 146). "It would later be discovered that Private Beall 'fell ill enroute to his station.'"¹⁰

On January 11, 1780, a marriage license was issued in Prince George's County to Christopher Beall and Ann Brooke: "Ann Brooke, of P. G. Co., dr of Henry Brooke and his wife, Margaret Darnell."¹¹

On April 23, 1819, Christopher Beall, age 66, a resident of Baltimore County, Maryland, Baltimore Co., Maryland deposed:

> ... that he the said Christopher Beall enlisted for the term of three years, on or about the month of September in the year Seventeen hundred and Seventy five, at the Town of Bladensburg, Prince George's County in the State of Maryland, in the Company commanded by Captain Barton Lucas of the first Regiment Maryland Line, commanded by Colonel William Smallwood, on the continental Establish-

ment; that he continued to serve in said Corps, or in the service of the United States until the 27th day of December in the year 1779, when he was discharged from service at Cambridge Farm, near Morristown in the State of New Jersey; that he was in the Battles of Long Island, Brandywine, German Town, Monmouth and at the storming of Stony Point; and that he is in reduced circumstances, and stands in need of the assistance of his Country for support, and that he has no other evidence in favor of his said services.

On September 1, 1820, Christopher Beall, age 68, a resident of Anne Arundel County declared: "...that he enlisted in Captain Barton Lucas's Company of the first Maryland Regiment who were in the service of the United States during the Revolutionary War, commanded by Colonel William Smallwood in the year seventeen hundred and seventy six as a private and that he continued in the service for the term of four years when he was discharged. That he follows the occupation of a Laborer and not able to obtain subsistence by his labor, that he has a wife Living with him who is sixty one years of age and who is too feeble to work, and that he has no children living with him to aid in his and wife's support." A schedule of property was attached showing the Christopher Beall owned two trunks valued by the court at two dollars.[12]

Christopher Beall died on July 17, 1831. On February 2, 1839, the children of Christopher Beall were paid from March 4, 1831, to July 17, 1831, the date of the soldier's death.[13]

On April 15, 1850, a letter was written to the War Office by Attorney E. Israel in which he said: "Mrs. Margaret Logan and Mr. James Beall are the only children and heirs at law of Mr. Christopher Beall who was a soldier of the Revolution and Pensioner on the Maryland Agency and received his Pension $8 per month to 4th March 1831 and died July 17th 1831. The arrears of his Pension to day of his death $35.47 were paid to his children Feb 7 1839. Mr. Christopher Beall was from Prince George's County, Maryland and enlisted to serve during the whole war. His children believe there was Bounty Land due him which he never received and which if he did not receive they are entitled to under the Pension Laws." The file does not contain a response.[14]

Christopher Beall was a descendant of Colonel Ninian Beall, born 1625 in Scotland. A family history relates the story of his passage from Scotland:

> Oliver Cromwell, an active leader in the Puritan cause, had risen to power in England, and in 1648 he repelled the Scottish Royalist invasion at Preston. Scotland had become Presbyterian, principally through the work of John Knox, although the Stuarts favored the Episcopal Church. In 1649, Cromwell's political power was enhanced by the removal of Presbyterian leaders from Parliament. In 1650, he invaded Scotland and defeated the Royalist Scots at Dunbar. More than 3,000 Scotsmen were slaughtered on the field and 10,000 prisoners were taken. The wounded among these were released, but 5,000 were sent into virtual slavery in

Northumbria, and the rest were shipped off to America and the West Indies. Among these was Ninian Beall who held a commission as a cornetist in the Scottish-English Army under Leslie raised to resist Cromwell, and fought and was made prisoner in the battle of Dunbar, September 3, 1650. He was sentenced to five years of servitude and, after a short stay in Ireland, was packed into the hold of a prison ship with 149 other Scotsmen and sent to Barbadoes, West Indies.[15]

About 1652, he was transferred, still a prisoner, to the Province of Maryland where he served five years with Richard Hall of Calvert County. "Then came Ninian Beall of Calvert County, planter, and proved his right to 50 acres of land for his time in service, as military prisoner, performed with Richard Hall of said county. This servitude which came to him through the fortunes of war was an Honor."[16]

During his lifetime Ninian Beall attained wealth and held many public offices. By the time of his death in 1717, he owned over 25,000 acres (part of which is now Washington, D.C.). He gave the land and founded the first Presbyterian church in Maryland at Upper Marlborough. Colonel Ninian Beall lived to be ninety-seven. He was buried on his home plantation near Georgetown [Washington, D.C.]. "On the town being expanded his remains were dug up. Then 'it was found that he was six feet seven inches tall and his Scotch red hair had retained all its fiery hue.'"[17]

Private Garret Brinkenhoof enlisted April 17, 1776 (MSA: 18, 10). No further records have been found for this soldier.

Private Richard Brookes enlisted February 3, 1776 (MSA: 18, 10). No further records have been found for this soldier.

Private John Brown enlisted January 22, 1776 (MSA: 18, 9). Private John Brown, First Regiment, enlisted on May 19, 1777, and was discharged on January 21, 1778. "Deserted" (MSA: 18, 80).

Private John Brown, First Regiment is shown as having served August 1, 1780 through November 1, 1783 (MSA: 18, 524).

Bounty Land Warrant Number 10956 for 100 acres in the name of Private John Brown of Maryland was issued August 14, 1793, to Francis Sherrard, assignee. A note at the bottom says, "Note: The Bounty Land Wt. Book shows also the following: Abijah Buxton, Pvt., Maryland Lind, Wt. 10956 issued Mrch 11, 1791 to Abijah Buxton."[18]

Sergeant Peter Brown enlisted January 20, 1776 (MSA: 18, 9). On July 9, 1776, he was commissioned ensign (MSA: 12, 16). He is listed among the prisoners taken on Long Island on August 28, 1776, and later returned to Maryland.[19]

Immediately upon his return with the prisoners, Ensign Brown reenlisted and was commissioned a second lieutenant on December 10, 1776. He resigned July 10, 1777 (MSA: 18, 80).

Peter Brown was born about 1750 in Germany. He died in Frederick County, Maryland, in 1823. "The records of the Maryland Society, Sons of the American Revolution, indicate that Sgt. Peter Brown was one of the famous Maryland 400 who fought at the Battle of Long Island on August 27, 1776 and saved Gen. Washington's Army from being totally destroyed."[20]

Sergeant James Burnes enlisted January 21, 1776 (MSA: 18, 9). On May 1, 1778, commissions were issued to "Truman Skinner app^d Lieut. Col. John Perry Capt Benjamin Wales first Lieut. James Burnes second Lieut Moses Orme Ensign Alex^r Howard Magruder" (MSA: 21, 62).

Private Abijah Buxton enlisted February 13, 1776. His surname was spelled Buxtone (MSA: 18, 10). Private Buxton reenlisted on December 10, 1776, and was discharged on December 27, 1779 (MSA: 18, 81). During this time he was shown on the muster roll of the "First Maryland Regiment in the First Battalion of Colonel Otho H. Williams' Regiment serving in the Southern Army of the United States for the Month of October 1780. North Carolina Camp Hillsborough November 1780." Enlistment date was given as March 4, 1778. "Abijah Buxton. Gone to camp. Men Inlisted in Fredk. Town for the 7th Md. Regt. from Jan. until April, 1780" (MSA: 18, 334). He reenlisted again in June 1780 and he was shown as being present on November 1, 1780 (MSA: 18, 190). "Bounty Land Warrant #10956 for 100 ac. issued to Private Abijah Buxton, March 11, 1791."[171]

Private Michael Catons enlisted January 27, 1776. It was noted that he was "Sick, in barracks" (MSA: 18, 10). No further records have been found for this soldier.

Private John Cissell enlisted January 20, 1776. "At the magazine" (MSA: 18, 9). No further records have been found for this soldier.

Private Francis Cole enlisted April 2, 1776 (MSA: 18, 10). No further records have been found for this soldier.

Private Patrick Collins enlisted May 18, 1776. His first name was spelled Patk. It was noted that Private Collins was "in the black hole." (MSA: 18, 11). "Patk. Collins in Capt. Thomas Bell's Company. Patk. Collins, under guard Sept '77" (MSA: 18, 303). The name of Patrick Collins was included in "A List of Recruits and Deserters Passed by Thomas Sprigg, Lieut. of Washington County, April 22nd, 1780" (MSA: 18, 336).

Private Josias Connally enlisted January 22, 1775 (MSA: 18, 9). No further records for this soldier have been found.

Private John Dunn enlisted January 22, 1776 (MSA: 18, 9). "Jno. Dunn (D.F.)" enlisted on December 10, 1776, and was discharged on April 15, 1777. "Non

Commissioned Officers and Soldiers of the Fifth Maryland Regiment left out of the Rolls February, 1778" (MSA: 18, 278).

Private John Enright enlisted January 27, 1776 (MSA: 18, 9). On December 10, 1776, Private John Enright reenlisted. He was discharged April 15, 1777, "ex. For A. Hughes" (MSA: 18, 106).

Private Thomas Ferguson enlisted February 25, 1776 (MSA: 18, 10). No further records have been found for this soldier.

Private John Fleming enlisted February 3, 1776. It was noted that he was "sick in barracks" (MSA: 18, 10). This soldier, his name given as "Jno. Flemming," reenlisted in the First Regiment on December 10, 1776. He was discharged on November 20, 1777 with the notation that he had died (MSA: 18, 108).

Private John Flint enlisted February 6, 1776 (MSA: 18, 10). The descendants of Private John Flint from Worcester County, Maryland, have claimed membership in the Daughters of the American Revolution using the enlistment information for this soldier stating that he enlisted in the Third Company, First Battalion of Maryland, commanded by Captain Barton Lucas: "John Flint, Pvt, 3rd Co., 1st Bttn., Maryland commanded by Capt. Barton Lucas; b. 7/6/1756 in MD and died 8/13/1841 in Union Co., IN. He married Elizabeth Johnson, 3/16/1789."[22]

The Bureau of Pensions, on an undated form, filed with the pension records of John Flint of Indiana, stated that there was only one soldier by the name of John Flint who served during the Revolutionary War from Maryland. It is the opinion of this writer that they are both wrong.

On October 13, 1835, John Flint, age 79, a resident of Bath Township, Franklin County, Indiana, deposed that in the spring of 1776 he enlisted and served under the command of Captain Ebenezer Handy; then under Captain Robert Handy; and, lastly, Captain John Dashiel [Dashiell]. This soldier stated specifically, "He was never marched out of the said State of Maryland was in no considerable engagements, his business being merely to prevent the encroachments of the enemy."[23]

The first John Flint who enlisted in the Third Company under the command of Barton Lucas is probably the same as John Flint whose estate was probated in Prince George's County, September 11, 1781.[24]

Private James Gardiner enlisted May 14, 1776 (MSA: 18, 11). "REGIMENTS AND DATES OF DESERTION NOT KNOWN. James Gardner." No date, but appears to be 1781 (MSA: 18, 416).

Private Zachariah Gray enlisted February 3, 1776. His name was given as Zacha. Gray (MSA: 18, 9). Private Gray was taken prisoner at the battle and later returned to Maryland.[25]

On September 17, 1777, it was "Ordered That the said Treasurer pay to Comfort Gray (the widow of Zachariah Gray who was lately killed in the Service) Twelve pounds for the Subsistance of herself and her five small Children till some Provision towards their support may be regularly made" (MSA: 16, 379).

Private John Halsey enlisted February 20, 1776 (MSA: 18, 10). This soldier is shown reenlisting on December 10, 1776, with his surname being spelled Holsey. No discharge date was given (MSA: 18, 117). In 1790, John Halsey was listed as head of household in Prince George's County.

Private George Hamilton enlisted January 31, 1776. This is the only time his surname was spelled Hamiltone (MSA: 18, 10). Private George Hamilton reenlisted on December 10, 1776, and was discharged on April 21, 1777 with the notation "ex. R. Green" (MSA: 18, 117). This soldier reenlisted a third time in June 1778 and was discharged in December 1779. It was noted that he had deserted (MSA: 18, 124). On July 18, 1793, Bounty Land Warrant #11,318 was issued in the name of Private George Hamilton of Maryland for 100 acres.

Corporal Samuel Hamilton enlisted January 31, 1776. This is the only time his surname was spelled Hamiltone (MSA: 18, 9). Sergeant "Saml. Hamilton" reenlisted on December 10, 1776, and was discharged on July 11, 1778, with the notation "joined Corny" (MSA: 18, 117).

The last record of this soldier was on August 16, 1792, when Maryland's auditor was "requested to issue Certificates for Depreciation of pay to Samuel Hamilton late a Serjeant in the first Maryland Regiment" (MSA: 72, 288).

Private Josias Hatton enlisted January 30, 1776. His name was erroneously given as Josiah Hattou (MSA: 18, 10).

Josias Hatton was born in Prince George's County, Maryland, on July 1, 1757. He was the great-grandson of William Hatton who, along with his siblings, was transported to Maryland in 1649 by his widowed mother, Margaret. William Hatton's uncle was Thomas Hatton, secretary of the Province of Maryland, who was executed by the Puritans after the Battle of the Severn, March 5, 1655.

Private Hatton married Mary Mitchell in Prince George's County, on February 22, 1793. On October 16, 1798, Josias Hatton died at the age of 42. He is buried in the Hatton family cemetery near Piscataway, Maryland.

Private Rhody Hously enlisted January 23, 1776 (MSA: 18, 9). No further records have been found for this soldier.

Private John Hughes enlisted February 27, 1776 (MSA: 18, 10). Private Hughes reenlisted on December 10, 1776, exchanged for R. Baily. His pension records reveal more about his service:

State of Virginia, Rockbridge County. On this 3rd day of September in the year 1832 Personally appeared in open Court, before the Justices of said Court, being a Court of Record, and now sitting, John Hughs a resident in said county of Rockbridge, State of Virginia, who being first duly sworn, according to Law, doth on his oath, make the following declaration in order to obtain the benefit of the Act of Congress, passed June 7th 1832. That he will be 82 years of age the 4th day of October 1832. That he enlisted as a soldier in the Town of Bladensburg in February 1775 — was in service in the Company of Barton Lucas, under whom he enlisted, in the city of Annapolis when National Independence was declared, and engaged in the celebration of that event. He further states that after that event, he marched under Capt. Lucas to the neighbourhood of Long Island in New York, at which place he enlisted as a United States soldier, under a certain Captain Ewing for three years. That he continued with Capt. Ewing until the Battle of the White Plains, where he was wounded having his thigh fractured. That he obtained a permit from his officer to return home, near Georgetown, until he was ready for further duty. That he did so return, but in consequence of his enfeebled health & strength, was never able to join his company again. That he went to Annapolis in hopes of meeting with some one of the officers who had known him in service, that he might procure a regular discharge, but meeting with none of them he made known his situation to the Governor Johnston and Council and obtained from them a writing or paper which he considered as substantially a discharge. That this paper has since been lost, having been kept until there seemed to be no prospect of it being worth any thing to him. This applicant also states that he was in the Battle of Long Island under the command of Capt. Lucas & before he had enlisted under Capt. Ewing. Lord Sterling commanding in that Battle, the United States forces.

Tombstone of John Hughes. This soldier is buried in the cemetery of the Neriah Baptist Church in Buena Vista, Virginia. He died in 1851 and by that time he was probably one of the last surviving Revolutionary War soldiers (photograph courtesy Wayne S. Combs).

This applicant has within the last three years been much & severely afflicted with sickness & the many distresses incident to old age & poverty & cannot recall, as he could, the particulars connected with his revolutionary service. He has never received a pension at any time, though he has often spoken of applying for one. And he hereby relinquishes every claim whatsoever to a Pension or annuity except the present, and declares that his name is not on the Pension Roll of the Agency of any State. Sworn to and subscribed the day and year above written. The Mark of John Hughs. Letter from A. D. Hiller, Bureau of Pensions, to the Quartermaster General, Memorial Branch, War Department, Washington, D.C., August 27, 1935.

Reference is made to your request for information in regard to John Hughes, private in the War of the Revolution from Maryland, died February 9, 1851 and buried Uriah [Neriah] Baptist Cemetery, Buena Vista, Virginia.

The data pertaining to John Hughes furnished herein was obtained from the papers on file in pension claim S 5594, based upon his service in the Revolutionary War. John Hughes was born October 4, 1750, place not shown, nor are the names of his parents given.

While a resident of Frederick County, Maryland, he enlisted in Bladensburg, Maryland, February 15, served in Captain Barton Lucas' company, Colonel Smallwood's Maryland regiment, was in Annapolis when "National Independence was declared," marched from there to Long Island, was in the battle there in August, the day after the battle he was transferred to Captain Ewing's company in same regiment, was in the battle of White Plains, where wounded by a cannon ball which fractured his left thigh; he had no more service after this accident and was discharged June 10, 1778. He was allowed pension on his application executed September 3, 1832, at which time he was a resident of Rockbridge County, Virginia.

There are no data in this claim concerning the family of John Hughes.

The application for headstone for John Hughes, a letter addressed to your office and signed by B. E. Patterson of Buena Vista, Virginia, and a questionnaire sent out by your office, are all returned herewith. Very truly yours, A. D. Hiller, Executive Assistant to the Administrator.[26]

"John Hughes, married, born in Virginia about 1743; died at the age of 107. Died in February, 1850 of old age in the 51st District, Rockbridge, Virginia."[27]

John Hughes is buried in Section B of the graveyard at Neriah Baptist Church. His tombstone inscription reads, "John Hughes, February 9, 1851, Pvt. Lucas' Co., Smallwood's Md. Regt."[28]

Private James Hurdle enlisted January 22, 1776 (MSA: 18, 10). No further records have been found for this soldier. He was probably a brother of Lawrence and Robert Hurdle, both of whom were Revolutionary War soldiers from Montgomery County, Maryland.

Private Zachariah Hutchins enlisted June 9, 1776. There is a question mark after his surname and no other records have been found for a soldier by this name (MSA: 18, 11).

Private Alexander Jackson enlisted February 5, 1776. His name was given as Alex. Jackson (MSA: 18, 11). No further records have been found for this soldier.

Private John Jackson enlisted February 8, 1776 (MSA: 18, 10). Private John Jackson, First Regiment, "not mustered after July 1779 (in Invalids, died 21 December 1779)" (MSA: 18, 125).

Private Basil Jenkins enlisted March 10, 1776. His first name was spelled Bazel (MSA: 18, 10). No further records have been found for this soldier.

Private Charles Jones enlisted January 29, 1776 (MSA: 18, 10). No further records have been found for this soldier.

Private Benjamin Kelly enlisted January 20, 1776. His name was given as Benjn. Kelly (MSA: 18, 9). No further records have been found for this soldier.

Private George Knott enlisted January 27, 1776 (MSA: 18, 9). He was taken prisoner at the battle and later returned to Maryland.[29]

Private George Ledburn enlisted January 22, 1776. His surname was spelled Leadbarn (MSA: 18, 10). On December 10, 1776, now as Private George Leadhurn of the First Regiment, he reenlisted and was shown as being discharged on August 12, 1777. He enlisted a third time in June 1780 and was shown as a prisoner on August 16, 1780 (MSA: 18, 32).

On January 19, 1780, an order was issued to the commissary of stores to "deliver to George Ledburn a recruit, a Blue Coat, green waistcoat Breeches and overalls, 1 Shirt, 1 hat, I p^r Shoes and I pair Stockings the Bounty allowed by the late Act of Assembly" (MSA: 43, 62). On February 4, 1780, another order was issued to the commissary of stores to deliver to, among others, "George Ledburn, of the 1 Reg^r 1 p^r of Shoes and one pair of stockings due them from the Continent" (MSA: 43, 78).

Private George Rex Leonard, Drummer enlisted January 22, 1776 (MSA: 18, 9). No further records have been found for this soldier.

Private John Rex Leonard enlisted January 25, 1776 (MSA: 18, 10). No further records have been found for this solder.

Private Robert Lesache enlisted January 22, 1776 (MSA: 18, 9). No further records have been found for this soldier.

Private Daniel McKay enlisted January 20, 1776 (MSA: 18, 9). He was taken prisoner at the battle and later returned to Maryland.[30] No further records have been found for this soldier. It is possible, however, that his surname was actually McCoy. There was a Daniel McCoy listed in the 1790 census of Prince George's County.

Private James Murphy enlisted January 26, 1776 (MSA: 18, 9).
"James Murphey, age 35, 1 Md. Regt., Lost one Legg, Aug 27, 1776, Long Island. Return of Invalid Pensioners" (MSA: 18, 632).

On October 23, 1779, it was ordered "...the western shore Treasurer pay to James Murphey a Soldier, late of Capt Lucas's Company of the old Maryland Regiment who lost one of his Legs in Consequence of a Wound received in the Battle on Long Island in 1776, two hundred Pounds so much allowed him up to the first Day of next Month by this Board by Virtue of the Resolution of the General Assembly of the 9th of August last. (MSA: 21, 566).

"I hereby certify that James Murphy enlisted under Capt. Barton Lucas of the 1st Maryland Regiment during the war and continued (in) the same. Signed by Peter Brown, June 14, 1789."[31]

"James Murphy, late a soldier in the 1st Maryland Regiment in the Continental Army, serving until the end of the war, do hereby authorized and empower Capt. Lloyd Beall to make application and receive from any person or persons, properly authorized to issue the same, the warrant or warrants for the land, which I may be entitled to as a soldier and after the reception thereof to locate and survey the same in any manner he may conceive conducive to my interest. Mark of James Murphy, June 15, 1789.[32]

On July 29, 1791, Ann Newton deposed that "she saw Mary Murphy (who was formerly Mary Craddock) married to James Murphy, who was an invalid soldier and is now dead and that said Murphy was entitled and did recover pay by order of the Montgomery County Orphan's Court."[33] A marriage license was issued to James Murphy and Mary Craddock on June 8, 1778, in Montgomery County, Maryland.[34]

On February 10, 1802, papers were filed by William Murphy, son of James Murphy, who stated that his father's leg was shot off at the battle of Long Island and that he had received a pension for some time. He also said that his father has been dead ten or twelve years.[35]

Private John Murphy enlisted February 8, 1776 (MSA: 18, 10). No further records have been found for this soldier.

Private Thomas Murray enlisted January 27, 1776 (MSA: 18, 9). No further records have been found for this soldier.

Private Jeremiah Owings enlisted February 3, 1776 (MSA: 18, 10). Private Jeremiah Owens was shown on the rolls, January 1, 1782 (MSA: 18, 455).

Private John Owings enlisted February 7, 1776 (MSA: 18, 10). He reenlisted on February 10, 1776, and was discharged on March 6, 1778, at which time it was noted that he had deserted (MSA: 18, 148).

Private Roddey Owings enlisted February 2, 1776 (MSA: 18, 10). No further records have been found for this soldier.

Private William Pearce enlisted January 29, 1776 (MSA: 18, 10). No further records have been found for this soldier.

Private Samuel Ray enlisted February 3, 1776 (MSA: 18, 10). Private Samuel Ray, First Regiment, enlisted January 1, 1780, and was discharged March 10 (no year), "dead" (MSA: 18, 155).

Ensign William Ridgley "Ensign of Smallwood's Maryland Regiment, 14th January, 1776; 2d Lieutenant, 1st Maryland, 10th December, 1776, but never joined the regiment, having been taken prisoner at Long Island, 27th August, 1776."[36] "A list of the killed and missing in the Maryland Battalion: Capt. Veazey, killed; Lt. Butler, said to be killed; Ensign Fernandes, Lt. Dent, Capt. Bowie, missing; Lt. Sterret, Coursey, and Wright, Ensign Ridge [Ridgely], 13 Sergeants, and 259 privates."[37] "At Long Island, early in the war, Capt. Daniel Bowie, Lts. William Steret, William Ridgely, Hatch Dent, Walter Muse, Samuel Wright and Joseph Butler were captured by the British and Edward Praul, Edward Courcy, Ensign James Fernandez and William Courts were wounded."[38]

Lieutenant Alexander Roxburgh was commissioned second lieutenant on January 3, 1776 (MSA: 18, 9). He was commissioned first lieutenant on July 9, 1776 (MSA: 12, 16). On December 10, 1776, Captain Alexander Roxburgh of the First Regiment reenlisted. He was discharged on April 1, 1780, and shown as major of the Seventh Regiment (MSA: 18, 164).

"Major Alexander Roxburgh, 2nd Regt., enlisted 4/7/1780. Promoted from 1st Regt" (MSA: 18, 476). Major Alexander Roxburgh served from August 1, 1780 to November 15, 1783 (MSA: 18, 518).

On Friday, August 17, 1781: Ordered that the western shore Treasurer pay to Major Alexander Roxburgh of the 4th Regim^t nine pounds of the Bills emitted under theAct for the Emission of Bills of Credit not exceeding two hundred thousand pounds &^{ca} of the money appropriated for the present Campaign for Stores on Account. That the said Treasurer pay to Major Alexander Roxburgh five pounds seventeen shillings and six pence of the same Emission of the money appropriated as aforesaid for Potts bought by him for the use of the 4th Regim^t per Account passed by the Aud. Genl That the Issuing Commissary deliver to Major Alexander Roxburgh Twenty four Gallons of Rum and ninety six pounds of sugar to the 1st Instant on Account" (MSA: 45, 568). Major Roxburgh received Warrant #1837 for 400 acres of bounty land in western Maryland. The warrant was issued on June 10, 1789.[39]

In relating a history of the Eastern Shore of Maryland, we are told that: "Alexander Roxburgh, a Scot who served with General Smallwood became Salisbury's Revolutionary hero. He was promoted to Captain for conspicuous gallantry in the Battle of Long Island and ended the war as a major. After the war, Roxburgh eloped with Frances Handy, granddaughter of Colonel Isaac Handy of Pemberton Hall."[40]

Major Roxburgh died in Somerset County, Maryland, in 1807. In his will dated July 19, 1805, he devised his bounty land to his children as follows:

Thirdly that the four lots of land of fifty acres each lying in Washington County and State of Maryland, and numbered as per tickets Three thousand two hundred and thirty four, Three thousand two hundred and thirty two and Three thousand two hundred and twenty six and Three thousand two hundred and twenty seven, granted by the commissioner for the State of Maryland for Military services during the American Revolution; and also four lots of land lying and being in the State of Ohio formerly called the North Western Territory, containing one hundred acres of land each granted unto me by the United States of America as may be fully by having recourse to the Patent thereof made to appear, Be sold or otherwise disposed off by my Executor hereafter named for the only use and benefit of my before mentioned children William Roxburgh Matthew Roxburgh and Elizabeth Roxburgh the equal rights interest and estate of them and their heirs and off spring forever after their arrival at lawful or full age.[41]

Private Joshua Saffell, Fifer enlisted April 19, 1776 (MSA: 18, 9). On July 24, 1777, Joshua Saffel and Verlinda Prather were married in Montgomery County, Maryland, by Rev. Thomas Reed.[42] The family was living in Montgomery County, Maryland, at the time of the 1790 census. Joshua Saffell was deceased and widow and family had moved to Iredell County, North Carolina, prior to 1812.[43]

Private Thomas Scott enlisted January 20, 1776 (MSA: 18, 9). "Commission issued to Thomas Scott, Ensign, June 21, 1777" (MSA: 16, 296). "Commission issued to Thomas Scott, Ensign, belonging to the Lower Battalion of Militia, Montgomery County, September 12, 1777" (MSA: 16, 373).

Private Thomas Shannen enlisted March 10, 1776 (MSA: 18, 10). No further records have been found for this soldier.

Private James Smith enlisted March 2, 1776 (MSA: 18, 10). "Private James Smith, First Regiment, enlisted February 22, 1777; Corporal, January 1, 1778; Sergeant, July 1779; discharged February 22, 1780" (MSA: 18, 160).

Lieutenant William Sterett was commissioned in the Third Company, January 3, 1776. His surname was spelled Sterrett. It was noted that he was on furlough (MSA: 18, 9). "At Long Island, early in the war, Capt. Daniel Bowie, Lts. William Steret, William Ridgely, Hatch Dent, Walter Muse, Samuel Wright and Joseph Butler were captured by the British and Edward Praul, Edward Courcy, Ensign James Fernandez and William Courts were wounded."[44]

Believing he was dead, a friend of Lieutenant Sterett wrote a poem that was published in the September 12, 1776, edition of the *Maryland Gazette*:

> On the death of Mr. WILLIAM STERET, who was killed in the engagement on Long Island.
>
> > Why throbs my heart? Alas, whence that sigh?
> > That sudden damps this cheerless hour?

> Is Steret dead? Relentless death, alas, why?
> So soon a victim to thy sullen pow'r?
> Could not his virtues guard him on that day
> From Death's too firm, too cold embrace?
> Ah! No! His virtues did his life betray,
> And led him eager to that fatal place.
> Ah luckless spot — that did the world bereave
> Or worth entreating to such height —
> Ah luckless spot — that caus'd a friend to grieve
> His Steret lost for ever to his sight,
> Alas! How fleeting are our youthful joys,
> My Steret's death can tell —
> Call'd forth to action by the public voice,
> He willing fought — and nobly fell.
> Oft hand in hand we've eager trac'd the wood
> Thoughtless and void of anxious care,
> Together oft in youth we've *stemm'd* the flood,
> Nor knew — not thought of trouble near.
> Adieu ye scenes of happiness — adieu —
> Which oft we joyous did explore,
> Now, Steret's gone for ever from my view —
> Oh scenes of happiness no more.

There must have been much joy among the family and friends when they found that William Sterett had not died after all. We have no way of knowing how long they mourned before he returned, but this notice appeared in several newspapers, including the April 20, 1777 edition of the *Pennsylvania Evening Post*:

> Maryland, Baltimore Town, January 29, 1777.
> William Sterett, Lieutenant in Captain Barton Lucas's company, and late Col. Smallwood's battalion of Maryland troops, being nineteen years of age, deposeth and saith,
> That he was taken prisoner, on the 27th August, on Long-Island, that many who were taken with him were robbed of their hats, shoes, buckles, &c. Many were stripped almost naked, particularly the wounded; the Hessian officers were somewhat kind and polite, and the Hessian soldiers, after committing robberies on the prisoners, were obliging; the allowance of provision not near a sufficiency, only two thirds of a British ration allowed to each one, the bread particularly was frequently exceeding bad; numbers slightly wounded, many of whom, through neglect of the surgeons, lost their lives; recruiting officers often were among the prisoners, some inlisted, chiefly Irish and English, but whether from persuasion or force is unknown. Sworn before GEORGE GOULD DRESBURY.

Just 24 years old, William Sterett died in Baltimore on August 16, 1782: "Baltimore, August 20. On Saturday evening last died, at his father's house in this town, much lamented, major William Sterett, in the prime of life. The bravery of this young gentleman in the field of battle, his steadiness as a patriot, his probity as a merchant, and his amiable deportment as a citizen and private gentleman, render his death a heavy loss to this country, as well as to his family and friends. The next day his remains were respectfully deposited in the burying ground belonging to the Presbyterian church."[45]

Private Absalom Stevenson enlisted February 7, 1776. His name was given as Absolarn Stevenson (MSA: 18, 10). No further records have been found for this soldier.

Private Richard Stone enlisted January 31, 1776 (MSA: 18, 10). No further records have been found for this soldier.

Sergeant Zachariah Tannehill enlisted January 29, 1776. His name was given as "Zacha. Tannahill" (MSA: 18, 9). Sergeant Tannehill was killed at the Battle of Fort Washington, November 16, 1776.[46]

Private Zachary Tilley enlisted January 20, 1776 (MSA: 18, 9). In 1777, he petitioned Smallwood for his discharge from the service:

> [Petition of Zachariah Tilley.] To the Honourable Brigadier General Smallwood. The petition of Zachariah Tilley humbly sheweth, That your petitioner has served during the last campaign, as a soldier in Capt. Barton Lucas's company, under your command; and is now absent from the army on Furlough. That your Petitioner having been bred to the business of a Ship Carpenter, conceives he can be of more service to his country by working for the Publick in that capacity, than by continuing as a soldier; as he understands that Ship Carpenters are much wanted in the public Dock yards. Your petitioner therefore most humbly prays that he may be discharged from the army, that he may be at liberty to serve the States in the business to which he was bred and your petitioner shall ever pray &c. February 5th 1777.
>
> We whose names are hereunto subscribed do certify that Zachariah Tilley was bred to the business of a Ship Carpenter, under his Father and brothers; and that he worked at that trade, until he enlisted into the army last winter (Signed) William Sydebotham, Henry Bradford, William Murdock, Chr^r Loundes, Robt. Dick, Richard Henderson, Peter Cams, Thomas Cramphin, Richard Ponsonby [MSA: 16, 119].
>
> "July 13, 1781. Zacha. Tilley. DRAFTS FROM THE CLASSES FOR FILLING UP THE QUOTA OF MEN FROM PRINCE GEORGE'S COUNTY" [MSA: 18, 382].
>
> "December 11, 1781. Zachariah Tilley a Draught from Prince Georges County to serve till the 10th of this Instant, is hereby Discharged" [MSA: 48, 18].

Private Richard Wade enlisted February 3, 1776. "On guard." (MSA: 18, 10). No further records have been found for this soldier.

Corporal Benjamin Warner enlisted January 29, 1776. "Sick in barracks" (MSA: 18, 9). No further records have been found for this soldier.

Private Leonard Watkins enlisted January 20, 1776 (MSA: 18, 9). Private

Leonard Watkins, First Regiment, reenlisted on February 10, 1776 (MSA: 18, 172). Sergeant Leonard Watkins reenlisted on May 2, 1778; discharged on May 11, 1780 (MSA: 18, 256). "Passed January 2, 1813. In favour of Leonard Watkins. RESOLVED, That the treasurer of the western shore be, and he is hereby directed to pay unto Leonard Watkins, a sergeant in the Maryland line, during the revolutionary war, or to his order, a sum of money annually in quarterly payments, equal to the half pay of a sergeant, as a further remuneration for those services rendered his country during the American war." (MSA: 192, 2969).

On April 22, 1818, Leonard Watkins, a resident of Anne Arundel County, Maryland deposed:

> That he entered into the Continental service in the American Revolution as a private in Capt. Barton Lucas' company, attached to Col. Smallwood's Regiment of Maryland troops on the 20th of January 1776; that he joined the Regiment at New York in the same year and was wounded in the foot at the battle of Long Island; that he was in the battle of York Island in the same year; that he returned to Annapolis and received a furlough for a few months; he reenlisted with the army in Capt. Joshua Miles' company attached to the 6th Regt. of Maryland troops commanded by Col. Otho H. Williams; that he joined the regiment, to the best of his recollection, at Valley Forge in the state of Pennsylvania in May 1778; that he was in the battle of Monmouth in June 1778; that he marched to White Plains to West Point Fort and other places and wintered with the regiment at Weeks' farm in Pennsylvania in 1778–1779; that he went to Washington county in Maryland in the recruiting service; that when the regiment marched to the southward in 1780, he was ordered to Frederick Town, Maryland from whence he received his discharge and returned home; his term of service for which he enlisted being extended on the 11th of May 1780.[47]

On November 17, 1820, Leonard Watkins, now a resident of Montgomery County, Maryland, age 66, deposed: "That he enlisted in January 1776 as a private in the company commanded by Captain Barton Lucas in the 1st Maryland Regiment commanded by Col. William Smallwood. He served in that regiment for two years and was then transferred to the 6th Regiment commanded by Col. Otho Holland Williams where he served as a Sgt. until the 10th day of May 1780 when he was discharged at Frederick Town by Maj. Henry Hartman. He was in the battle of Long Island on the 27th day of August 1776 and was there wounded through the right foot; he was in the battle of York Island; the battle of White Plains; and in the battle of Monmouth Court House in New Jersey."[48] "February 28, 1839: Resolved by the General Assembly of Maryland, That the Treasurer of the Western Shore be, and he is hereby directed to pay to Mary Watkins, of Montgomery county, widow of Leonard Watkins, a sergeant of the revolutionary war, or to her order, the half pay of a sergeant of the revolution during her life, in quarterly payments, commencing the first day of January, eighteen hundred and thirty-nine" (MSA: 598, 455).

Private Philip Weller enlisted March 10, 1776 (MSA: 18, 10). He reenlisted on December 10, 1776 and was discharged on December 27, 1779 (MSA: 18, 173). This soldier was taken prisoner at the Battle of Long Island. His surname was spelled erroneously as Wellen. He was later returned to Maryland with a group of others soldiers taken prisoner at the battle.[49]

"Private Philip Weller was the son of John Weller and Catherine Ambrose of Frederick County, Maryland. He married Mary Magdalen Firor and they emigrated to Kentucky in middle life. He was born in Frederick County on April 16, 1754 and died March 1, 1830 in Bardstown, Nelson Co., KY.[50]

Sergeant Levin Wilcoxon enlisted January 30, 1776. His name was listed erroneously as Levin Will Coxen. He was born in Prince George's County, Maryland, on October 15, 1744.

On April 12, 1777, "Levin Wilcoxon a Serjeant in Colonel Stone's Regiment discharged from the service, the facts in his Petition being proved." The petition referred to was not found in the records (MSA: 16, 209). Sergeant Wilcoxon married Mary Brashears February 11, 1780.[51]

In 1783 Levin Wilcoxon was one of the signers of a petition to the Continental Congress asking for help in getting Virginia and Pennsylvania to agree on state boundary lines. From a map included with the petition, the area where the petitioners were then living was described as being to the west of the Allegheny Mountains.[52]

Private Zachariah Willing enlisted February 3, 1776 (MSA: 18, 10). He was one of those taken prisoner the day of the battle and later returned to Maryland.[53]

Private Thomas Windham enlisted March 16, 1776. His surname was erroneously spelled Windom (MSA: 18, 10). Corporal Thomas Wyndham, First Regiment, reenlisted on December 10, 1776, and was discharged on December 27, 1779. He is shown enlisting a third time as Sergeant Thomas Wyndham, January 10, 1780, and was discharged on November 1, 1780 (MSA: 18, 173). A fourth enlistment for Thomas Wyndham occurred on January 14, 1783, when he enlisted for three years.

Thomas Windham was born September 12, 1750, in Prince George's County, Maryland. He died in 1795. On July 21, 1785, a marriage license was issued in Anne Arundel County to Thomas Windham and Sarah Lamb, widow of a fellow soldier of the First Regiment, Joshua Lamb.

A letter dated October 11, 1924, to Silas W. Mack, U.S. Commissioner, Monterey, California from Commissioner, Revolutionary and 1812 War Section states:

> I have to advise you that from the records of this Bureau it appears that Sarah Windham of Annapolis, Maryland, aged 89 years, was allowed pension on account of the Revolutionary War services of her husband, Thomas Windham, on a certificate

which was issued August 25, 1838, and was allowed pension by Special Act of Congress dated March 3, 1839 on account of the Revolutionary War services of her former husband, Joshua Lamb.

From the papers in her two claims for pensions, it appears that she was a widow, Mrs. Sarah Slicer, with a son, Andrew Slicer, when she married at Annapolis, Maryland in June 1777, Joshua Lamb, who was drowned in 1780 or 1781 on 1782, on a voyage to the West Indies in the Schooner Dispatch; she had but one child by Joshua Lamb, a son John, born January 17, 1780.*

She married in 1785 (marriage license dated July 21, 1785) at Annapolis, Maryland, Thomas Windham and he died in May 1795.

They had children — George Washington, born January 29, 178_; Charles, b. May 16, 1790; and Eleanor, born February 16, 1794.

It appears that Joshua Lamb enlisted December 10, 1776 and served as Corporal in the 1st Maryland Regiment; was promoted to Sgt. August 1, 1777 and discharged December 27, 1779.

It appears that Thomas Windham enlisted December 10, 1776, served as Corporal in the 1st Maryland Regiment and was discharged December 27, 1779. He reenlisted January 10, 1780, served as Sgt. in the 1st Maryland Regiment and was discharged November 15, 1783.

A careful search of the records of this Bureau fails to show a claim for a pension filed by a Sarah Windham (all spellings of that name searched), who is reported on the census of pensioners of 1840, as a resident of Goshen, Belmont County, Ohio, on account of the services of any soldier in any War, or at any period prior to 1840.

It is proper to add that said volume was compiled from the reports of the marshals of the several judicial districts, under the Act for taking the Sixth Census, (see title page) and without reference to the archives of this Bureau, and it is not always possible to verify the statements made therein.[54]

Corporal Benedict Woodward enlisted February 3, 1776 (MSA: 18, 9). No further records have been found for this soldier.

Private George Wright enlisted April 11, 1776. No further records have been found for this soldier.

The names of seven soldiers, who were originally listed, have been removed from the roster of the Third Company. In addition to Captain Barton Lucas who was sick the day of the battle, they were:

Private Timothy Collins was apparently transferred to the Third Maryland Battalion prior to the battle. On April 30, 1818, he applied for a pension. At that time,

---

*Joshua Lamb drowned in 1780 on his third voyage to the West Indies in the schooner Dispatch when "all hands, with the vessel and cargo were lost." He had one child, John Lamb, whose birth was recorded in the family Bible in the handwriting of Joshua Lamb. He wrote: "John Lamb, son of John and Sarah, was born January 17, 1780 when people walked across the Chesapeake Bay on the ice (I believe persons were never known to cross the Bay at that part of it any other time than the aforesaid) and Indian meal sold for 5 pounds a bushel (This was Continental money when it had depreciated to almost nothing)."[55]

he deposed that he had enlisted as a private in Captain Daniel Dorsey's Company for five months and was honorably discharged on December 1, 1776, and that he had served in the battles of White Plains, York Island, Brandywine, German Town, Paulus Hook, and in various other skirmishes. Timothy Collins filed another deposition on June 1, 1820, again stating that he had served only under Captain Daniel Dorsey. This soldier, therefore, was not one of The Maryland 400.

Private Hugh Conn was transferred to Captain John Fulford's Company of Artillery. He was, therefore, not one of The Maryland 400.

Private George Evans. This name exists only in the index of volume 18 of the Archives of Maryland. There is no enrollment or other information. It must conclude that there was no soldier by this name.

Private Nathan Peake applied for a pension on November 1, 1819. His application states that he was at the battles of Long Island (crossed through), White Plains, Trenton, and Princeton. In subsequent applications, he mentioned White Plains, Trenton, and Princeton, but never Long Island. Why Private Peake was not at the battle that day is unknown, but he said that he was not, therefore, he must be excluded as one of The Maryland 400.

Private Obediah Summers, whose surname on previous lists was incorrectly shown as Sumers, was transferred to the Second Independent Company of Somerset County under the command of Captain John Gunby by June 26, 1776. He was, therefore, not one of The Maryland 400 (MSA: 18, 641).

Private John Wood is shown to have deserted by May 8, 1776 (MSA: 18, 10). There is no indication that he had returned to his company prior to the battle and, therefore, he would not have been one of The Maryland 400.

Summary

Eighty soldiers were originally shown as enlisted in the Third Company. Of those, 70 are presumed to have gone into battle (excluding the nine men listed above and Captain Lucas who was sick the day of the battle). Forty-two of these men are known to have survived and 28 are unaccounted for. Thirteen men from this company were taken prisoner the day of the battle.

Sixth Company

The soldiers of the Sixth Company were primarily from the Eastern Shore, that is, Queen Anne's, Caroline, and Kent counties. They served under the command of Captain Peter Adams. Unfortunately Captain Adams would not lead his men into battle on August 27 as he was sick. He was, therefore, not one of The Maryland 400. "Major Guest (sic) commanded the Maryland battalion (the col. and lt. col. being both at York). Capts. Adams and Lucas were sick."[1]

Captain Adams, a resident of Great Choptank Hundred, Caroline County, was commissioned on January 3, 1776 (MSA: 18, 13). His brothers, William and Nathan Adams, also served during the war, enlisting in Kent County, Delaware.

On December 10, 1776, Captain Adams attained the rank of lieutenant-colonel. He served throughout the war, retiring on April 12, 1783.[2] He died prior to September 5, 1785, when his will was probated in Caroline County. His brother, William Adams, was executor and sole legatee of his estate.[3]

Captain Adams served under General Smallwood throughout the war, but he was not one of his favorites. On September 12, 1781, Smallwood wrote to Gov. Thomas Sim:

> I arrived early the next Morning after I left Annapolis, at George Town, Col° Adams had marched the day before from Cameron and crossed the Ferry at Colchester, I detached an Officer after him with Orders to leave at Dumfries the covered Waggon for the Officers of the first and second Regiments, Thirty five Tents, and two Waggons for use of the 4th Regiment, urging the necessity of this distribution that the Troops might fare alike, and that the State was making every exertion to forward Supplies to them, but as he paid no Attention to the former Order respecting the covered Waggon, it is doubtful whether he will comply with this, as he is more commonly actuated by caprice and invincible Obstinacy, than that propriety of Conduct which should ever mark and distinguish the Officer, but I haveleft it optional with him to comply with the order or subject himself to an Arrest.[4]

Little data has been compiled about the services of African Americans during the Revolutionary War. We have been taught in the past that they were precluded from enlisting, but the obituary of Thomas Carney who served under Captain Peter Adams would seem to contradict this:

Died on June 30, near the village of Denton, Md., Thomas Carney, a colored man, age 74. At the commencement of the Revolution, he enlisted as a soldier under Col. Peter Adams and was in the battle of Germantown. When the Maryland and Delaware lines were ordered to the south, Tom marched with his regiment; at the battle of Guilford Court House, he bore a conspicuous part as a soldier and has often persisted that when the Maryland troops came to the charge, he bayoneted 7 of the enemy. At Camden, Hobkirk's Hill, and Ninety-Six, he bore his part under Howard. At Ninety-Six, his Captain, the late Maj. Gen. Benson, received a dangerous wound. Tom carried him on his shoulders to the place where the surgeon was stationed.[5]

Private William Aitken enlisted May 7, 1776 (MSA: 18, 15). No further records have been found for this soldier.

Private James Barclay enlisted May 7, 1776. His surname was spelled Barkley (MSA: 18, 15). James Barclay of the First Regiment is shown as having been discharged June 1778 with the notation that he had deserted (MSA: 18, 82).

Private James Bell enlisted January 30, 1776 (MSA: 18, 14). No further records have been found for this soldier.

Private Joseph Bootman enlisted January 30, 1776 (MSA: 18, 14). Sergeant Joseph Bootman reenlisted in the First Regiment on December 10, 1776, and was discharged on February 7, 1777, and it was noted that he was dead (MSA: 18, 81). Sergeant Joseph Bootman was killed February 7, 1777.[6]

Private John Bryan enlisted February 15, 1776.[7] Private John Bryan, Seventh Regiment, enlisted on June 10, 1777, and was discharged on November 1, 1780 (MSA: 18, 188). In 1778 John Bryan is noted as having been "taken by prior enlistment. Reenlisted in State Regiment" (MSA: 18, 86).

On September 6, 1781, it was ordered "that the Commissary of Stores deliver to John Bryan late a soldier in the Extra Regiment a suit of Cloaths Complete, one hat, one pair Shoes one pair Stockings and two shirts" (MSA: 45, 604).

John Bryan married Elizabeth Carroll on January 18, 1780, in Frederick County, Maryland.[8] The family moved to Adams County, Ohio, by 1810 and John Bryan died there on November 20, 1827.

Private Carberry Burns enlisted January 23, 1776. His name was given erroneously as Carbry Burn (MSA: 18, 14). It is assumed that Private Burns was taken prisoner by the British at the Battle of Long Island and after undoubtedly being starved and mistreated by his captors and facing death, he enlisted with the British.

Sometimes listed as Private Carbry Burns and others as Carberry Burns, this soldier was shown on the muster rolls of Captain Francis Stephenson's Light Infantry Company, Queen's Rangers beginning April 24, 1778, and ending August 24, 1781.[9]

Private James Carmichael enlisted February 24, 1776 (MSA: 18, 15). Private Carmichael reenlisted in the First Regiment on December 10, 1776, and was discharged on July 10, 1777 (MSA: 18, 91). On July 13, 1778, it was ordered "that the said Treasurer pay to James Carmichael fourPounds fifteen shillings amount of Account passed by the Auditor General" (MSA: 21, 158).

Private John Clark enlisted January 22, 1776 (MSA: 18, 14). No further records have been found for this soldier.

Private William Clark enlisted May 7, 1776 (MSA: 18, 15). He reenlisted in the First Regiment on December 10, 1776, and was discharged in July 1777 at which time it was noted that he had deserted (MSA: 18, 91).

Crisenberry Clift enlisted May 15, 1776 (MSA: 18, 15). He was one of the soldiers taken prisoner at the battle. On February 14, 1777, his name, spelled erroneously as Christenburry Cuff, was listed on the payroll for "prisoners taken on Long Island from 27th August to the 10th December, 1776" as being returned to Maryland.[10]

Private Henry Clift enlisted February 6, 1776 (MSA: 18, 14). No further records have been found for this soldier.

Private Thomas Cooper enlisted February 6, 1776 (MSA: 18, 14). Private Cooper was taken prisoner at the battle. His name appeared on the payroll for "prisoners taken on Long Island from 27th August to the 10th December, 1776" being returned to Maryland.[11] "Thos. Cooper, Private, died 1 Apl '82" (MSA: 18, 442).

Private Henry Covington enlisted January 22, 1776 (MSA: 18, 14). He reenlisted in the First Regiment on December 10, 1776, was promoted to corporal on July 1, 1779, and was discharged on January 12, 1780 (MSA: 18, 192). On April 20, 1780, a commission was issued to "1st Lieut. Henry Covington" (MSA: 43, 146).

Private James Craig enlisted February 22, 1776 (MSA: 18, 14). No further records have been found for this soldier.

Private George Dowling enlisted May 7, 1776. His name was given as Geo. Dowling (MSA: 18, 15). No further records have been found for this soldier.

Corporal Daniel Dwiggins enlisted January 22, 1776. His name was given as Danl. Dwigens (MSA: 18, 14). The name of Sergeant Daniel Dwigins appeared on the payroll for "prisoners taken on Long Island from 27th August to the 10th December, 1776" being returned to Maryland.[12]

Corporal Samuel Dwiggins enlisted January 24, 1776. His name was given as Saml. Dwigens (MSA: 18, 14). This soldier was one of those taken prisoner at the battle. His name, erroneously given as Corporal Samuel Durgins was on the payroll for "prisoners taken on Long Island from 27th August to the 10th December, 1776" being returned to Maryland.[13]

Sergeant Thomas Dwyer enlisted January 30, 1776 (MSA: 18, 13). "Thomas Dwyer, drummer, 1st Regiment, enlisted March 16, 1778" (MSA: 18, 105).

Sergeant Edward Edgerly enlisted February 15, 1776 (MSA: 18, 13). He was commissioned as a second lieutenant in the Second Regiment on January 14, 1777; appointed regimental adjutant on April 3, 1778; commissioned as first lieutenant on May 27, 1778; and ultimately captain on September 10, 1779. He was transferred to the Fifth Regiment on January 1, 1781. Captain Edward Edgerly was killed at the battle of Eutaw Springs (South Carolina) on September 8, 1781.[14]

"Wednesday, May 22, 1782. A representation from major John Davidson and lieutenant Christopher Richmond, on behalf of the natural son of major Edward Edgerly, who fell at the Eutau, was preferred and read, and referred to Mr. Stone, Mr. Forrest, and Mr. Rowland, to consider and report thereon."[15]

> Friday, May 24, 1782. THE committee, appointed to take into consideration the representation of major Davidson and Mr. Richmond, in behalf of a destitute child, beg leave to report, that your committee, from circumstances, are of opinion, that a child now in the city of Annapolis, and commonly called and known by the name of Edward Edgerly, was the natural son of captain Edward Edgerly, a respectable and brave officer in the Maryland line, who fell at the battle of Eutau; that captain Edgerly, by acts of attention and parental care, sufficiently manifested his affection for the child, and an opinion that he was his son; that the child is at present almost entirely destitute of maintenance and support; that captain Edgerly has no legal representative in this country; Therefore it is the opinion of this committee, that affection for officers who have died for their country, political gratitude to a virtuous citizen, humanity for an helpless infant, are considerations superior to those which arise from the distinctions the law has raised between legitimate and natural born children; that therefore the interest of the account of the money which the legal representatives to captain Edgerly would have been entitled to receive from this State, shall go to the maintenance and education of the said child, who shall be named Edward Edgerly; that the age of twenty-one years, or day of marriage, the principal of the money aforesaid shall belong to the said Edward Edgerly, but if he shall die before he arrives to the age of twenty-one years, and without being married or leaving issue, then the money as aforesaid shall be vested in the State. All which is submitted to the honourable house. By order, J. KNAPP, clk.[16]

Sergeant Joseph Elliott enlisted January 30, 1776 (MSA: 18, 13). No further records have been found for this soldier.

Lieutenant Nathaniel Ewing was commissioned second lieutenant on January 3, 1776 (MSA: 18, 13).

On June 18, 1776, Lieutenant Nathaniel Ewing was paid "six Pounds four Shillings for Expences incurred in guarding a sick Prisoner sent from the Colony of

North Carolina, from the City of Annapolis to Pennsylvania. Ordered That the said Treasurer pay to said Nathaniel Ewing thirty nine Shillings for thread for the use of the Troops" (MSA: 11, 497).

Captain Nathaniel Ewing of Maryland was erroneously shown as having died in 1780 in *Known Military Dead during the American Revolutionary War* by Clarence S. Peterson.[17]

Captain Ewing lived in St. Mary's County, Maryland, after the war until 1809 when he moved to Franklin County, Tennessee. He married, first, Catherine, widow of John Reeder, on February 24, 1784, and, second, Elizabeth, widow of William Cartwright, on June 16, 1807.[18]

His death notice reads: "February 23, 1818. Col. Nathaniel Ewing died Dec. 28, 1817 in Winchester, Tennessee in his 73rd year. He was one among many who stepped forward in the Revolutionary struggle for independence in which he entered as Lt. in the U.S. Army, and continued in the service of his country until the conclusion of the war in 1783, during which time he obtained the grade of Colonel."[19]

Private Thomas Fisher enlisted January 30, 1776 (MSA: 18, 14). Thomas Fisher was listed on the payroll for "prisoners taken on Long Island from 27th August to the 10th December, 1776" being returned to Maryland.[20]

Corporal Daniel Floyd enlisted January 23, 1776 (MSA: 18, 14). No further records have been found for this soldier.

Private Elijah Floyd enlisted January 23, 1776 (MSA: 18, 14). No further records have been found for this soldier.

Private John Floyd enlisted January 23, 1776 (MSA: 18, 14). Private John Floyd is showing enlisting in the Fifth Regiment on May 29, 1777. He was discharged on September 24, 1777 (MSA: 14, 279).

Private Moses Floyd enlisted January 23, 1776 (MSA: 18, 14). This is probably the same Moses Floyd who married Drucilla Rumbley in Caroline County, Maryland, in October 1775.[21] No further records have been found for this soldier.

Private Alexander Fulton enlisted February 3, 1776. His name was shown as Alex. Fulton (MSA: 18, 14). Private Alexander Fulton of the First Regiment was discharged December 27, 1779 (MSA: 18, 108).

Private Hugh Galway enlisted May 7, 1776 (MSA: 18, 15). On December 10, 1776, Private Hugh Galloway (*sic*) is shown having enlisted in the First Regiment. He was discharged March 15, 1779, and it was noted that he had deserted (MSA: 18, 112).

Private Jonathan Galway enlisted February 24, 1776 (MSA: 18, 15). No further records have been found for this soldier.

Private James Gibson enlisted February 24, 1776. His name was given as Jas. Gibson (MSA: 18, 15). No further records have been found for this soldier.

Private William Glover enlisted February 15, 1776 (MSA: 18, 14). "William Glover. Passed by Col. Orme." Undated, but appears to be in 1778 (MSA: 18, 341). "Pvt. William Glover, 6th Co., Capt. Lloyd Beall." No date.

Private John Hatton enlisted January 23, 1776 (MSA: 18, 14). This soldier reenlisted on October 26, 1779, and was discharged on July 1780 (MSA: 18, 124).

Private William Holmes enlisted February 15, 1776. His name was given as William Holms (MSA: 18, 14). Private Holmes was taken prisoner at the battle. His name, given as William Holme, was listed on the "payroll for prisoners taken on Long Island from 27th August to the 10th December, 1776" being returned to Maryland.[22] He reenlisted in the First Regiment on December 10, 1776, and was discharged on December 27, 1779 (MSA: 18, 117).

On January 22, 1780, the commissary of stores was ordered to deliver to, among others, William Holmes, "1 pʳ Overalls, 1 pr. Shoes 1 pʳ Stockings, 1 Coat, 1 vest and 1 Shirt in part of the Cloathing due them from the Continent" (MSA: 43, 65).

On February 17, 1781, the treasurer of the Western Shore was ordered to "pay to William Holmes Twenty eight pounds eight shillings and nine pence of the same Emission in lieu of eleven hundred and thirty seven pounds ten shillings due him per Account passed by the Aud. Gen" (MSA: 45, 314).

Private George Jackson enlisted January 22, 1776 (MSA:18, 14). No further records have been found for this soldier.

Private John Johnston enlisted January 25, 1776 (MSA: 18, 14). His surname was erroneously spelled as Johnson.

According to family tradition, John Johnston was born in Annandale, Scotland, and was part of the Johnston family to whom Sir Walter Scott referred saying, "Among the glades of Annandale The gentle Johnston's ride; They have been there a thousand years. A thousand more they'll bide."[23]

This member of the Johnston family, however, would not remain in Annandale. He ran away from home at the age of 16 and eventually made his way to Baltimore where he lived quietly until the outbreak of the war.

As the soldiers were marching to Philadelphia, they passed through Path Valley, Maryland, stopping at the Almony farm for water. "The young daughter of this house Ann Almeny by name stood in the doorway and after taking one good look at her, John Johnston vowed that if he returned alive from the war, he would make her his wife. And it is pleasing to relate, that after receiving his discharge he was able to make good his vow."[24]

In 1798, John Johnston moved his family to Steubenville, Ohio, where he bought a large farm. Private Johnston died at his home on March 19, 1838. Members of the family with whom the author has spoken state that his death was recorded in the Devine family bible, location now unknown, and that he died at the age of 106 years and 3 months.

Ensign John Jordan was commissioned January 3, 1776 (MSA: 18, 13). By December 10, 1776, when he reenlisted, he had been promoted to the rank of lieutenant of the First Regiment (MSA: 18, 126). Just a little over a year later on December 20, 1777, he was commissioned captain and transferred to the Second Regiment where he served through the remainder of the war (MSA: 18,126, 363, 379).

John Jordan was the son of John Jordan of St. Mary's County and his wife, Eleanor Dent. Like many of the soldiers, he put his life on hold until after the war. On December 27, 1787, he married Sarah Harrison, daughter of Robert Hanson Harrison and Elizabeth Chapman of Charles County. Their only child, Maria Jordan, was born on October 21, 1788, but John Jordan would have only a little bit of time to get to know his daughter as he died on November 8, less than three weeks later. Maria died in 1792 at the age of four.

Sarah (Harrison) Jordan married her second husband, Adam Craik, son of Dr. James Craik, one of the physicians who attended George Washington at his death: "There were three physicians in attendance at the time of the death of George Washington in 1799. One was Dr. Elisha Cullen Dick and the other two were Dr. Richard Gustavus Brown of "Rose Hill" at Port Tobacco and Dr. James Craik of La Plata. Dr. Brown is buried at Rose Hill while Dr. Craik is buried at the Old Presbyterian Meeting House at Alexandria, Virginia."[25]

In October 1796 Sarah was married for the third and last time to David Easton. He died in 1835. Sarah applied to the General Assembly of Maryland asking for a pension based on the service of John Jordan. "Resolution No. 26, in favour of Sarah Easton. Passed January 1835. Resolved by the General Assembly of Maryland, That the Treasurer of the Western Shore pay to Sarah Easton, who was the widow of Captain John Jordon, in quarterly payments, during her life a sum of money equal to the half pay of a Captain in consideration of the services rendered by her said husband, during the revolutionary war" (MSA: 214, 719–720).

Private James Kelly enlisted January 26, 1776. His name was given as Jas. Kelly (MSA: 18, 14). Private James Kelly of the First Regiment reenlisted on December 10, 1776, and was discharged on August 22, 1777. No reenlistment was shown, but he was said to be a prisoner on December 27, 1779 (MSA: 18, 129). "Deserters Sent to Chester Town. Wm. Lock and James Kelly, deserters taken up in Harford Co. for two of the Classes of this Co. and delivered to Col. Dallam, October 17, 1780" (MSA: 18, 346).

Private John Kirby enlisted February 24, 1776. His surname was spelled Kerby (MSA: 18, 15). On December 10, 1776, Private John Kirby of the First Regiment reenlisted. He was discharged on August 22 (year not given) and it was noted he was a prisoner (MSA: 18, 129).

Private James Kirk enlisted February 15, 1776. His name was given as Jas. Kirk (MSA: 18, 129). On May 19, 1781, "Jas." Kirk enlisted for three years (MSA: 18, 429).

Private Thomas Laffy enlisted February 15. 1776 (MSA: 18, 14). No further records have been found for this soldier.

Private William Layton enlisted January 22, 1776. His name was spelled Wm. Laighton. This surname appears to have been spelled Layton by the families of the Eastern Shore.

> Kentucky, Fleming County Sct. On this 9th day of August 1832 personally appeared in open court sitting, William H. Layton, resident of Fleming County Kentucky aged seventy seven years who being first duly sworn according to law doth on his oath make the following declaration in order to obtain the benefit of the act of Congress passed June 7th 1832.
>
> That he enlisted in the service of the United States in the month of January 1776 in the State of Delaware and County of Kent for one year as a common soldier in the company commanded by Capt. Adams in the Regiment commanded by Colo. Haselet marched to Lewistown from thence to Philadelphia and from thence to Long Island and there fought a battle with the British, the Americans commanded by General Southerland and was whiped and had to retreat to the City of Philadelphia there he marched to Trenton and fought and was at the Battle and taking of the Hessions, the Americans commanded by General Washington, attached to Capt. Moors Company, discharged January 1777 at Philadelphia where he received an Honorable and written discharge signed by Capt. James Moore and then returned home to Kent County Delaware. He enlisted in the month of June 1781 for three years or during the war in the Company of Capt. Beasey in the Fourth Maryland Regiment commanded by Colo. Carvell Hall, was marched and fought at the Battle of the Cowpens: General Green commanded and was no other engagement until the Siege of York at the Surrender of Cornwallis. Some time after the Siege was discharged on account of the white swelling*; and received an unlimited furlow and written discharge lost having got wet and worn out in his pocket. He further states that he knows of no person whose testimony he can provide who can testify to his service and further he states he resided in Maryland until the last thirty years.
>
> He hereby relinquishes every claim whatever to a pension or annuity except the present, and declares that his name is not on the pension roll of the agency of any State.
>
> Sworn to and subscribed the day and year aforesaid in open court. Signature of Wm. H. Layton.[26]

By the time of the 1840 census, William H. Layton, age 83, Revolutionary War pensioner, was living in Harrison County, Kentucky, in the home of James Whiteaker.

Tuberculosis of the bones and joints.

Private William Leeson enlisted February 15, 1776 (MSA: 18, 14). I believe this to be the same man listed as Sergeant William Leamon, who enlisted in the First Regiment on April 22, 1777, and was discharged on April 22, 1780 (MSA: 18, 135).

Private William Locke enlisted February 24, 1776. His name was given as Wm. Lock (MSA: 18, 15). Private Locke was taken prisoner at the battle. His name, given as William Look, was listed on the "payroll for prisoners taken on Long Island from 27th August to the 10th December, 1776" being returned to Maryland.[27]

As Corporal William Lock, this soldier reenlisted the same day he was returned from captivity, December 10, 1776, was discharged May 23, 1778, and was noted as "deserted" (MSA: 18, 132). Although no record is found, he must have reenlisted yet again because on August 4, 1780, William Lock, First Maryland Regiment, appeared on a list of deserters submitted by Richard Dallam, Lt., Harford County (MSA: 18, 344). "Deserters Sent to Chester Town. Wm. Lock and James Kelly, deserters taken up in Harford Co. for two of the Classes of this Co. and delivered to Col. Dallam, October 17, 1780" (MSA: 18, 346).

Private John Lowrey enlisted February 22, 1776. His name was given as John Lowry (MSA: 18, 14). Private Lowrey was taken prisoner at the battle. His name, given as John Lowrey was listed on the "payroll for prisoners taken on Long Island from 27th August to the 10th December, 1776" being returned to Maryland.[28]

John Willis Barlow, a descendant of John Lowrey, provided the following information from the Orphan's Court of Harford County, Maryland:

> June Court, 1785 — Court ordered that John Lowrey, a wounded soldier of the 1st Maryland Regiment and Capt. Adams' Company, who having a regular discharge which is lost or mislaid, on the testimony of Ignatius Wheeler, Jr., Esq. be allowed fifteen pounds for two years up to June 27, 1785.
>
> August Court, 1787 — Court granted John Lowrey, a maimed soldier of the First Maryland Regiment, half pay of 7 pounds, 10 shillings, up to June 27, 1787. Order given to Ignatius Wheeler, Esq., on August 14, 1787.
>
> January Court, 1790 — John Lowrey, a soldier, to make known to the Court where he was wounded, at what place, and who commanded. Appeared in Court and said that he served in 1st Maryland Regt. under Colonel Smallwood and he was wounded through the groin in the Battle of Long Island on August 27, 1776.
>
> January 23, 1805: A petition of John Lowry, of the county of Harford, in the State of Maryland, was presented to the House and read, praying an augmentation of the pension heretofore granted to the petitioner by law, in consideration of a wound received at the battle on Long Island, in the State of New York, during the Revolutionary war with Great Britain, which hath rendered him incapable of obtaining a livelihood by labor.
>
> Ordered, That the said petition be referred to the Committee of the Whole House to whom was committed, on the second instant, the bill in addition to "An act to make provision for persons that have been disabled by known wounds received in the service of the United States, during the Revolutionary war."[29]

According to a letter written by Margaret Willis, John Lowrey's daughter, it was stated that her father, "...enlisted in the year 1775 for 7 years or during the war in the 7th Regiment of the Maryland Line. He was in the Battle of Long Island and there received a wound by a ball entering the calf of his leg from which he soon recovered and entered he again received a ball entering the groin and extracted and the wound became a running sore for life. He lay 19 months in the hospital and was honorably discharged by his officers and approved by his doctors on the 20th day of April 1781, he was a cripple for life and received a small pension of 60 dollars per annum."[30]

John Lowry (Lowrey) was born on April 27, 1750, in Cecil County, Maryland. His parents were James Lowry and Mary Veazey, who were married in St. Mary Anne's Parish in Cecil County, Maryland, on April 27, 1748. He married Hannah Finney, daughter of Manassah Finney of Harford County, Maryland. The birth, marriage, and death dates of Hannah Finney Lowrey are unknown, but the will of Manassah Finney includes his daughter Hannah Lowrey and her husband John Lowrey.[31]

John Lowrey died intestate prior to September 6, 1815, as recorded in the registry of administrations granted in Baltimore County. The administrator was his son-in-law, Cornelius Willis, who married his daughter, Margaretta, in Baltimore on April 13, 1797. The registry had the names of two securities, but there was nothing to secure or claim.[32]

Private John Lynch enlisted February 24, 1776 (MSA: 18, 15). This soldier reenlisted in the First Regiment on August 5, 1777, and was discharged on November 1, 1780 (MSA: 18, 135). On December 1, 1789, Corporal John Lynch of the First Maryland Regiment, a resident of Kent County, was shown on a return of invalid pensioners. It was noted that his pension had commenced in 1786 (MSA: 18, 632).

"August 17, 1791: List of Orders drawn by the Orphans Courts in the several Counties in favor of Invalid Pensioners, discounted by the Collectors and allowed by the western shore Treasurer from the first of November 1790 to the first of July 1791. When drawn: Novem'r. 12; in whose favor: John Lynch; in what County: Kent; when allowed: April 1791; Sums: 8:5:0" (MSA: 72, 215).

> February 5, 1807: THE committee to whom was referred the petition of John Lynch, of Kent county, late a soldier in the revolutionary war, report, that they have had the same under consideration, and find, from ample testimony that the petitioner was wounded when fighting the battles of his country, which secured liberty and independence to America, the effects of which have rendered him unable, in his advanced age, to procure a support for himself and children, who are dependent on him for their subsistence; with this view of his case, your committee, under the impression that it becomes the duty of this state to provide for the unfortunate and meritorious soldier, who has spent the prime of his life, and nobly shed his blood, in her cause, recommend the following resolution:

RESOLVED, That the treasurer of the western shore be and he is hereby directed and required to pay to John Lynch, of Kent county, late soldier in the revolutionary war, or to his order, in half yearly payments, a. sum of money equal to the half pay of a corporal. All which is submitted [MSA: 555, 46].

"November 10, 1808. A petition from John Lynch, of Kent county, stating that he had been a revolutionary soldier, and praying the pay of a corporal during life, was preferred, read, and referred to Mr. Moffitt, Mr. Welch and Mr. Frazier, to consider and report thereon" [MSA: 556, 6].

November 15, 1808: Mr. Moffitt, from the committee, delivers to the speaker the following report: THE committee to whom was referred the petition of John Lynch, of Kent county, beg leave to report, that they have had the same under consideration, and are of opinion that the facts therein stated are true, and that the sum heretofore allowed him under his late misfortune, has become inadequate for his support; and under the impression that it becomes the duty of the state to provide for the unfortunate and war-worn soldier, who spent the prime of his life, and shed his blood, in fighting the battles of his country, beg leave to recommend the following resolution:

RESOLVED, That the treasurer of the western shore be and he is hereby directed and required to pay John Lynch, of Kent county, late a soldier in the revolutionary war, or to his order, the sum of thirty-three pounds, the full pay of a corporal, annually, in half yearly payments, instead of the half pay heretofore allowed him. All which is submitted [MSA: 556, 13-14].

Private Robert Man enlisted February 22, 1776 (MSA: 18, 14). No further records have been found for this soldier.

Private Hugh McClain enlisted February 24, 1776 (MSA: 18, 15). Private Hugh McLane, First Regiment, enlisted on December 10, 1776 and was discharged on April 25, 1779 (MSA: 18, 137). "December 1, 1789: Private Hugh McClean, 1st Regiment. Invalid pensioner; pension commenced in 1785" (MSA: 18, 632).

"June 12, 1792: The Auditor is requested to issue a Certificate for the Depreciation of pay to Frederick Mire late a soldier in the first Maryland Regiment and deliver the same to the Treasurer of the western shore, who is Ordered to pay it to Hugh McClean Administrator of the said Frederick Mire" (MSA: 72, 276).

Private John McClain enlisted January 23, 1776. "Absent, on furlough" (MSA: 18, 14). Private McClain was taken prisoner at the battle. His name, given as John McLaine, was listed on the "payroll for prisoners taken on Long Island from 27th August to the 10th December, 1776" being returned to Maryland.[33] "Corporal Jno. McLane, 1st Regiment, enlisted O.S.; discharged December 27, 1779" (MSA: 18, 137). As Private John McClaine, he enlisted again on August 1, 1780, and was discharged on September 7, 1783 (MSA: 18, 548).

Private John McClain (of Harford) enlisted February 22, 1776 (MSA: 18, 14). He was from Harford County and identified as shown to keep his identity separate from John McClain above. No further records have been found for this soldier.

Private Samuel McCubbin enlisted February 15, 1776. His name was given as Sam'l. McCubbin (MSA: 18, 14). No further records have been found for this soldier.

Private William McDaniel enlisted January 22, 1776. His name was given as Wm. McDaniel (MSA: 18, 14). No further records have been found for this soldier.

Private William McDaniel, 2nd enlisted January 30, 1776. His name was given as Willm. McDaniel (MSA: 18, 14).

Private William McGregor enlisted January 30, 1776. His name was given as Willm. McGreger (MSA: 18, 14). On October 17, 1780, William McGreagor's name was shown on a list of deserters sent to Chester Town (MSA: 18, 346).

Sergeant Thomas McKeel enlisted January 30, 1776 (MSA: 18, 13). He was taken prisoner at the battle. His name, given as Sergt. Thomas McKee, was listed on the "payroll for prisoners taken on Long Island from 27th August to the 10th December, 1776" being returned to Maryland.[34]

Private John Morrow enlisted May 7, 1776 (MSA: 18, 15). No further records for this soldier have been found.

Lieutenant Alexander Murray was commissioned as second lieutenant on January 14, 1776. His name was given as Alex. Murray (MSA: 18, 13). He was commissioned first lieutenant in August 1776 and then captain of the First Maryland Regiment on December 10, 1776. He resigned on June 10, 1777, and joined the navy.[35]

Alexander Murray was born on July 12, 1754, in Chestertown, Queen Anne's County, Maryland. He was the son of Dr. William Murray, a native of Scotland, and Ann Smith. He was the grandson of James Murray who fled to Barbados with his

Alexander Murray. Lieutenant Murray's preference had been for sea duty, but with no ships available, he entered the army. By the end of the war, he had participated in 13 engagements on sea and shore and had been taken prisoner twice. On July 8, 1813, he was appointed as the first commandant of the Philadelphia Navy Yard (originally published in *The Port Folio Magazine,* Philadelphia, Pennsylvania, May 1814).

family after he was banished and his estates confiscated during the Jacobite rebellion of 1745.

Lieutenant Murray wanted sea service, but at the time of his enlistment there were no vessels available so he elected to enlist in the First Maryland Regiment instead. "The bursting and several pieces of cannon on the New-York battery, did such injury to his sense of hearing, as to impair it through life."[36] "On October 20, 1777 he commanded the brig Saratoga owned by Samuel and Robert Purviance of Baltimore, mounting 12 carriage-guns and 8 swivels. On April 5, 1779 he commanded the brig Columbus, owned by the Purviances, mounting 10 guns and 6 swivels. On June 24, 1780, he commanded the brig Revenge owned by John Muir and others of Baltimore, mounting 12 guns and 2 swivels."[37]

By the end of the war, Alexander Murray had participated in thirteen engagements on sea and shore and had been taken prisoner twice. With the organization of the U.S. Navy in 1798, he was commissioned captain and participated in the Quasi War with France and the Barbary Coast Wars. From 1808 until his death on October 6, 1821, Murray was superintendent of gunboats at Philadelphia. On July 8, 1813, he was appointed as the first commandant of the Philadelphia Navy Yard.[38]

In 1815 Alexander Murray was the Navy's most senior officer, but he was bypassed when Stephen Decatur was promoted to command the navy in the war against Algiers. Leiner writes, "When he had last served in the Mediterranean a dozen years before, William Eaton, the United States consul at Tunis, had sneered that the United States might as well send out Quaker meeting houses to float about the sea, as frigates with Murray in command."[39]

Alexander Murray died on October 6, 1821. "He died on the 6th instant, at his residence near Germantown, with the prevailing fever, and though his sufferings were acutely painful, he bore them with his characteristic patience and firmness. When his death was announced in the navy yard, all labour was instantly arrested, and a silent gloom clouded the countenance of all, from the highest to the lowest. They felt that they had lost a kind protector — a just and generous commander."[40]

> His funeral was solemn and imposing, and altogether corresponding with his rank, character, and services. Flags were displayed at half mast at the navy yard, and by the merchant shipping of the port. The corpse was conducted from the house of Benjamin Chew, Esq., in Philadelphia, by a numerous escort, and a large concourse of respectable citizens, to the burying-ground in Market Street.
>
> During the movement of the procession, which was arranged in the following order, minute guns were fired from the North Carolina and marine barracks.
>
> Military escort under the command of Lieutenant Broom. A veteran Tar bearing the broad pendant at half mast. The Reverend Clergy. The Body borne by sailors dressed in white. Pall Bearers. General Scott, General Cadwallader, Captain Biddle, Captain Brown, Major Gamble, Captain Dallas. Mourners. Attending Physicians. Cincinnati Society. Officers of the Navy. Officers of the Army. Officers of the First Brigade of Pennsylvania Volunteers. Citizens.[41]

The U.S. Navy has named two ships in honor of Alexander Murray. The first was the USS *Murray* (DD-97, 1918–1922) and the second, DD-576 (1943–1965) was named for him and his grandson, also named Alexander Murray, who had a long and distinguished career in the navy, retiring as a rear admiral in 1876.[42]

Private William Nagle enlisted February 24, 1776. His name was given as Wm. Nagle (MSA: 18,15). He reenlisted in the 1st Regiment on December 10, 1776, and was discharged on February 4, 1777, at which time it was noted that he was dead. His name was given this time as William Neagle (MSA: 18, 146).

Private Zachariah Nicholson enlisted January 22, 1776. His name was given as Zacha. Nicholson (MSA: 18, 14). No further records have been found for this soldier.

Private Joseph Perkins enlisted January 30, 1776. His name is given as Joseph Pirkens (MSA: 18, 14). No further records have been found for this soldier.

Private John Phelps enlisted May 20, 1776 (MSA: 18, 15). No further records have been found for this soldier.

Private John Powell enlisted January 30, 1776 (MSA:18, 14). No further records have been found for this soldier.

Private Patrick Quigley enlisted February 22, 1776, and it was noted he was in the "*black hole.*" His first name was spelled Patk (MSA: 18, 15). No further records have been found for this soldier.

Private William Ray enlisted February 15, 1776. His name was given as Wm. Ray (MSA: 18, 14). No further records have been found for this soldier.

Private Robert Ritchie enlisted February 24, 1776. His name was given as Robt. Ritchie and it was noted that he was "sick in barracks" (MSA: 18, 15). No further records have been found for this soldier.

Corporal James Rogan enlisted January 30, 1776. His name was given as Jas. Rogan (MSA: 18, 14). No further records have been found for this soldier.

Private Robert Ross, Drummer enlisted February 15, 1776 (MSA: 18, 14). No further records have been found for this soldier.

Private William Temple enlisted May 7, 1776. His name was given as Wm. Temple (MSA: 18, 15). No further records have been found for this soldier.

Private Hugh Wallace enlisted January 30, 1776 (MSA: 18, 14). No further records have been found for this soldier.

Private Thomas Williams enlisted February 24, 1776 (MSA: 18, 15). This soldier reenlisted in the First Regiment on December 10, 1776. "Corpl 1 Aug 77 redd. 10 feb 78 discharged left out of musr. taken in April 80" (MSA: 18, 173).

Private Alexander Wright enlisted January 23, 1776. His name as given as Alex. Wright (MSA: 18, 14). No further records have been found for this soldier.

The names of three soldiers, who were originally listed, have been removed from the roster of the Sixth Company. In addition to Captain Peter Adams who was sick the day of the battle, they were:

Private John McFadden, whose surname had originally been shown as McFadon, applied for a pension on August 31, 1838:

> August 31, 1838: Declaration of John McFadden of Sugar Creek Township, Venago County, Pennsylvania, age 83, born in Cecil County, Maryland and was living there in 1776 when he entered the service of the United States. He enlisted in March of that year for 12 months in the infantry company commanded by Captain Peter Adams. The company rendezvoused at Annapolis where we joined by several other companies and went under the command of Colonel Small (sic), Major Price was an officer of the regiment and Captain Stone commanded another company and Captain Scott another company. I was retained in Captain Adams' Company.
>
> From Annapolis, we were marched to Philadelphia (went by water to the head of the Elk) under Colonel Small (sic) as aforesaid. From thence, we marched to New York. We lay at New York a few days until the battle of Long Island took place. **Applicant was not in that engagement, being confined by fever to his tent.** [Emphasis added.] At the battle of Long Island, the company the applicant belonged to was so much reduced that but 14 or 15 men remained and they were attached to Captain Ramsay's infantry company of the same regiment and were then marched up the North river to Kingsbridge and lay there some time and applicant in company with Lt. Ewing went to Newark in Jersey where he remained with the lieutenant in consequence of ill health, where the lieutenant and applicant joined their regiment at Trenton soon after which an engagement took place between the British and our army under Washington. After dark, the fires were lighted and we were marched to Princeton where an engagement took place. Petitioner was engaged in this battle and in the hottest part of the engagement, and was within a few rods of General Mercer when he fell. After this engagement, the term of his enlistment having expired, Petitioner returned to his place of residence in Maryland, with his comrades.[43]

Fifer Charles McKeel was discharged on June 7, 1776, well over two months before the battle and should have never been listed as one of The Maryland 400 (MSA: 18, 14).

Summary

Seventy-two soldiers were originally shown as enlisted in the Sixth Company. Of those, 69 are presumed to have gone into battle (excluding the two men listed above and Captain Adams who was sick the day of the battle). Thirty-five of these men are known to have survived and 34 are unaccounted for. Ten men from this company were taken prisoner the day of the battle.

Ninth Company

The men of the Ninth Company were almost, without exception, from Frederick County, Maryland, created from Prince George's County in 1748. Most of them were of German ancestry.

Frederick County was truly frontier territory where families lived under the daily threat of Indian attacks. Either they or their fathers had fought in the French and Indian War and they became known for their ability to fight "Indian style," their superior marksmanship, and for their patriotic zeal.

Maryland had problems with Tories throughout the war, but none were dealt with more harshly than those who lived in Frederick County:

> While there were a number of Tories among the citizens of Maryland there were very few to be found among the German settlers. These, as a rule, were ardent patriots, and there were few instances where Germans were arrested as Tories. There was, however, one notable exception. In 1781 another plan was formed by the British and Tories for dividing the northern colonies from the southern. According to this scheme Cornwallis was to march inland from the Chesapeake and meet the bands of Tories which were to be raised and armed in the interior. In maturing their plans it was arranged that a disguised British officer was to meet a Tory at a point in Frederick county to put him in possession of all the plans of the conspirators. But it so happened that an American officer was at the appointed place and the Tory's papers fell into his hands, revealing the plot and the names of the conspirators. The latter were arrested. Among them were a number of Germans: Peter Sueman, Nicholas Andrews, John George Graves, Yost Flecker, Adam Graves, Henry Shett, and Casper Fritchie. On July 25 these seven were placed on trial before a special court at Frederick, consisting of Alexander Contee Hanson, afterwards Chancellor of the State, Col. James Johnson and Upton Sheredine. The seven were found guilty of high treason in "enlisting men for the service of the king of Great Britain and administering an oath to them to bear true allegiance to the said king, and to obey his officers when called upon." Judge Hanson then sentenced the men as follows:
>
> Peter Sueman, Nicholas Andrews, John George Graves, Yost Flecker, Adam Graves, Henry Shett, Casper Fritchie, attend. It has been suggested to the court that notwithstanding your guilt has been ascertained by an impartial jury, you consider the proceedings against you nothing more than solemn mockery, and have adopted a vain idea, propagated by the enemies of this country, that she dare not punish her unnatural subjects for engaging in the service of Great Britain. From

the strange insensibility you have heretofore discovered, I was indeed led to conclude that you were under a delusion, which might prove fatal to your prospects of happiness hereafter. I think it is my duty, therefore, to explain to you your real situation. The crime you have been convicted of, upon the fullest and clearest testimony, is of such a nature that you cannot, ought not, to look for a pardon. Had it pleased heaven to permit the full execution of your unnatural designs, the miseries to be experienced by your devoted country would have been dreadful even in the contemplation. The ends of public justice, the dictates of policy, and the feelings of humanity all require that you should exhibit an awful example to your fellow-subjects, and the dignity of the State, with everything that can interest the heart of man, calls aloud for your punishment. If the consideration of approaching fate can inspire proper sentiments, you will pour forth your thanks to that watchful Providence which has arrested you at an early date of your guilt. And you will employ the short time you have to live in endeavoring, by a sincere penitence, to obtain pardon from the Almighty Being, who is to sit in judgment upon you, upon me, and all mankind. I must now perform the terrible task of denouncing the terrible punishment ordained for high treason.

You, Peter Sueman, Nicholas Andrews, Yost Plecker, Adam Graves, Henry Shett, John George Graves, and Casper Fritchie, and each of you, attend to your sentence. You shall be carried to the gaol of Fredericktown, and be hanged therein; you shall be cut down to the earth alive, and your entrails shall be taken out and burnt while you are yet alive, your heads shall be cut off, your body shall be divided into four parts, and your heads and quarters shall be placed where his excellency the Governor shall appoint. So Lord have mercy upon your poor souls. Four of these men were pardoned, the other three being executed in the court-house yard at Frederick. One of those executed was Casper Fritchie, the father of John Casper Fritchie, who was the husband of Barbara Fritchie,* the heroine of Whittier's poem.[1]

The men of Frederick County were called upon to show their patriotism early in the war. In January 1776, Captain George Stricker "raised a company comprising many of the youth of his neighborhood which went soon into active service."[2]

On July 17, 1776, Captain Stricker was commissioned lieutenant-colonel of the German Regiment and therefore was no longer in charge of this company. He was replaced by Lieutenant Benjamin Ford, formerly of the Second Company, who had been commissioned captain in May 1776. In speaking of Captain Stricker, it was said that "the fate of his company was disastrous; at the battle of Long Island so great was the havoc in its ranks, in the conflict and during the retreat, that scarcely none of its members escaped death or a wound."[3]

*In 1862, then aged 92, Barbara Fritchie is said to have defied Confederate troops under the command of Stonewall Jackson, as they marched through her hometown of Frederick, Maryland, by continuing to fly the Union flag outside her door. The story has been debunked, but the fable lives on. General Jackson, in John Greenleaf Whittier's poem, is supposed to have said: "Shoot, if you must, this old gray head, / But spare your country's flag," she said. / A shade of sadness, a blush of shame, / Over the face of the leader came; / The nobler nature within him stirred / To life at that woman's deed and word; / "Who touches a hair of yon gray head / Dies like a dog! March on!" he said.

Captain Benjamin Ford was commissioned as a first lieutenant in the Second Company on January 14, 1776. His name was given as Benj. Ford (MSA: 18, 7). This soldier's name has been erroneously given in the past as Benjamin Floyd. As stated previously, Benjamin Ford was commissioned captain in May 1776 and placed in charge of the Ninth Company.[4]

Fourteen of his men are documented as having been taken prisoner the day of the battle. There were probably many more. "Payroll for prisoners taken on Long Island from 27th August to 10th December, 1776: Sergt. Alex. Porter; David Gibeny; Valentine Lynn; Isaac Rue; Philip Hern; John Good; Frederick Myer; John Coater; Samuel Denny; Beall Holland (corporal); Jacob Greenwald. I hereby certify that the above-named soldiers, belonging to the Company of Maryland Regulars under my command last campaign, and taken prisoners in the action on Long Island on the 27th August last, are returned to Maryland. Signed by Benjamin Ford."[5]

On December 10, 1776, Captain Ford was commissioned major in the Second Regiment and just four months later, on April 17, 1777, he was commissioned lieutenant-colonel of the Sixth Regiment. He was transferred to the Fifth Regiment in January 1781.[6]

On April 25, 1781, only four months after his transfer to the Fifth Regiment, Benjamin Ford was wounded in the elbow at the battle of Hobkirk's Hill (South Carolina). He died as a result of his wounds on June 15, 1781, in Charlotte, North Carolina. While we will never know the particulars of his death, he was probably the victim of a botched amputation or gangrene.

Brigadier General Otho Holland Williams wrote to his son Elie Williams on June 23, 1781, that his "worthy little friend Coll. [Benjamin] Ford died a few Days since of the wound he received before Camden [South Carolina]."[7] Also among the papers of Otho Holland Williams is a letter written to General Williams by Edward Giles of Annapolis dated August 29, September 2, 1781, in which he said: "Capt. [John?] Swan delivered Williams' letter of July the moment he arrived in the city; Giles showed the letter to their mutual friends, and gave a part of it to the printer, a liberty he hopes Williams will excuse; the operations of the Southern Army since Gen. [Nathanael] Greene took command would have reflected additional Lustre on the military Character of ... Caesar; Williams had told him of the deaths of [Benjamin] Ford, [William] Beatty [Jr.] and [Archibald] Anderson; has written a poem to the memory of Anderson; Ford deserves to be immortal; Beatty was a promising youth, engaged to marry an amiable girl; George Armstrong was distinguished in his fall and is justly regretted."[8]

> Battle of Hobkirk's Hill. As they moved slowly up the slope, Campbell and Ford were ordered to turn the flanks of the British, while the first Maryland regiment, under Gunby, was ordered to make an attack in front. Rawdon perceived this movement, and, ordering the Irish corps into line, strengthened his position by extending his front.

The battle opened from right to left with great vigor. The two Virginia regiments, led by Greene in person, aided by Huger, Campbell, and Hawes, maintained their ground firmly, and even gained upon the enemy. At the same time, Washington, with his cavalry, was sweeping every thing before him upon the right flank of the British. The artillery was playing upon the center with great execution, and Gunby's veteran regiment rushed forward in a deadly charge with bayonets. Notwithstanding their inferiority of numbers and disadvantage of position, the British maintained their ground most gallantly until Gunby's charge, when they faltered. Hawes was then descending the hill to charge the New York Volunteers, and the falchion that should strike the decisive blow of victory for the Americans was uplifted. At that moment, some of Gunby's veterans gave way: their commander was killed. Colonel Williams, who was near the center, endeavored to rally them, and Gunby and other officers used every exertion to close their line. In this attempt, Colonel Ford was mortally wounded and carried to the rear. Gunby, finding it impossible to bring them into order, directed them to rally by retiring partially in the rear.[9]

Benjamin Ford was born in Charles County, Maryland, and was the son of Allanson Ford and his wife, Hepzibah Beall. He was a descendant of Edward Ford, a cordwinder, who married Elizabeth Allanson, daughter of Thomas Allanson, Gentleman, who in 1659 received a special warrant for 1,000 acres in Charles County that he named Christian Temple Manor.

On July 22, 1825, forty-four years after the death of Captain Ford, his heirs at last laid claim to his bounty land. The papers were filed by Henrietta (Lowe) Ford, the widow of Captain Ford's nephew, Charles Allanson Ford, Jr.:

> Henrietta Ford, guardian to Robert and Susan Ford, children of Charles Allison Ford, deceased, upon oath testifies and declares that to the best of her knowledge and belief, Lt. Col. Benjamin Ford died in battle or died of wounds received in battle during the War of the Revolution and that he was a single and unmarried man, having one brother named Charles Allison Ford, father to the first named Charles Allison Ford who is also dead and that he, the said Charles Allison Ford, as she believes, never during his lifetime received the Bounty land due him as heir of the said Benjamin Ford. Neither has his son, the last named Charles Allison Ford, since the death of his father, Charles Allison Ford received said land or possessed of it to any person as she firmly believes. I, Henrietta Ford, guardian as aforesaid for and in behalf of my said wards, Robert and Susan Ford, do hereby constitute and appoint Col. Joseph Wathen of Washington City, my true and lawful attorney for me and in the name of my wards aforesaid to demand and receive from the Secretary of War of the United States, a warrant for the bounty land to which they are entitled as heirs at law to Lt. Col. Benjamin Ford, dec'd. Wit.: Stephen Adams, Jr., Stephen Dice. Sworn before Stephen Martin, Justice of the Peace.[10]

Corporal Jacob Alexander enlisted January 20, 1776 (MSA: 18, 18). He reenlisted in the German Regiment with the rank of sergeant in February 1778 and was discharged on August 1, 1780 (MSA: 18, 184).

"Jacob Alexander was one of the early settlers of Middletown, Frederick Co.

Capt. Jacob Alexander was among those who raised companies and participated in the battle of Bladensburg (War of 1812)."[11] This soldier died sometime prior to January 30, 1836, when his widow, Mary Alexander, petitioned the Maryland Legislature to be placed on the pension rolls. Her request was approved and she received "a sum of money equal to the half pay of a sergeant in consideration of the services of her husband" (MSA: 214, 719).

Private James Beale enlisted February 8, 1776 (MSA: 18, 20). No further records have been found for this soldier.

Many individuals have claimed that this soldier was James Beall, son of Roger Brooke Beall, and that after the Battle of Long Island he enlisted in Hartley's regiment, which was transferred to the Pennsylvania Line. They claim that after the war, he married and settled in New Jersey where he died in 1831. They spell the soldier's surname as Bell. The soldier named James Bell who died in New Jersey was not the same one who served at the Battle of Long Island. That soldier applied for a pension and deposed that he enlisted in 1777, making no mention of the battle at all.

Private Alexander Boston enlisted January 25, 1776 (MSA: 18, 19). No further records have been found for this soldier.

Private Peter Breat enlisted January 31, 1776 (MSA: 18, 20). No further records have been found for this soldier.

Private Meicher Brobeck enlisted January 21, 1776 (MSA: 18, 18). No further records have been found for this soldier.

Private Adam Bromcord enlisted January 22, 1776 (MSA: 18, 19). Private Adam Bromgart, First Regiment, enlisted on May 28, 1777, was discharged on October 9, 1777, deserted, and joined again on April 9, 1779 (MSA: 18, 81). While it is believed these men are the same, no further records have been found to confirm the surname.

Sergeant William Bruce enlisted January 26, 1776 (MSA: 18, 18). "Bruce, William (Md). 2d Lieutenant 1st Maryland, 10th December, 1776; 1st Lieutenant, 10th June, 1777; Regimental Adjutant, 6th June, 1778; Captain, 1st August, 1779; transferred to 5th Maryland, 1st January, 1781; retained in Maryland Battalion, April, 1783, and served to 15th November, 1783."[12]

"September 21, 1779: Power of attorney from William Bruce (Lt. in the First Regt. of Foot from Maryland) to his trusty brother, John Bruce of Charles County to recover debts, money, etc. Wit.: John Gwinn and Richard Harrison Reeder."[13]

> December 9, 1812: THE Committee to whom was referred the petition of William Bruce, of Charles county, report, that they have taken the same into consideration, and find from the documents accompanying the same, that he served in the Maryland line from the commencement of the revolutionary war to the end thereof; and

that he was a brave and meritorious officer; they are therefore of opinion that from his infirmities and old age, and having a wife and a numerous offspring, it will be humanity in the legislature to afford him the relief prayed for; they therefore submit the following resolution: Resolved That the treasurer of the western shore be, and he is hereby directed, to pay unto William Bruce, late a captain in the Maryland line, during the revolutionary war, or to his order, a sum of money annually in quarterly payments, equal to the half-pay of a captain, as a further remuneration for those services rendered his country during the American war.[14]

RESOLVED, That the treasurer of the western shore be, and he is hereby directed, to pay unto William Bruce, late a captain in the Maryland line during the revolutionary war, or to his order, a sum of money annually, in quarterly payments, equal to the half pay of a captain, as a further remuneration for those services rendered his country during the American war. Passed December 30, 1812 [MSA: 192, 2966].

On March 30, 1818, William Bruce of Charles County applied for a pension from the federal government saying:

That he the said William Bruce of the county and state aforesaid inlisted and entered as a soldier early in the Army of the State of Maryland in a company of riflemen commanded by Captain George Stricker attached to Colonel William Smallwood's Regiment of regular troops issued for the Defense of the State of Maryland in January 1776; and continued in that Regiment as a soldier until December of the said year, when he as appointed a second Lieutenant in Captain John H. Bean's Company in the first regiment of Continental troops commanded by Colonel John H. Stone and continued in the said command until the year 1780 when he was promoted to a captaincy in the said Regiment, and ordered to join the Southern army in which service he continued until after the defeat at Camden when he was ordered and marched to the northward and served in a detachment of Continental troops under the command of Major Thomas Lansdale consisting of five companies in the year 1782 and marched to join General Washington to the eastward and (after the cessation of hostilities between the United States and Great Britain) marched to the State of Maryland and was in November 1783 disbanded when the Maryland line of the army of the United States was discharged and that he is in reduced circumstances.[15]

John Rousby Plater, associate judge of the First Judicial District, apparently felt compelled to write to John C. Calhoun, secretary of war, on behalf of Bruce saying: "I have in preference of the directions of the act of Congress of the present session inclosed a certificate and the oath of a meritorious revolutionary soldier distinguished for his long faithful and constant duties during that glorious contest. His advanced age and reduced circumstances bring him within the provisions of the law; and all Maryland knows his worth valour and services, and it affords me pleasure in transmitting the necessary documents. I am Sir with great consideration and respect, Yr. Obt. Sert., JRPlater."[16]

A writer in the *Maryland Gazette* reflected on William Bruce's death:

Communicated. Another soldier of the Revolution gone! On Wednesday, the 25th ultimo, Colonel William Bruce, departed this life, at his residence in Charles

County. He was in the 73rd year of his age, and, during his long and varied life, there was no one action, the remembrance of which could embitter his parting hour, or stain the cheek of his surviving family with shame. He entered Army of the Revolution in the spring of the year '76 as a private, fought through the whole war, and finally came out a Captain of the 1st Maryland regiment. From these trying scenes of hardship, hunger, and bloodshed, he returned to the quietude and duties of private life, and as he had been a brave soldier, so he became an excellent citizen. In this domestic relations, as husband, father, and master, he was affectionate, indulgent, and humane; as a neighbor, urbane and friendly; as a citizen, frank and patriotic, and as a man, strictly and sternly honest. This tribute is paid by one who had been early taught to revere Col. Bruce, and the sentiments it expresses will find an echo in the bosom of all who knew him.[17]

William Bruce was the son of Charles Bruce and Jane Yates of Charles County, Maryland.

*Private **William Casbear*** enlisted January 26, 1776 (MSA: 18, 19). Private William Casser, First Regiment, enlisted April 28, 1778, and was discharged in July 1779. "Not heard of" (MSA: 18, 91). While it is believed these men are the same, no further records have been found to confirm the surname.

*Corporal **Robert Chandler*** enlisted January 31, 1776. "Sick in hospital" (MSA: 18, 18). No further records have been found for this soldier.

*Private **John Cobeth*** enlisted April 17, 1776. "On Guard" (MSA: 18, 20). No further records have been found for this soldier.

*Private **Andrew Conslean*** enlisted January 22, 1776 (MSA: 18, 19). No further records have been found for this soldier.

*Private **George Crutsinger*** enlisted January 29, 1776 (MSA: 18, 19). No further records have been found for this soldier. He was the brother of Solomon Crutsinger, below, and they were the sons of George Crutsinger and wife, Elizabeth of Washington County, Maryland. The surname is also spelled Kretsinger or Krutsinger.

*Private **Solomon Crutsinger*** enlisted February 10, 1776 (MSA: 18, 20). This soldier moved to Tennessee where he applied for a pension in 1832.

> Declaration, State of Tennessee, Sullivan County. On this twenty third day of August in the year 1832 personally appeared before me John Anderson a Justice of the Peace for said County, Solomon Crutsinger a resident of said County of Sullivan aged eighty five years who being first sworn according to law doth on his oath make the following declaration in order to obtain the benefit of provision made by the act of Congress paper June the 7th 1832 that the said Solomon Crutsinger in the 1777 enrolled himself as a volunteer for one year under a Captain Striker of Smallwoods Regiment in Maryland, that he served in the Continental Service the period of his

enrollment being one year as you said & then went home & he then enlisted in the Continental Service in the Revolutionary War at little York State of Pennsylvania for the during the Revolutionary War under Captain Walker in General Waynes Brigade of the Pennsylvania line.

Colonel Hartly was Colonel of said Regiment that he the said Solomon states that after his enlistment he helped to take the convey a company of Hessians to Philadelphia, was then marched to Paris & Wick where the Regiment joined the principal Army & he was again attached from the Army & sent to Sausburg on the frontiers of Pennsylvania to check the Indians & after having made many excursions through the Indian country & had many engagements with them at length said regiment was attacked by a Company of British forces & Indians on the Susquehannah and in the heat of the engagement this applicant was twice wounded to wit one in the right arm with a Rifle ball & one in the right shoulder with a musket ball which prevented him from serving for six months during which time he lay in the Hospital at Sausburg & when he had recovered sufficiently from his wounds he again joined his regiment commanded by Col. Hartly & after several excursions against the Indians was taken prisoner by said Indians & was kept prisoner by them until Gen. Sullivan drove back the Indians to Niagara at which time this applicant was taken and after acts of Savage cruelty being repeatedly exercised toward him & his life threatened was sold by the Indians to the British & kept until restoration of peace for which reason he never obtained a discharge as he was only liberated from imprisonment on the return of peace this applicant states that he did serve in the Revolutionary war first & last together with the time he was a prisoner as above stated for a period of three years. He also states that he never has received any annuyity or pension under the law of the United States, he further state that he is very sickely & stands in great need of the assistance of his Country for support.

The within applicant further states that he has no living or documentary evidence of his serving & that he knows of no person whose testimony he could procure to testify to his service as aforesaid. Sworn to & subscribed this day and year aforesaid. Mark of Solomon Crutsinger.

Declaration — April 1844 In order to obtain the benefit of the act of Congress of the 7 July 1838 entitled an act granting half pay and pension to certain widows in the State of Tennessee, Sullivan County. On this 11 day of April 1844 personally appeared before the subscriber, a trustee of the now Mrs. Katherine Crutsinger, a resident of Sullivan County and State of Tennessee aged 80 years the 21st day of June next who being first duly sworn according to law doth on her oath make the following declaration in order to obtain the benefit of the provision made by Congress proposed July 7, 1838, entitled an act granting half pay and pension to certain widows.

That she is the widow of Solomon Crutsinger who was soldier in the War of the Revolution. That he enrold himself as a volunteer for twelve months, he entered the service in the year 1777 under Captain Stuker of Smallman's Regiment in the State of Maryland the he served in the Continental Service the period of enlistment being twelvemonths and returned home and did enlist in the Continental Service in the Revolutionary War at Little York State of Pennsylvania for during the Revolutionary War to wit under Captain Walker in General Wayne's Brigade of the Pennsylvania that her husband, the before said Solomon Crutsinger was wounded in the right arm with a rifle ball and again in the right shoulder with a musket ball which prevented him from service for six months during which time he lay in the hospital at Sausburg and when recovered sufficiently from his wounds, he again joined said regiment commanded by Col. Hartley. That she cannot recollect of anything more of his service as it has been a long time since she heard him talk.... Claimant further declairs that her husband, the afforesaid Soloman Crutsinger, drew a pension of $80 per annum for the above service, the proof of which she would refer us to the records of the books and she further declairs that she was married to the said Solomon Curtsinger on the 21st day August 1787. And her husband, the aforesaid Solomon Crutsinger, died May the 17th, 1837, that she was not married to him prior to his leaving service. But that the marriage took place previous to the first January seventeen Hundred and ninety four (1794) and she above states that she still remains a widow that the family record herto anint [attached] is a true record. Mark of Katherine Crutsinger.[18]

Private Michael Curtz enlisted January 22, 1776 (MSA: 18, 19). No further records have been found for this soldier.

Private Notley Davis enlisted June 7, 1776 (MSA: 18, 20). Private Davis was born in Trinity Parish, Charles County, Maryland on February 9, 1746–1747. He was the son of Joseph Waters Davis and Mary Barker. According to family tradition, Notley Davis died on a British prison ship during the Revolutionary War.

Private Miseal Deaver enlisted January 31, 1776. His name was given as Michael Deaver (MSA: 18, 20). "A Return of the Recruits, Draughts and Substitutes in Anne Arundel County under the Act to procure Recruits passed October Session, 1780. 'Misail Deavour, 'til 10th Dec Draught'" (MSA: 18, 369).

> February 25, 1780. [Sam Gadman A. A County, Elk Ridge Landg To his Excellency Thomas Sim Lee, Governor of Maryland, & his Hble Council] Whereas information has been made to me, one of the justices assigned to keep the Peace, in said the County, that a certain John Hobbs, in the County aforesaid, being pursuant to an Act of Assembly of this State, appointed a Recruiting Officer, for the said County has frequently and in diverse manner abused the Trust reposed in him, by Misting of Men for the Army of the United States, and suffering them, for certain considerations paid him to be at Liberty, taking advantage of unguarded men wl families, by making them Drunk, and inlisting them, with a view of making them Ransom themselves at a very high rate those that had not money tn dn it, he'd take an Indenture on, and sell them for 2, 3 or 4 years during the continuance of the Substitute Law, he recruited a number of Men, which he sold to different People for Substitutes at a very advanced Price, it appears from the general Tenor of his Conduct, since his commencement, that he has continued an entire prostitution of the publick Money, in such, and the like egregious enormities. The better to make this appear, the summoning of John Horn Benjamin Stevens John Ellicot & Misael Deaver, all of this County (except Jno Ellicott) will shew the matter very clearly. Presupposing it was to your Honorable Board the information ought to be given, I have taking the Liberty to present the above [MSA: 43, 432–433].

Private Deaver was born on June 6, 1752, in Frederick County, Maryland. He was the son of Basil Deaver and Chew Pierpoint, both of Anne Arundel County.

"Basel DEAVER & Chew his wife, 'accepted in marriage' Abraham, b. 13 of eleventh mo. 1749. Misal, b. 6 of 6 mo. 1751. Mary, b. 15 of ninth mo.1753."[19] (Quaker Records of Northern Maryland).

On January 22, 1819, Miscal Deaver, age 66, a resident of Frederick County, Maryland, deposed that he had enlisted in Frederick Town in the company commanded by George Stricker in January 1776 and that he had served more than two and nearly three years, when losing the use of an eye, he was discharged in Annapolis. Private Deaver deposed that he had fought in the battles of Long Island, Harlem, White Plains, and also in several skirmishes.

His pension application was rejected. At his request, Frederick County officials sent a letter dated August 9, 1819, to his brother, Abraham Deaver, then living in Muskingum County, Ohio:

> Sir, At the request of your brother and with the view of subserving his interests I inform you that through my agency a regular application has been made by him to the War department of the United States for a pension and that his application has been returned rejected by reason of his name not appearing on the Maryland pay rolls. This circumstance he must acquiesce in the rejection or prove his service by previous acquaintances with it. He has diligently sought in this quarter for some of his old associates, but time has left so few remaining that not one could be discovered here whose recollections were sufficient. In this exigency he has to request of you to ratify for him and to this end I have annexed a blank affidavit comprising such proof as will be needful and as your knowledge will enable you to furnish. It will be necessary that the affidavit be made before some Justice of the peace or Judge, the blanks filled up and a certificate of the county clerk with his seal of office as to the Justice or Judg being duly commissioned and qualified be annexed and also that the Justice or Judge who takes this affidavit certify as to your credibility, for which purpose I have also annexed a form. You will return by post the affidavit as speedily as possible directed to your brother. I am, Sir, your obdt. Servant, A. Showing.[20]

Abraham Deaver complied with his brother's request on October 8, 1819, deposing that: "...he is well acquainted with Miscal Deaver of Frederick County and State of Maryland and knows well of his own knowledge that the said Miscal Deaver enlisted in the service of the United States in the early part of the year 1776 in the company commanded by Captain George Stricker of the regiment commanded by Colonel William Smallwood of the Maryland line and that the said Miscal Deaver continued in the service considerably longer than one year, but does not recollect the exact time."[21]

In a second application dated July 21, 1820, the soldier stated that he was a blacksmith by occupation but that he could not work by reason of him being palsied and having very weak eyes. He provided a schedule of property showing that he owned only one table, two iron pots, and one bake oven. His household consisted of himself, age 69; his wife, Sarah, about 70; and a son, Henry, who was about seventeen.

Private Deaver's application was approved this time, retroactively to September 1819. He died in Frederick County, Maryland, on March 29, 1823.

Private Samuel Denny enlisted January 26, 1776 (MSA: 18, 19). Private Denny was one of those taken prisoner at the battle. His name appeared on a list of soldiers "belonging to the Company of Maryland Regulars under my command last campaign, and taken prisoners in the action on the 27th August last, are returned to Maryland. Signed by Benjamin Ford."[22]

"Sgt. Samuel Denney, enlisted March 2, 1778; discharged March 2, 1781. Muster Roll of the late Capt. Beatty's Company under command of Lt. W. Lamar, in the 1st Maryland Regiment Serving in the Southern Army of the United States, made this — Day of August, '81. [For Jan., Feb., Mch., Apl., May, June and July, '81.]" (MSA: 18, 202, 388).

"Samuel Denny, Pvt., 7th Regt., Lot. #1232. (In 1787, An act was passed by the General Assembly to dispose of the reserved lands westward of Ft. Cumberland. This land was allotted to Revolutionary War soldiers. Each officer was assigned 4 lots and each private 1 lot."[23]

Ensign Hatch Dent, Jr. was commissioned January 3, 1776 (MSA: 18, 18). On July 9, 1776, he was commissioned first lieutenant (MSA: 12, 16).

"Dent, Hatch (Md). Ensign of Smallwood's Maryland Regiment, 14th January, 1776; Lieutenant, March, 1776; taken prisoner at Long Island 27th August, 1776; exchanged 20th April, 1778; 1st Lieutenant 1st Maryland, 10th December, 1776; Captain 2d Maryland, 17th April, 1777; resigned 13th November, 1778."[24]

Lieutenant Dent was taken prisoner at the battle. He was confined on one of the British hulks anchored in Wallabout Bay for a little over two years and was finally exchanged on April 20, 1778 (MSA: 18, 616).

Hatch Dent was promoted to the rank of captain on April 17, 1777, while still in captivity. According to Joseph Balkoski, command historian for the Maryland National Guard, "It's entirely possible that Dent could have been promoted while in captivity. At some point, it might have been arranged that he was going to be exchanged, and at some point he might have even been paroled and free to travel as he wished as long as he did not take up arms until exchanged. Therefore, the regiment might have promoted him under the expectation that in a few months he was going to return."[25]

After he resigned his commission, Dent returned to his home in Charles County, Maryland, where he married Judith Poston on December 17, 1778. In 1785 he became an ordained Episcopal minister. In 1794, he led a group of settlers from St. Mary's County and Charles County, Maryland, to Rowan County, North Carolina:

About the year 1794, a number of Episcopal families removed from Maryland to the western part of Rowan, among them two families of Barbers, and other families by the name of Gardner, Chunn, Harrison, Alexander, Lightell, Mills, Swan, Reeves, Burroughs, and c., & c. The Rev. Richard W. Barber of Wilkesboro, is descended from Elias Barber, the patriarch of one branch of the Barber family, and the Rev. Samuel S. Barber of Hyde county, is descended from Jonathan Barber the patriarch of the other branch.

Mr. Chunn was the grand father of the Chunns of this county, Mrs. Susan W. Murphy, Mrs. Betty Murphy and many others. The late Archibald Henderson was often heard to remark that Rev. Thomas F. Davis, later the Bishop of South Carolina, said to him that Mr. William Chunn, the father of Mrs. Susan W. Murphy, was "God's Gentleman," meaning thereby that he was endowed by nature with all the traces and genuine characteristics of a true, cultured christian gentleman. A very high compliment indeed, coming from such a man as Bishop Davis.

Mr. Samuel R. Harrison, of Salisbury, and many others are descendants of those who first came out with the Maryland colony, and the Turners of Rowan and Iredell are also descended from one of this colony. Mr. Charles Nathaniel Mills, with his family, removed soon after his arrival to Iredell county, where his descendants, including a portion in the Northwestern States, and a few in Salisbury, now number several hundred.

The Rev. Hatch Dent, an Episcopal clergyman, and an uncle of the Barbers, came out with this colony. He purchased 661 acres of land, in Mt. Ulla township, where Dent's mountain is situated, being that part of the Boyden and Henderson plantation called "the Dent Tract." The Reverend gentleman remained but a few years only. Parson Dent and Jonathan Barber had married two Misses Swan [sic], aunt and niece, and the parson on returning to Maryland, left his nephew in charge of this tract of land, just mentioned, giving him the use of it rent-free for ten years.

Jack Turner, whose wife was a Dent, was the father of Wilson and Joseph Turner and others. Wilson Turner (brother of Jack) was the father of Wilfred Turner and others. Samuel Turner came into the county ten or twenty years later than the first colonists. Had Parson Dent made Rowan his permanent residence, and if he had been ordinarily zealous and successful in his ministrations, it is believed by many that the Episcopal Church would have been at his time numerically as strong as any religious denomination in the county. An opportunity presented itself at that early day which can never occur again.[26]

Reverend Dent returned to Maryland by 1796 when he was appointed the first principal of Charlotte Hall School. This school was founded in 1774 but, with the onset of the war and the financial difficulties afterward, it would be 22 years before the school actually opened its doors on January 19, 1797.[27] Reverend Dent served as principal until his death on December 30, 1799. He was buried at Trinity Episcopal Church in Charles County.

In 1883, Dent Chapel was erected at Charlotte Hall School in his memory and his remains and his tombstone were moved to this site. His tombstone reads:

> The Rev Hatch Dent (son of Hatch, grandson of John,
> and great grandson of John Dent of Yorkshire England.
> One of the early settlers of the Province of Maryland).
> Born May 20, 1751 Died December 30, 1799
> An Honored Officer in the Army of the Revolution of 1776
> and an Eminent teacher and minister of the church.
> Ordained by Bishop Seabury in 1785.
> First Principal of the Charlotte Hall School.
> Removed from the Gelbe of Trinity Parish.

[Last line added at the time the stone was relocated].

Ironically, Hatch Dent is buried on property that was originally owned by his great-grandfather, Captain John Dent. The property, called Coole Springs, was said to contain "waters of exceptional purity and reputed healing quality [that] led to the establishment near here of one of the earliest hospitals in the North American Colonies, authorized by the General Assembly, October 20, 1698."[28]

Corporal Adam Everly enlisted January 20, 1776 (MSA: 18, 18). This soldier was born in Frederick County, Maryland about 1750. His parents, Johan Eberle and Eva Maria Peckinpaugh, were German immigrants. By the time of the Battle of White Plains on October 28, 1776, this soldier was serving under the command of General Anthony Wayne in the Pennsylvania Line. He may have transferred prior to the Battle of Long Island, but that has not yet been determined. He married Barbara Smith about 1780 and they eventually moved to Greene County, Pennsylvania, where Corporal Everly died on December 14, 1802. He is buried in the Everly Cemetery, Dunkard Township, Greene County, Pennsylvania.

Private Jacob Fisher enlisted January 29, 1776 (MSA: 18, 19). No further records have been found for this soldier.

Private Stephen Fluharty enlisted January 31, 1776. His surname was spelled Fleehearty (MSA: 18, 19). Private Fluharty (his surname spelled Floharty) reenlisted in the First Regiment on December 10, 1776, and by August 1, 1779, when he enlisted a third time, he had risen to the rank of corporal. He was discharged on December 27, 1779 (MSA: 18, 208).

Sergeant Stephen Fluharty, "5 CO., 1 B. CAPT. LLOYD BEALL. LT. EDWARD M. SMITH," on the rolls January 1, 1782" (MSA: 18, 437). "Sergeant Stephen Flaharty, In Hospital 19 June and July. Muster Roll of the late Capt. Beatty's Company under command of Lt. W. Lamar, in the 1st Maryland Regiment Serving in the Southern Army of the United States, made this — Day of August, '81 [For Jan., Feb., Mch., Apl., May, June and July, '81.]" (MSA: 18, 389).

Stephen Fluhart, Sergeant of the First and Seventh Regiments was included in a 1788 "List of Officers and Soldiers Entitled to Lots Westward of Fort Cumberland."[29]

On July 20, 1818, Stephen Fleeharty, a resident of Harrison County, Virginia, deposed that he had: "...enlisted in the year 1775 in the State of Maryland in the company commanded by Captain George Stricker of the first Maryland Regiment commanded by Col. Smallwood for the term of during the war, that he continued to serve in the said Corps or in the Service of the United States until the Close of the war when he was discharged from service at Annapolis in the State of Maryland in the year 1782. That he was at the battles of Long Island, White Plains, Trenton, Princetown, Germantown, Monmouth, Camden, Guilford, Eutaw Springs, Cowpens, and at the Siege of 96."

On August 21, 1820, Stephen Fluharty, aged 74 years, a resident of Harrison County, Virginia, declares "...that he enlisted in the year 1775 in the first Maryland Regiment, commanded by Colonel Smallwood, in Captain George Stricker's Company, Maryland line." After taking the prescribed oath, Fluharty stated that he owned no property and that he was "by occupation a farmer but from infirmities unable to labour. [I] have no family."[30]

The pension papers of this soldier state that he died on January 28, 1825.[31]

According to Roy Fluharty, one of the descendants of this soldier, Stephen Fluharty was a member of the surveying party of Michael Cresap on the Ohio River in 1774 when Cresap was wrongly accused of the murders of the family of Mingo Chief Logan. These murders were a prime cause of Lord Dunmore's War against the Shawnee of Ohio. Stephen was then a member of a company of scouts commanded by Cresap in this war. He was discharged at Fort Pitt (Pittsburgh, Pennsylvania) late in 1775 and shortly thereafter enlisted in the 1st Maryland Regiment of Infantry. Stephen Fluharty was buried somewhere along East Run in Marion County, West Virginia. The grave is unmarked.[32]

Private Jacob Gardner enlisted January 20, 1776 (MSA: 18, 18). No further records have been found for this soldier.

Private John Gerrish enlisted January 22, 1776 (MSA: 18, 19). No further records have been found for this soldier.

Sergeant David Gibony enlisted January 20, 1776. His surname was given as Giveny (MSA: 18, 19).

The name of David Gibeny appeared on a list of soldiers "belonging to the Company of Maryland Regulars under my command last campaign, and taken prisoners in the action on the 27th August last, are returned to Maryland. Signed by Benjamin Ford."[33]

Private John Glatz enlisted January 22, 1776 (MSA: 18, 19). No further records have been found for this soldier.

Sergeant John Good enlisted January 20, 1776 (MSA: 18, 18). The name of John Good appeared on a list of soldiers "belonging to the Company of Maryland

Regulars under my command last campaign, and taken prisoners in the action on the 27th August last, are returned to Maryland. Signed by Benjamin Ford."[34] On July 18, 1777, it was ordered: "that the western shore Treasurer pay to John Good twenty seven pounds, seven shillings and six pence due on Account passed. John Good who was of the Light Infantry Company of Smallwoods Battalion being unable for further Duty is hereby discharged" (MSA: 16, 312).

Private Jacob Greenwald enlisted January 29, 1776. His surname was given as Grenewald (MSA: 18, 19).

His name, given as Jacob Greenwald appeared on a list of soldiers "belonging to the Company of Maryland Regulars under my command last campaign, and taken prisoners in the action on the 27th August last, are returned to Maryland. Signed by Benjamin Ford."[35] No further records have been found for this soldier.

Private Michael Hackethorn enlisted January 21, 1776 (MSA: 18, 18). No further records have been found for this soldier. This writer believes that he was a son of Reinhard Jacob Heckendorn, born June 6, 1715, in Memmelshoffen, Germany, who immigrated to Frederick County, Maryland, between 1741 and 1744. Some of the descendants spelled their surname Hackethorn.

Private Michael Hahn enlisted March 10, 1776. His surname was spelled Haun (MSA: 18, 20).

On August 6, 1833, Michael Hahn, age 85, the 15th of this present month, a resident of Stark County, Ohio, deposed that:

> In the spring of 1775 in Fredericktown, Md. where he then resided, he enlisted in the U.S. service as a private to serve in the Army of the revolution and was in a battalion commanded by one Gen. Smallwood and having a major by the name of Price.
>
> The sd. battalion immediately after its organization marched to Annapolis and remained there probably 4–5 months for the purpose of being disciplined. From Annapolis, the battalion marched to New York, passing through Philadelphia and some other places. While in Philadelphia, Capt. Stricker, who commanded the company, was promoted to the office of Lt. Col. and transferred to another regiment and the company to which the deponent belonged was marched to New York along with the first mentioned battalion under the command of an ensign in the company previously commanded by sd. Capt. Stricker.
>
> In marching from Philadelphia to New York, the battalion passed through Trenton and Princeton and some other places not recollected and Morristown in which latter town the Battalion remained through the winter of 1775 and 1776.
>
> In the spring of 1776, the battalion marched to New York and when they arrived there were attached to the brigade commanded by Brig. Gen. Stirling. After remaining in New York about two months, the whole brigade moved to Long Island and was there when the Declaration of Independence was proclaimed in 1776.
>
> While in New York, Benjamin Ford was appointed Captain of the company of this deponent. Deponent was engaged in the battle of Long Island and the company to which he belonged consisted of 74 and only 15 escaped.

After this battle, the American forces and this deponent retreated to a fort on Long Island near New York and there remained 2–3 weeks and then returned to the city of New York.

On leaving New York, the Army marched to White Plains in New York. At Kingsbridge, that part of the battalion to which the deponent belonged, which had escaped from the battle of Long Island was engaged in a skirmish with the British — a small party thereof — after which nothing of note occurred til the Army arrived in White Plains.

Deponent states that he was present at the battle at that place. After the battle, the battalion marched to Morristown, thence to Fort Lee, thence to Princeton and was proceeding onward when between Princeton and Trenton, the battalion was dismissed by the Colonel verbally and no written discharge was given.

Hahn stated that he served 1 year and 8 months. He had enlisted for 1 year and 9 months, but they were dismissed early because of the losses sustained in battle.

In the summer of 1777 in Northumberland Co., Pa., where the deponent then resided, he enlisted as a substitute for his father, Michael Hahn, as a private in the Militia of Pennsylvania into a company commanded by Capt. Casper Reid and 1st Lt. Baker. The regiment to which he was attached had no Colonel but was commanded by a Major whose name he doesn't recall. In this regiment he served three months. The regiment was engaged in scouting expeditions against the Indians and guarding the frontiers but was in no battle, though constantly in service.

In the latter part of the spring of 1778, he was drafted to serve as a private in the Militia of Northumberland Co., Pa. in the same company he served previously as a substitute for his father, commanded by the same officers and for the same purpose as before — that of resisting the aggression of the Indians. He was in no engagement, but continued in service for two months making the while period of his service 2 years and 1 month.[36]

Hahn deposed that he was born in Bucks County, Pennsylvania, on August 15, 1748, and that there was a record of his age in Bucks County, Pennsylvania, but none with him. When he enlisted, he lived in Fredericktown, Maryland. The next two times when he entered the Pennsylvania Militia, he lived in Northumberland County, Pennsylvania.

Private Hahn stated that since the war, until 12–13 years before, he lived in Northumberland County, Pennsylvania, and then moved to Jefferson County, Ohio, where he lived for one year. From there he moved to Wayne County, Ohio, were he lived about six years and from there he moved to Tuscarawas Township in Stark County, Ohio, where he was then residing.

He stated that the first time he entered the service, he volunteered; the second time he entered as a substitute for his father; and the third time he was drafted. He stated that during his enlistment, he served under General Washington; Brigadier General Stirling; Colonel Smallwood; Major Price; Captain Stricker, afterward promoted to a lieutenant colonelcy; Captain Benjamin Ford who succeeded Captain Stricker; Lieutenants Smith and Ringgold. While in the Pennsylvania troops, the only names he recalled were Captain Casper Reid and First Lieutenant Baker.

On May 20, 1853, Nancy Hahn, 77, a resident of Fredericksburg, Wayne County, Ohio, deposed that she was the widow of Michael Hahn and that they were married in July or August in 1801 near Harrisburg, Pennsylvania, and that Michael Hahn died in August 1844.[37]

Private Andrew Hardy enlisted January 22, 1776. No further records for this soldier have been found.

Private Jacob Harman enlisted January 29, 1776 (MSA: 18, 19). On December 3, 1776, it was "Ordered That the said Treasurer pay to Jacob Harman sixteen Pounds eight Shillings" (MSA: 12, 501).

Private George Hellmold enlisted January 28, 1776 (MSA: 18, 19). He is shown as Private George Heldmole when he reenlisted on December 10, 1776. Private Hellmold was discharged on October 31, 1777. It was noted that he had deserted (MSA: 18, 117).

Private John Heywood enlisted January 22, 1776 (MSA: 18, 19). No reenlistment date is shown for this soldier, but Private John Heywood of the First Regiment was discharged on July 25, 1777. It was noted that he had deserted (MSA: 18, 117).

Private Causamer Hill enlisted January 26, 1776 (MSA: 18, 19). Private Casemar Hill discharged July 26, 1779. "Pay Roll of Capt. Michael Bayer's Company in the German Regiment, Continental Troops in the United States. Commanded by Lt. Col. Ludwick Weltner. For the months of July, August, September and October, 1779" (MSA: 18, 262).

Private Casimir Hill enlisted for three years. "A List of Recruits belonging to the German Regiment. Commanded by Lieut. Colonel Weltner. White Plains, Sept. 5th, 1778" (MSA: 18, 267). "Cosomer Hill, passed 2/27/1778. A Return of Recruits for the Continental Army. Passed by Charles Beatty, Esq., Lieut. of Fredk. Co. March 10th, 1778" (MSA: 18, 314).

Private John Hite enlisted February 8, 1776 (MSA: 18, 20). No further records have been found for this soldier.

Private Basil Holland enlisted in the Ninth Company of Light Infantry, February 12, 1776 (MSA: 18, 20). The name of Corporal Beall Holland appeared on a list of soldiers "belonging to the Company of Maryland Regulars under my command last campaign, and taken prisoners in the action on the 27th August last, are returned to Maryland. Signed by Benjamin Ford."[38] It is believed that Basil Holland and Beall Holland were the same man and that this soldier is the same as Basil Holland, born June 18, 1755, in Frederick County, Maryland, son of Abraham Holland and Asenath Spires.

Basil Holland was living in Montgomery County, Maryland, at the time of the

1800 census. Shortly thereafter he moved his family to Trigg County, Kentucky. This soldier died in Trigg County, Kentucky, on June 25, 1829.

Private John Hoofman enlisted January 26, 1776 (MSA: 18, 19). No further records have been found for this soldier.

Private John Kasler enlisted January 28, 1776 (MSA: 18, 19). It is believed that this soldier is identical to the one erroneously called John Coater on the list of soldiers "belonging to the Company of Maryland Regulars under my command last campaign, and taken prisoners in the action on the 27th August last, are returned to Maryland. Signed by Benjamin Ford."[39] He may also be the man listed as John Kesler in Frederick County, Maryland, at the time of the 1790 census.

Private Frederick Keller enlisted January 21, 1776. His name was given as Fredk. Keller. No further records have been found for this soldier.

Private Philip Kern enlisted January 28, 1776 (MSA: 18. 19). It is believed that this soldier is identical to the one erroneously called Philip Hern on the list of soldiers "belonging to the Company of Maryland Regulars under my command last campaign, and taken prisoners in the action on the 27th August last, are returned to Maryland. Signed by Benjamin Ford."[40]

Philip Kern was listed in the tax assessment records of Washington County, Maryland in 1783.[41]

Private George Kephart enlisted January 31, 1776. His name was given as George Kipheard (MSA: 18, 19). He reenlisted, this time in the German Regiment on February 13, 1778 and was discharged on August 1, 1780. His name was given as George Keephart (MSA: 18, 223).

George Kephard enlisted for three years. "Deserted. A List of Recruits belonging to the German Regiment. Commanded by Lieut. Colonel Weltner. White Plains, Sept. 5th, 1778" (MSA: 18, 267).

George Kepphard was shown on the "Pay Roll of Capt. Michael Bayer's Company in the German Regiment, Continental Troops in the United States. Commanded by Lt. Col. Ludwick Weltner. For the months of July, August, September and October, 1779" (MSA: 18, 262).

> August 31, 1819, Jackson Co., Indiana: Letter to the Undersecretary of War: The undersigned, George Keiphart, now of Jackson Co., Indiana, states he is a native of Maryland and that in 1776 he enlisted as a private in Capt. George Stricker's Rifle Company and served one year in the Regiment commanded by General Smallwood. He states that he was in the Battle of Long Island in 1776 and also in the Battle of White Plains and was then permitted to go home. On February 22, 1777, he enlisted in the U.S. service for three years in Capt. Boyer's (Bowyer) Company of Infantry, in Col. Wiltner's Independent Regiment. That in 1778 he joined

General Sullivan's army in the northern frontier in the state of New York and served the term of three years.

He states that he was in the battle called the Catherinetown on the Tioga River and was discharged on 2/28/1780 in Fredericktown, Maryland by Col. Wiltner who promised to see that he had land for his services and that the Colonel died two days afterwards. He has never had any land or money for his service. He is now 65, infirm, and unable to support himself.[42]

On June 24, 1820, George Kephart, age 67, of Jackson County, Indiana, deposed that he enlisted for one year as a private in Captain Stricker's company, commanded by Colonel Smallwood. He stated that his occupation was that of a brewer and baker but that he was unable to work and that his wife Margaret was 64 years old and that "she is unable to make a support."[43]

Private Martin Kephart enlisted January 22, 1776 (MSA: 18, 19). He was discharged on December 27, 1779 (MSA: 18, 129).

On March 26, 1821, in Stark County, Ohio, Martin Kephart, age 60, deposed that he served in the Maryland Line. He stated that he enlisted in 1775 in the First Regiment commanded by Colonel William Smallwood in the company commanded by George Stricker, being a Rifle Company and served one year until the company was made a Musket Company and continued to serve in the same company and regiment for four years. When he was discharged, he went to the office in Philadelphia with the intention to draw his pay and left his discharge papers there.

Martin Kephart deposed that he was in the Battle of Long Island, Battle of White Plains, Battle of Trenton (when Washington conquered the Hessians), Battle of Princeton, Battle of Monmouth, Battle of Brandywine, Battle of Germantown, and "a number of inferior skirmishes." A cooper by profession, he was unable to work from old age and infirmity, being severely attacked with the palsy and was frequently confined to his bed. His wife, nearly 60, was unable to work but very little from age and general infirmity. "Our daughter, my oldest child, is blind and has been since her infancy, is a constant charge, not being able to support herself. Our other daughter, about 15, is unable to support herself."

In a previous deposition dated June 10, 1818, Martin Kephart stated that he enlisted in Fredericktown, Maryland, and was discharged in 1780 in Morristown, New Jersey. He stated that he was wounded in the thigh with a musket ball at Princeton and that the shot was still in his body.[44]

Private Peter Kline enlisted January 29, 1776 (MSA: 18, 19). No further records have been found for this soldier.

Private Valentine Lynn enlisted January 22, 1776 (MSA: 18, 19). The name of Valentine Lynn appeared on a list of soldiers "belonging to the Company of Maryland

Regulars under my command last campaign, and taken prisoners in the action on the 27th August last, are returned to Maryland. Signed by Benjamin Ford."[45]

Shown as Sergeant Valen Linn, he reenlisted in the First Regiment on December 10, 1776, and was discharged on December 27, 1779 (MSA: 18, 131).

Valen Linn reenlisted in the First Regiment on December 10, 1776; was promoted to corporal April 12, 1777; discharged October 11, 1777; rejoined July 1778; reduced to private on September 15, 1778; and was discharged on December 27, 1779.[46]

On September 21, 1795, a marriage license was issued in Prince George's County, Maryland, to Valentine Lynn and Elizabeth Johnson.[47]

> November 18, 1796: "THE committee to whom was referred the petition of Valentine Linn, of Prince-George's county, report, that they have taken the same into their consideration, and are of opinion that the facts therein set forth are true; they therefore recommend the following resolution: RESOLVED, That the auditor be and he is hereby authorised and directed to adjust the depreciation due to Valentine Linn, late a soldier in the first Maryland regiment, and that the treasurer of the western shore issue to said Valentine Linn a certificate for the same, bearing an interest of six per cent. from the time of issuing the said certificate [MSA: 105, 78].
>
> By the HOUSE of DELEGATES, November 21, 1796. RESOLVED, That the treasurer of the western shore pay to Valentine Lynn the sum of sixty-eight pounds thirteen shillings and one penny current money, it being the amount of depreciation due him as a soldier in the first Maryland regiment, as ascertained by the auditor-general [MSA: 105, 8].
>
> By the HOUSE of DELEGATES, December 5, 1796. GENTLEMEN OF THE SENATE, WE return you the resolution in favour of Valentine Lynn, and hope that upon reconsideration it will meet with your concurrence. The ground of your dissent, we presume, was the want of indifferent testimony to establish the fact of the petitioner's absence from the state of Maryland. As this testimony is now procured, we flatter ourselves all objections to the relief prayed for will not be effectually removed [MSA: 105, 108].
>
> December 7, 1796: "On motion, ORDERED, That the senate reconsider the resolution in favour of Valentine Lynn; and upon reconsideration the said resolution was assented to." [MSA: 206, 18].

Unfortunately, no information was provided as to the exact reason why there was an objection to the relief sought by Valentine Lynn nor was there any information provided as to where he was then living.

Private William Lynn enlisted January 22, 1776 (MSA: 18, 19). No further records have been found for this soldier.

Private Pacel Martin enlisted January 29, 1776 (MSA: 18, 19). No further records have been found for this soldier.

Private Dennis May, Fifer enlisted January 28, 1776 (MSA:18, 18). "Private Dennis May, fifer, discharged August 22, 1777." No reenlistment date is shown. "*Prisoner.*"

It is believed that this soldier was taken prisoner at the battle and was still being held as of the date of discharge (MSA: 18, 137).

Sergeant Peter McNaughton enlisted January 12, 1776 (MSA: 18, 18). This soldier would serve throughout the war in various regiments. His surname was given several times as McNorton.

Sergeant McNaughton reenlisted in the First Regiment on December 10, 1776, and was discharged on November 1, 1780 (MSA: 18, 138). "A List of the Officers and Soldiers of the 8th Company of the Maryland Line who were in Service from the first of August, 1780, until the first of January, 1781. Sgt. Peter McNaughtan" (MSA: 18, 357).

On May 8, 1781, Sgt. Peter McNaughton of the Fourth Regiment was shown on a list of Maryland troops at the garrison of Whetstone Point (MSA: 18, 626).

"Sgt. Peter McNaughton, a member of the Seventh Company, Third Regiment on August 28, 1781" (MSA: 18, 396).

"An Acct. of Pay due the Non Commis'd Officers and Privates of the Maryland Line, from Jan'y 1st, 1782, to Jan'y 1st, 1783. 2 CO., 1 B. CAPT. EDWARD PRALL. LT. WM. RAISIN. ENSIGN BASIL BURGESS. Peter McNorton, Sgt" (MSA: 18, 431).

"Serjt. Peter McNorton [Dischd. 29 Nov '83]" (MSA: 18, 545).

Corporal William McPherson enlisted February 4, 1776 (MSA: 18, 18). No further records have been found for this soldier.

Private Frederick Miles enlisted January 22, 1776. "Sick in hospital." He reenlisted on April 25, 1778, and was discharged on May 1, 1781. His name was given as Private Fredk. Miles (MSA: 18, 19, 140). Another record shows his rank as corporal and states that he was discharged on May 1, 1781 (MSA: 18, 545).

A marriage license was issued to Frederick Miles and Ruth Brashears in Prince George's County on February 11, 1784.[48]

Private Henry Miller enlisted January 21, 1776 (MSA: 18, 18). No further records have been found for this soldier.

Private James Miller enlisted January 22, 1776 (MSA: 18, 19). No further records have been found for this soldier.

Private Michael Miller enlisted January 22, 1776 (MSA: 18, 19). He is shown to have reenlisted on December 10, 1776, and was discharged on August 22 (no year). The same entry says "Dept. joined 15 Sept 78, present 1 Nov 80" (MSA: 18, 137). He was still in the service on January 1, 1782 (MSA: 18, 432).

Michael Miller was shown in Frederick County as head of household at the time of the 1790 and 1800 censuses. By 1820 he was living in Coshocton County, Ohio.

FRANKLIN TOWNSHIP. The list of earliest settlers in Franklin township includes the names of James Robinson, Benjamin Robinson, John Robinson, Wm. J. Robinson, Michael Miller, Jacob Jackson, James Tanner, John Walmsley, William Taylor, Abraham Thompson, Joseph Scott, John G. Pigman, Obadiah Davidson, Valentine and Jane Johnson, Geo. Littick, Isaac Shanbaugh, Phillip Hershman, and Lewis Roderick. One half of the township was originally owned by Michael Miller, Sr., and the Robinsons, each having a four-thousand-acre tract.[49]

The State of Ohio, Coshocton County, SS:. In the matter of claim for bounty land for Michael Miller a Revolutionary Soldier; On this 16th day of September A. D. 1909 personally appeared before me Solomon Mercer, deputy Clerk of the Court of Common Pleas in and for said County duly authorized to administer oaths, John H. Rice, aged 38 years, a resident of Coshecton in the County of Choshocton and State of Ohio, whose Post Office address is 941 Main Street, Coshoctor, Ohio, well known to me to be respectable and entitled to credit and who being duly sworn, declared that he is a son and heir at law of Irvin Rice and Caroline Rice, now deceased that the said Caroline Rice was the daughter of Isaac Miller and Mary Miller, his wife, both now deceased. The said Isaac Miller was the son of Charles Miller and Nancy Miller, both now deceased and that the said Charles Miller was the son of Michael Miller and Margaret Miller, his wife, now deceased and further that Michael Miller was a private in the 2nd Maryland Regiment[sic] and served as a soldier in the Revolutionary War, and that said Michael Miller had not claimed the bounty land allowed to him for such military service prior to the 16th day of January A.D. 1826, and in the year 1839, he departed this life his only wife Margaret having previously died. Signed by John H. Rice, September 16, 1909.[50]

Private George Morriner enlisted January 31, 1776 (MSA: 18, 19). No further records found for this soldier.

Private John Mugg enlisted January 21, 1776. "On Guard." No further records have been found for this soldier.

Private Michael Mullen enlisted January 22, 1776. "Sick in hospital." His name was given as Michl. Mullen (MSA: 18, 19). "Sgt. Michael Mullen, 6th Regiment enlisted 4/30/1778; joined 10/2/1778, private; discharged 12/3/1778. Deserted" (MSA: 18, 233).

Private Frederick Myers enlisted January 29, 1776. His name was given as Frederick Myre (MSA: 18, 19). His name, given as Frederick Myer, was on the list of soldiers "belonging to the Company of Maryland Regulars under my command last campaign, and taken prisoners in the action on Long Island on the 27th August last, are returned to Maryland. Signed by Benjamin Ford."[51] On December 10, 1776, Private Frederick Mire is shown reenlisting in the First Regiment. He was discharged on December 27, 1779 (MSA: 18, 137).

This soldier reenlisted a third time. "Fredk. Moyer, enlisted in the Maryland Line, 8 Aug 1781" (MSA: 18, 405). He was shown on the rolls of the Fourth Regiment as Fredk. Meyers on September 10, 1781 (MSA: 18, 397). "Frederick Myers, Myirs

P. deserted 11 Apl '82. 2 Co., 4 B. Capt. John Mitchell, Lt. John McCoy, Ensign Joseph Cross" (MSA: 18, 458).

Frederick Myers was listed as head of household in Frederick County, Maryland, at the time of the 1790 census. He was deceased by June 12, 1792, when the state's auditor was requested to "issue a Certificate for the Depreciation of pay to Frederick Mire late a soldier in the first Maryland Regiment and deliver the same to the Treasurer of the western shore, who is Ordered to pay it to Hugh McClean [sic] Administrator of the said Frederick Mire" (MSA: 72, 276). Hugh McClain was a fellow soldier from the Sixth Company, First Regiment.

Private Peter Myers enlisted February 10, 1776. His name was given as Peter Myre. He reenlisted on May 3, 1778; Cpl., March 1, 1780; discharged August 16, 1780 and it was noted that he was "missing." This entry gives his name as Peter Moire (MSA: 18, 137).

This soldier moved to Monroe County, New York, where he died on June 28, 1843. He is buried in the Pine Hill Cemetery, Rush, New York. His tombstone reads "Peter Myers from Hagerstown, Maryland, Died June 28, 1843, ae. 95. Rev. Sold." There is a notation that "record taken earlier says ae. 85."

Private Alexander Naylor enlisted January 21, 1776. His name was given as "Alex. Nailor" (MSA: 18, 18). The name of Sergeant Alexander Porter appears on "the list of prisoners belonging to the Company of Maryland Regulars under my command last campaign, and taken prisoners in the action on Long Island on the 27th August last, are returned to Maryland. Signed by Benjamin Ford." There was no soldier enlisted at that time by the name of Alexander Porter and the author believes this name should actually be Alexander Naylor.[52]

On December 10, 1776, he reenlisted in the First Regiment and was shown as "Sgt. Alexr. Naylor." It was noted that he had transferred (MSA: 18, 146).

"Sergt. Alex. Nailer was at Valley Forge in May and June of 1778 under the command of Col. John H. Stone and Capt. Alexander Roxburgh"[53] It is presumed that on December 10, 1776, Alexander Naylor had enlisted for three years. By the end of 1779, he would have been discharged.

The next record found of him is in Pennsylvania in 1782 when he was shown as being enlisted in "Capt. George Brown's Company of Washington County Militia on the Sandusky Expedition Commanded by Col. William Crawford Commencing 18 May 1782 and Ending 10th June 1782 Both Days Included." He served as a private in this expedition.[54]

The Crawford expedition, under the command of Colonel William Crawford, occurred in 1782 in present day Ohio, then the western front of the American Revolutionary War. Their objective was to destroy enemy Indian towns along the Sandusky River thereby ending Indian attacks on American settlers. Crawford, with a force of about 500 volunteer militiamen, marched deep into American Indian territory, hoping to surprise the Indians. The Indians and their British allies from Detroit, however, had already learned of the expedition and were ready.

Before the end of the first day of fighting, the Americans were surrounded and attempted to retreat. Most were successful and made their way back to Pennsylvania, but at least 70 were killed. Colonel Crawford and a small number of his men were captured by the Indians. The Indians executed many of these captives in retaliation for the Gnadenhutten massacre that occurred earlier in the year, in which about 100 Indian civilians were murdered by Pennsylvanian militiamen. Crawford's execution was particularly brutal: he was tortured for at least two hours before being burned at the stake.[55]

Alexander Naylor was married for the first time to Magdalena about 1785. They had a son, Samuel, who was born on 2 January 1786. Magdalena apparently died shortly after Samuel's birth. He married, second, Mary Mills on 9 March 1786 at the German Reformed Church in Frederick, Frederick County, Maryland. His son Samuel was christened on 18 March 1788 at the Evangelical Lutheran or Lutheran Congregation of Middletown, Frederick Co., Maryland. Alexander Naylor was listed as head of household in Frederick County at the time of the 1790 census. The last record found of him is a 1796 voting record in Frederick County.[56]

Private Nicholas Naylor enlisted January 22, 1776 (MSA: 18, 19). He is shown re-enlisting on December 10, 1776, as *"Sgt. Nicholas Naylor, 1st Regt., Q.M.S. Corpl."* (MSA: 18, 146).

Nicholas Naylor survived the battle and was promoted to corporal. He went with Gen. Mercer's Brigade as they retreated from New York through New Jersey and into Pennsylvania for two weeks before re-crossing the Delaware River to take the town of Trenton, followed by another victory at Princeton. In 1778, while still in the Quartermaster Service, and still under the command of Colonel John Hoskins Stone, one of his jobs was to transport wagons to and from Valley Forge.[57]

On February 15, 1783, a marriage license was issued in Prince George's County to Nicholas Naylor and Mary Selby. The family was living in Green County, Kentucky, by 1800; Barren County, Kentucky, by 1810; and by 1820 they had moved to Pike County, Indiana.

Private Samuel Price enlisted January 26, 1776. "Absent on furlough May 27" (MSA: 18, 19). No further records have been found for this soldier.

Private Henry Ramsburg enlisted January 31, 1776. His name was given as Henry Remsburg (MSA: 18, 20). Although no additional records were found for this soldier in the Archives of Maryland, it is believed that he survived the war. He was the son of Stephen Ramsburg of Frederick County, Maryland, whose will dated April 14, 1788, devised part of his estate to his son, Henry.[58]

Private Isaac Rice enlisted January 22, 1776 (MSA: 18, 19). The name of Isaac Rue appears on the list of soldiers "belonging to the Company of Maryland Regulars under my command last campaign, and taken prisoners in the action on Long Island on the 27th August last, are returned to Maryland. Signed by Benjamin Ford."[59] The name should have read Isaac Rice.

Private John Ross enlisted January 28, 1776 (MSA: 18, 19). No further records have been found for this soldier.

Private John Row, Drummer enlisted January 28, 1776 (MSA: 18, p. 18). No further records have been found for this soldier.

Private William Smith enlisted January 29, 1776. His name was given as Willm. Smith (MSA: 18, 19). Private Smith reenlisted in the First Regiment on December 10, 1776 and was discharged on November 1, 1780 (MSA: 18, 159).

On September 30, 1818, William Smith, a resident of Berkeley County, Virginia, age 66, deposed:

> ... that some time in the Spring of 1776 he enlisted in Frederick County, Maryland as a private to serve one year in a company of Rifle in the service of the U.S. and afterwards attached to a Maryland regiment commanded by Col. Smallwood, that the company he enlisted in was commanded by Capt. Stricker. That he served in the sd. Corps through the time of his enlistment and was then discharged. That afterwards, sometime in the spring of 1778 he again enlisted for three years in Philadelphia, Pennyslvania in a company commanded by Capt. Roxburgh in the 1st Maryland Regt. on Continental establishment. That he continued to serve in the sd. Corps until the expiration of three years, when he was discharged in Salisbury, SC. He was in the battles of Long Island, White Plains, and Camden.[60]

In 1821 William Smith was living in Morgan County, Virginia (created from part of Berkeley County, Virginia). He referred to his wife, age 55, and two children but did not name them. Private Smith died June 27, 1830.[61]

Private William Tarrance enlisted January 22, 1776 (MSA: 18, 19). No further records have been found for this soldier.

Private James Taylor enlisted January 28, 1776 (MSA: 18, 19). Private James Taylor, First Regiment "enlisted March 24 ___; deserted same month." (MSA: 18, 168).

Private John Taylor enlisted April 11, 1776. "Sick in barracks" (MSA: 18, 20). Private Taylor reenlisted in the First Regiment on December 10, 1776, and was discharged in June 1780. It was noted that he had deserted (MSA: 18, 168).

Private Levean Todd enlisted March 4, 1776 (MSA: 18, 20). No further records have been found for this soldier.

Private Robert Tune enlisted January 22, 1776 (MSA: 18, 19). No further records have been found for this soldier.

Private William Witner enlisted January 22, 1776. "Sick in barracks" (MSA: 18, 19). No further records have been found for this soldier.

Private Samuel Workman enlisted January 28, 1776 (MSA: 18, 19). No further records have been found for this soldier.

Private Henry Young enlisted January 21, 1776 (MSA: 18, 18). "'Private Henry Young. Date passed: June 2, 1778. Williams' Regiment. Enlisted for 9 mos.' A List of Substitutes Furnished by the Different Battalions After their being Classed in Order for the Draught. Frederick County" (MSA: 18, 324). A third entry shows "Private Henry Young, 6th Md. Regt., enlisted July 1, 1778; discharged 2/1779. Left out 7/1/1778, joined Ghislen's Company" (MSA: 18, 259).

On July 27, 1855, Mary Hoffman, age 72, a resident of Frederick County, and daughter of Henry Young deposed that her father was a private in the Revolutionary Army, having enlisted in the Fifth Regiment, Maryland Line, on July 1, 1778. He died in 1795. Her mother, Mary Young, survived her husband for about 52 years, dying on February 17, 1845, after a second marriage by which there was no issue.

Deposition of Mary M. Joy (age 79) and Stephen Joy (age 85), July 27, 1855:

> Mary Joy states that she was born in Middletown, Frederick County. Stephen Joy states that he was born in St. Mary's County and had lived in Frederick County since 1788. They both declare that they were acquainted with Henry Young who since died near Middletown and that the same Henry Young, in or about the year 1776 enlisted as a private in the army of the Revolution in the Maryland Line. They further declare that the sd. Henry Young died in 1793 and that he was married before he went to War in the year 1776 to Mary Girish and continued to live with her, his wife, until his death. Mary Young was married again in May 1818 to Vincent Sander and had no children by her last marriage. She died on the 17th of January 1845 and the sd. Vincent Sanders died on the 22nd day of July 1845.
>
> They further depose that the sd. Mary had by the sd. Henry Young, her first husband, 10 children named George, Casper, Jacob, Catherine, Henry, Dewalt, Nancy, Elizabeth, Mary, and Conrad, all deceased except Mary (now married to George Hoffman) and Dewalt & ____ Young.[62]

The names of six soldiers, who were originally listed, have been removed from the roster of the Sixth Company. They include the name of Captain George Stricker, who was replaced by Captain Benjamin Ford.

Cadet Larkin Dorsey was initially shown on the rolls of the Ninth Company of Light Infantry; however, by July 18, 1776, he had been transferred to Captain Daniel Dorsey's Company (MSA: 12, 76). This soldier was, therefore not one of The Maryland 400.

Cadet Richard Dorsey was initially shown on the rolls of the Ninth Company of Light Infantry, but he was transferred to another company. On July 16, 1776, "Richard Dorsey was appointed 3ᵈ Lieutenant of Capᵗ Nathaniel Smith's Company of Matrosses" (MSA: 12, 53). This soldier was, therefore, not one of The Maryland 400.

Private John McCabe was discharged from the service on May 11, 1776 (MSA: 18, 19).

Lieutenant Thomas Smyth, Jr. was commissioned Captain of the Fourth Maryland Battalion of the Flying Camp in July 1776.[63] He was, therefore, not one of The Maryland 400.

Private Dewalt Stottlemyer whose name was erroneously shown as Davall Stottlemeir, was shown to have been sent on detachment duty (MSA: 18, 18). There are no further records for this soldier, and since he appears to have been sent on detachment duty he is not believed to be one of The Maryland 400.

Captain George Stricker was commissioned lieutenant colonel of the German Regiment on July 17, 1776.[64] He was replaced by Captain Benjamin Ford.

Summary

Eighty-one soldiers were originally shown as enlisted in the Ninth Company. Benjamin Ford was transferred from the Second Company to replace Captain Stricker, which caused no gain in the number of soldiers. Of the 81 soldiers, 76 are presumed to have gone into battle (excluding the five men listed above). Forty-one of these men are known to have survived and 35 are unaccounted for. Fourteen men from this company were taken prisoner the day of the battle.

Total for All Companies

Three hundred eighty-three soldiers are shown as enlisted, of which 356 are presumed to have gone into battle. Of this number, 213 soldiers are known to have survived. A total of 142 are unaccounted for and 40 soldiers were taken prisoner.

Unsung Heroes

As mentioned earlier, at the request of General Smallwood, General Washington agreed to send additional men to rescue the beleaguered men of the 400, who by now had been instructed by Lord Stirling to make their way to safety as best they could while he personally surrendered to the Hessians. Marylanders would take the lead in this rescue mission with a company of Connecticut soldiers serving as their backup.

Captain John Allen Thomas and the men of the Fifth Independent Company, from St. Mary's County, Maryland, made their way to the mouth of the Gowanus Creek with two field pieces, which "silenced the six pieces of the enemy, which were firing upon the fugitives, all but 12 of whom waded or swam to safety, helped especially by Thomas's men."[1]

Captain Thomas was a native of Talbot County, Maryland, who moved to St. Mary's County prior to 1774. He was always an advocate for his men, ensuring they had adequate medical care, and he often used his own funds to ensure they had the necessary uniforms and equipment.

There were approximately 104 men in this company based on the number of canteens and hunting shirts that were ordered for them. Unfortunately, the rolls of this company are missing and only a handful of these soldiers have been identified to date. They were:

SERGEANT JOHN BLACKISTONE, Private, St. Mary's County Militia. "Sgt., 5th Independent Co., 1776. Participated in Battle of Brooklyn on August 27, 1776. Promoted to Ensign, 2nd Md. Line in March 1777 and commissioned 1st Lt., Upper Battalion on 11/18/1779. Died November 11, 1806."[2] The author's research indicates he died in 1801.

Family lore says that "Lt. John Blackistone of the American Army in 1776–7, then in New Jersey after the Battle of Trenton and after the army had gone into winter quarters at Morristown, obtained permission to visit home on the Potomac in St. Mary's. He had to pass thru enemy lines — he was espied and pursued. He broke a spur switch off a nearby pear tree, by aid of which with a fleeter horse, he escaped capture. At home he planted the pear switch. It lived, bore fruit. He requested to be buried under the pear tree. He said, 'It saved me from a prison ship.'"

CADET HENRY CARBERRY served first in the Maryland Line and later in the Pennsylvania Line. He would ultimately achieve the rank of captain during the Revolutionary War. This soldier certainly had an interesting career. He not only witnessed, but also participated in many historical events.

In June 1783 the Commonwealth of Pennsylvania sought to secure his arrest as one of the leaders in a planned revolt of the officers of the Continental Army the previous March over nonpayment of salaries, bonuses, and pensions.

1784 Apr. 28: O[tho] H[olland] WILLIAMS, Baltimore. To [Uriah] FORREST. [252]. [George Washington] will be in Baltimore this week on his way to Philadelphia for the Cincinnati meeting which he called for the first Monday in May; as a representative of Maryland, he [Williams] will set off with [John Eager] Howard in a day or two; will inform Forrest of anything material that happens; a committee of the Massachusetts General Assembly, appointed to enquire into the nature and tendencies of the Cincinnati, has made an unfavourable and plausable report; Rhode Island is said to be going to disfranchise all her citizens who join the order; all the eastern seaboard states are clamorous against half pay commutation, impost, the Cincinnati, and old uniforms; the people being what they are, this is not to be wondered at, but what does Forrest think of a prejudice in Congress against the order; Williams had thought that because the army is disbanded and the officers returned to their private lives, they were responsible only to the governments under which they were living; in this he is mistaken; the mutiny at Philadelphia last summer produced a quarrel between Congress and the state of Pennsylvania; Capt. [Henry] Carbury [Carbery] of Maryland was in the mutiny; he entered the service against the wishes of his father who disinherited him for doing so; when the Pennsylvania line was reduced, Carbery was put out of the army with nothing more to live on than a good military name; he [Carbery] was at the barracks in Philadelphia when the Northern Army was afraid it was going to be disbanded without pay or any settlement of its accounts; the troops at Philadelphia, encouraged by some of the citizens, decided to practise upon the fears of the general Assembly then sitting, hoping to extract money; the troops in the barracks at Lancaster [Pa.] heard of this, though not through Carbery, and some eighty or so of them marched upon the city; they insulted Congress and Congress left the city; after Congress had gone, the president of the State [John Dickinson] ordered out the militia; Carbery and [?] Sullivan, an accomplice, advised the soldiers to submit and went off; in a military view, Carbery's action was criminal; after peace was restored, Carbery came back to Maryland and was trying to get himself a pardon; Congress, hearing that he was in Baltimore, appointed a committee to go into the circumstances, and that committee signed a warrant for his arrest; an unsigned postscript to the warrant was in the hand of an able lawyer, one of our representatives, and some more was added by a member from Carolina verbally; Mr. [?] Gassaway was to take Carbery into custody, with the help of Sergeant [?] Dove, and carry him to Annapolis before one of the judges of the general court there, though there was a judge of that court in Baltimore then; Gassaway let Carbery go unattended to Annapolis on his parole; Mr. [?] Golds-borough, one of the judges has gone down for the occasion, and Mr. Harrison is already there; the issue will show whether citizens who have been soldiers are liable to arrest by Congress or like other citizens, they are subject to the laws of their own state only; Baltimore is generally afraid that a power has been exercised that is not warranted by the Confederation of the States; Carbery will probably not be executed; will write again when the matter is settled; hopes that the committee [of Congress] is wrong, at least in the manner of the arrest, for it would be hard if the soldiers should be the only class not entitled to the privileges of freemen; asks Forrest to send to Stoddert for him [Williams] a very plain neat, middlesized gold Wa[t]ch of Wagstaffs make value 20 or 25 G[uinea]s and I will give him the Clinkers.[3]

Henry Carberry would survive this debacle unscathed, although at one point, he thought of fleeing to France. Not only did he survive, he later served as Maryland's first adjutant general from 1794 to 1807.[4]

By the time the War of 1812 came along, Henry Carberry had achieved the rank of colonel in the Maryland Militia. "The 36th Infantry, under Col. Henry Carberry was removed from St. Mary's County by order of President Monroe in 1813 to defend Washington, Baltimore, and Annapolis."[5]

Col. Carberry was in Washington, D.C., when it was burned by British troops on August 24, 1814.

> In typical Armstrongian footdragging and dismissal, the Secretary of War told Col. Minor that the Quartermaster, a Col. Henry Carberry, would take care of all his supply needs in the morning. Members of today's armed forces will recognize the classic "hurry up and wait" situation the Virginia Militia faced of running eight miles to Washington and then being put off. You will see that this deserves at least two "U.S. failures" marks. You can also see how the mere attitude of one person in authority can null the heroic efforts of many. But you will also see how this childish, momentary attitude will cascade into other effects. Col. Minor did not know what greater effects this would have and it is just as well, for he was outraged enough for the moment. He returned to his troops at the Capitol. This author questions whether Winder was aware of the presence of these soldiers. No such mention is made in any historical source. Yet it might be assumed he did from his actions later that night.[6]

By the time of his death in 1822, Henry Carberry had achieved the rank of general. The May 29, 1822, edition of the *National Intelligencer* newspaper contained his obituary: "Died on May 26 at his seat near Georgetown, in his 66th year, Gen. Henry Carberry, an officer of the Revolution. He received a severe wound in the side from a musket ball, which could not be extracted and it was no doubt the cause of his death after remaining in him 40 odd years.[7]

CADET ROBERT CHESLEY applied for sea service in 1776 in St. Mary's County and was recommended by Captain John Allen Thomas as a cadet on March 8, 1776. "Commissioned 3rd Lt., 5th Independent Co. on August 7, 1776 and fought in the Battle of Brooklyn. Saw action in both the northern and southern campaigns. Capt., 2nd Maryland Line from June 10, 1777-October 25, 1781 when he retired."[8]

PRIVATE CHARLES CHILTON had also earlier applied for sea service and would later serve aboard ship, but first he would serve in the land forces. The April 23, 1824, edition of the *Baltimore Patriot* reported his death:

> Died on the 10th of April, at his residence in St. Mary's county, Charles Chilton, Esq., in the 69th year of his age. He was a patriot of the revolution, and was Purser on board the Virginia Frigate, when she was captured by the British fleet. He was a member of the State Convention, when she ratified the Federal Constitution, and an associate Judge of St. Mary's County, when he was appointed by Gen. Washington, about 35 years ago, "surveyor of the Port of Town Creek," which he held till his death, notwithstanding the violent conflict of party feeling while in office; and yet he was always a dedicated federalist, and among the last men in the world that would ever succumb to those in power. He has left a chasm in his neighborhood, that no human being can fill, unless they lived as he did, and did as he did. He lived and died a bachelor, although he lived not alone; for he was daily visited by the poor, the maimed, the halt (?), the blind, as well as by the rich, and they never left his dwelling without leaving a blessing behind them. He seemed to live for others and not for himself, and of all men the writer of this notice ever knew, he surely was, most emphatically, the poor man's friend.[9]

PRIVATE WILLIAM COE, a native of Calvert County, Maryland, enlisted February 1, 1776, in Captain Thomas's Company. According to his pension application, he "mustered at Leonardtown. Upon joining his company, he marched to Annapolis where the 5th remained until August of that same year. They were then ordered north. The company saw action both on Long Island and in New Jersey."

William Coe further stated that he participated in the Battle of Long Island, where the Maryland Line covered the retreat of the American forces. In the spring of 1777 he was transferred to a company of artillery, commanded by Captain William Campbell. He was promoted to corporal and served as a matross, assisting the gunner in loading, firing, and sponging the guns. He also carried flintlocks and marched as a guard with the storewagons.[10]

Private Coe was discharged on August 11, 1779, by furnishing two men to serve in his place until the end of the war. Prior to 1790 Coe moved to Annapolis where he operated a tailor shop on the north side of Main Street, not far from the waterfront, near the city tavern. When Thomas Jefferson was in Annapolis for a session of Congress from November 23, 1783 to May 11, 1784, he contracted with William Coe to handle his clothing needs. (Jefferson and James Monroe boarded together in a small rented house owned by a Mr. Dulany).[11]

About 1830 he moved to Baltimore, where he operated a tailor shop at 62 South Charles Street. He died in Baltimore on November 5, 1832. William Coe was the father of Dr. William Gwynn Coe, a bishop in the Baltimore Conference of the Methodist Episcopal Church and was said to have been the greatest preacher the conference ever produced.[12]

LIEUTENANT JOHN DAVIDSON "enlisted as a 2nd Lt., 5th Independent Md. Co., St. Mary's County, January 2, 1776. Saw action during Dunmore's invasion of St. Mary's County in July 1776 and was promoted to 1st Lt. on August 6, 1776; to Capt. on December 10, 1776; and later a Maj. in the 2nd Md. Line. Reported to the Gov. on August 26, 1777 that 'relapse of fever prevented his arrival at camp.' Participated in the Battle of Brooklyn and served in the Northern and Southern Campaigns. Served as a major, 5th Md. Line from January 1, 1781–January 21, 1783 when he was appointed Comptroller of Maryland by Gov. William Paca."[13]

PRIVATE ANTHONY DAVIS applied for a pension on May 11, 1818. At that time he stated that he was 63 years of age and that he enlisted in the spring of 1776 as a private in the company commanded by Capt. John Allen Thomas attached to the regiment of Maryland under the command of Colonel William Smallwood. In 1777 he was transferred to the artillery company commanded by Captain William Campbell and served until the summer of 1778 when he was discharged at Annapolis. "Is in reduced circumstances and stands in need of assistance for support."[14]

His pension application did not state the battles in which he had participated; however, the application of Jesse Thompson below states that these two men served together.

PRIVATE JOHN GARDINER, for reasons unknown, was discharged early. On December 5, 1776, the Council of Safety ordered that the paymaster "pay John Gardiner of Capt. John Allen Thomas's Company for four and a half months Service and that the sd. John Gardiner be discharged from the Service."[15]

PRIVATE JESSE JORDAN initially applied for sea service early in 1776. As there were no ships available, he, together with the others, served in the militia instead. He enlisted in this company on July 28, 1776.[16]

PRIVATE THOMAS LYNCH, at about age 59, applied for a pension on April 23, 1818. He deposed that he "enlisted in January 1776 in the company commanded by Capt. John Allen Thomas of the regt. commanded by Col. William Smallwood of the Maryland Line. He served in the sd. corps in the service of the U.S. until September 1777 when he was discharged from service at Leonardtown." Private Lynch stated that he was in the Battle of Long Island.[17]

LIEUTENANT HENRY NEALE served as a third lieutenant, Fifth Independent Maryland Company, St. Mary's County, January 2, 1776, and as a second lieutenant on August 9, 1776. He participated in the Battle of Brooklyn and the New York campaign in 1776. "Oath, 1778. Promoted to Lt. Col. in the St. Mary's County Militia in 1794."[18] Additional service records show that he served as "Captain 2d Maryland, 20th February, 1777; resigned 15th March, 1777."[19]

Henry Neale died in 1815. His obituary appeared in the December 27, 1815, issue of the *Centinel of Liberty*. "Departed this life on the 12th inst. at his seat in St. Mary's Co., Md., Col. Henry Neale (one of the few remaining veterans of '76) in the 64th year of his age, after a short but severe illness, thro' which was exemplified, that patient fortitude and christian resignation, the strong characteristics of his protracted and well spent life; leaving an affectionate wife and children, with a numerous and most respectable acquaintances to lament the awful separation."[20]

PRIVATE JOHN BAPTIST PRATT was an invalid by October 8, 1776. On this date, it was ordered "That Charles Wallace Esqr Paymaster advance one month's pay to John Pratt of Captn Thomas's Company" (MSA: 12, 326).

On November 22, 1776, "John Pratt of Capt. Thomas' Company (5th Independent Co)., being an invalid, ordered that he be discharged from the Service. Also ordered that the Paymaster discharge the pay of the sd. Pratt from the 8th of October to this day" (MSA: 12, 471). Private Pratt was deceased prior to February 1778 when his widow, Susanna, and his son, Zepheniah, administered his estate.[21]

PRIVATE AARON SPALDING, later promoted to sergeant, moved to Washington County, Kentucky, after the war. On January 23, 1816, it was "RESOLVED, That the treasurer of the western shore be and he is hereby directed to pay to Aaron Spalding, or to his order, annually in quarterly payments, during his life, a sum of money equal to the half pay of a sergeant" (MSA: 192, 2981).

On July 10, 1820, Aaron Spalding of Washington County, Kentucky, aged 68 deposed that he enlisted in St. Mary's County, Maryland in the beginning of January 1776 in Captain John Allen Thomas's company as a private, and in Colonel William Smallwood's regiment and served until the 6th of July 1783 when he was honorably discharged at James Island in South Carolina. He deposed that he was in the battles of Long Island, White Plains, Brandywine, Staten Island, German Town, Camden, Cowpens, Guilford Court House, Eutaw Springs, and Monmouth.[22]

The last record found of Aaron Spalding is in a deposition he made on June 30, 1828, in which he stated that Edmund Howard was a lieutenant in the First Regiment of the Maryland Line and that Spalding had served as a sergeant under him. Spalding was still residing in Washington County, Kentucky, at that time.[23]

PRIVATE HENRY SPALDING obviously fell on hard times after the war. On December 21, 1811, it was "Resolved, That the treasurer of the Western Shore be, and he is hereby directed and required to pay to Henry Spalding, late a private in the revolutionary war, or to his order, in quarterly payments, a sum of money equal to the half pay of a private, as a provision to him in his indigent situation and advanced life" (MSA: 614, 260–261).

On April 24, 1818, Henry Spalding, aged about 62 years, a resident of St. Mary's County, deposed that he enlisted in January 1776 in the company commanded by Captain John Allen Thomas of the First Maryland Regiment and he served until the

10th of January 1780 when he was discharged at Baltimore. He stated that he was in the battles of Long Island, White Plains, and Monmouth Court House.[24]

He filed additional papers on March 18, 1825. At this time he identified himself as Henry Spalding (of Peter) and stated that he was aged about 67 years. This time he stated that he enlisted for three years on the ___day of February in the year 1776 in the company commanded by Captain John A. Thomas in the regiment commanded by Colonel Smallwood in the line of the State of Maryland in the continental establishment, that he continued to serve in the said corps until the winter of 1780 when he was discharged from the service in Annapolis. He stated that he was a farmer by occupation but due to age and infirmities he was not able to work.[25]

On November 2, 1830 William Floyd made oath that Henry Spalding of Peter died about November 1, 1829.[26]

LIEUTENANT JOHN STEWART was likely one of the most colorful characters of the Revolutionary War. He was young, impetuous, hot tempered, headstrong, but very, very brave.

He was commissioned as a "1st Lieutenant of Thomas' Independent Maryland Company, 14th January, 1776; Captain 2d Maryland, 10th December, 1776; Major, 17th April, 1777; taken prisoner on Staten Island, 22d August, 1777. By the Act of 26th July, 1779, it was 'Resolved, unanimously, that Lieutenant-Colonel Fleury and Major Stewart, who, by their situation in leading two assaults (on Stony Point), had a more immediate opportunity of distinguishing themselves, have by their personal achievements, exhibited a bright example to their brother soldiers, and merit in a particular manner the approbation and acknowledgment of the United States; that a silver medal of this action be struck and presented to Major Stewart'; Lieutenant-Colonel 1st Maryland, 10th February, 1781. Died — December, 1782."[27]

If there was anything that Lieutenant Stewart couldn't stand it was a coward, especially after witnessing and participating in the events of August 27, 1776. On September 17, 1776, Stewart was leading a scouting party of Marylanders when they met and joined forces with a small group of Connecticut soldiers. They soon encountered an advanced guard of British soldiers. As the first shot was fired, Sergeant William Phelps of the Connecticut troops ran away. The events of this day would lead to charges and counter-charges being made and a court-martial was conducted on September 26 against both parties. According to the testimony of Captain [William] Hubbel,

> Last Wednesday morning Lt. Stewart came to my hut and inquired of Ensign Phelps, calling him a damned coward. I sent for the man, who is a Sergeant in my company; he came up, and Lt. Stewart told him he wanted to know his name to report him for a coward, for he had behaved like a damned coward the day before, and told him he was not fit for an Ensign; on which Phelps replied he was as fit for an Ensign as he (Stewart) was for a Lt. Upon which Lt. Stewart immediately struck

him in the face with the flat of his hand. I went off and complained to Col. Silliman, and Lt. Stewart came up with the Adjutant of our regiment, when Col. Silliman very mildly talked with Lt. Stewart, and told him he ought to have taken another course; Lt. Stewart grew warm, when Col. Silliman ordered him under an arrest. On this, Lt. Stewart took his hat and flung it on the ground, and said "I'll go to my tent—all you can do is take my commission, but I am a gentleman, and will put it out of your power, for I will resign it, and in less than two hours will be revenged on you, God damn you." He soon went off. He damned Col. Silliman several times.

At the court-martial, the Marylanders backed the testimony of Lieutenant Stewart while the Connecticut men backed Sergeant Phelps. The court found Lieutenant Stewart guilty of striking Sergeant Phelps but were of the opinion that he was provoked to do so. He was found not guilty. Sergeant Phelps was also acquitted.[28]

PRIVATE JEREMIAH TARLTON, according to his widow's application for a pension on March 18, 1829, served under Captain Thomas's company and then under Major Stewart. She stated that he enlisted at Leonardtown, St. Mary's County, at or near the commencement of the Revolution and that he served at least three years and nine months. Mrs. Eleanor Tarlton, then aged 75 years of age and a resident of Scott County, Kentucky, also said that her husband was promoted to corporal on June 1, 1778, and was discharged on January 10, 1780. She further stated that she had heard her husband say that he was in the battles of Bunker Hill, Quebec, Long Island, White Plains, Fort Washington, Germantown, Brandywine, Quaker Hill, Stony Point, and that he was at the capture of Cornwallis. Jeremiah Tarlton was married January 20, 1782, in St. Mary's County to Eleanor Medley. He died July 6, 1826, in Scott County, Kentucky.[29]

PRIVATE NATHAN THOMAS, 1758–1822. "Private, Capt. Allen Thomas' Co., SMC, 1776. He married Margaret _____ in 1782 or 1785 and they had six children. In 1818, aged 60, he applied for a pension in Mason Co., KY. In 1821, he was in Fleming Co. and again stated he was aged 60 and his wife was between 40 and 50 and his oldest child was aged 15. He died on 7/24/1822 and his wife died in April 1841."[30]

On May 18, 1818, Nathaniel Thomas, aged 60 years, a resident of Mason County, Kentucky, deposed that he enlisted in the month of February 1776 in the State of Maryland, and in the company commanded by Captain Allen Thomas of the regular army. He enlisted for twelve months and one day and was marched from Maryland to New York and joined the Continental Army on Long Island. The company to which he belonged was attached to the regiment commanded by Colonel Smallwood. He served until February 1777 to the end of the time for which he enlisted, one year and one day and was regularly discharged at Annapolis. He said that he was in the battles of Long Island, Kingsbridge, White Plains (where he was wounded in the leg) and at the taking of the Hessians at Trenton.[31]

On March 13, 1821, Nathan Thomas, aged 60 years of thereabouts, a resident of Fleming County, Kentucky deposed that he served in Captain Allen Thomas's company and in Colonel Smallwood's regiment as set forth in his original declaration dated about the 18th of May 1818. He further stated that he was a common laborer or farmer by occupation, but he has not been able to labor any for three years passed, "from having the dropsey on him, besides being a cripple from having his left leg broke by a musket ball in the battle of the White Plains, which has always been a running sore, and as I get older, it gets worse. My right leg is also much injured by a musket ball passing through the flesh of it in the same battle."[32]

On January 28, 1856, Solomon Applegate, of Fleming County, Kentucky, deposed that he was "the administrator of Margaret Thomas, dec'd who was the widow of Nathan Thomas, dec'd, or as he was sometimes called Nathaniel Thomas. Nathan Thomas died about the ___day of July 1820. The sd. Margaret Thomas was married to sd. Nathan Thomas on the ___day of ___1782 as he is informed. Margaret Thomas died on or near the County line between the counties of Fleming and Mason, part of the farm being in both counties on or about the ___day of April 1841."[33]

In a September 26, 1913, letter to Howard Clark of the Smithsonian Institute, the Pension Office wrote that Nathan Thomas died on July 24, 1822.

PRIVATE ELECTIOUS THOMPSON applied for a pension on June 1, 1833. He was then living in Morgan County, Alabama. Private Thompson said that he

> ... enlisted the first of April 1776 under the command of Capt. Allen Thomas in Leonard Town, St. Mary's Co., Maryland and served in the Regt. of Maryland under the command of General Smallwood. He stayed at Leonardtown until July and from there he marched to Cherry Fields near Blackistone's Island and from there we were marched to Annapolis on the Chesapeake Bay and from there to Baltimore and from Baltimore to Philadelphia and to New York and joined General Washington and joined the troops on their retreat from the Battle of Long Island and from there to White Plains at which place I was in a battle under the command of General Smallwood and same Captain, which battle I think was in the last of August 1776. I remained with the main army until it retreated near Philadelphia where I was taken sick and after laying sick three weeks, I was taken to the hospital in Philadelphia where I remained until sometime near Christmas of that year and from Philadelphia I got to Annapolis to which place I was taken on board a vessel and taken to the hospital at that place at which place I lay sick until some time in January of the next year. From there I returned to Leonard Town at which place whilst there, my time of service expired. In the fall of 1777, he thinks September, he entered the service of the United States. There was a draft among the militia of Maryland and John Compton of Capt. White's Company was drafted and I took his place. I was marched on by Capt. Shaw from Maryland near Bladensburg to Baltimore and from there to Philadelphia and from there we joined the main army under Gen. Washington a few weeks before the Battle of Germantown. I served three months. I was in the Battle of Germantown. I was born in Prince George's County, Maryland in 1755. After the war, I lived in St. Mary's County and then moved to Loudon

County, Virginia; from there to North Carolina; to Floyd County, Kentucky; and then to Morgan County, Alabama where I now live."[34]

PRIVATE JESSE THOMPSON would later be promoted to sergeant and transferred to another company. He was, however, with Captain Thomas's company at the time of the battle.

On January 1, 1813, it was "RESOLVED, That the treasurer of the Western Shore be, and he is hereby directed to pay to Jesse Thompson, late a serjeant in the Maryland line during the revolutionary war, or to his order, a sum of money annually, in quarterly payments, equal to the half pay of a sergeant, as a further remuneration for those services rendered his country during the American war" (MSA: 618, 245).

Jesse Thompson, aged 62 years, applied for a pension on May 12, 1818. He stated that he enlisted in the company commanded by Captain John Allen Thomas in February 1776 attached to the regiment of Maryland commanded by Colonel William Smallwood during the war and in the year 1777 was transferred to the artillery company under the command of Captain Filford. He declared that he was discharged at Annapolis on or about October 1783 and that he was in the battles of White Plains, Brandywine, Trenton, Camden, the Seige of Camden and '96, Guilford and Eutaw [Springs].[35]

On August 15, 1820, Jesse Thompson, aged 64 years, a resident of St. Mary's County stated that in February 1776 he enlisted as a private in the company commanded by Captain John A. Thomas, attached to a regiment commanded by Colonel Smallwood. In 1777 he was transferred from Smallwood's regiment to the artillery and was regularly discharged at the end of the war at Annapolis. He deposed that he served in the following battles: Long Island, White Plains, Camden, Guilford Court House, and Eutaw Springs. Thompson said that his occupation was a brick layer but that he is now very old and infirm and totally unable to perform his occupation.[36]

PRIVATE CHARLES TURNER, 1745–1796, enlisted in 1776 in the Fifth Independent Company of St. Mary's County.[37] Private Turner died January 24, 1796 leaving a widow and ten children.[38]

The Marylanders Fight On

The Battle of Long Island was not the end of fighting for many of the surviving soldiers of The Maryland 400. Rather, it was only the beginning. The Marylanders fought bravely in every major battle of the Revolutionary War.

> General Washington, knowing that he could rely upon the Marylanders in his army often chose them for the post of danger. He evinced no want of confidence, and often acted as if in command of veteran troops, whose resolution he had tried and on whom he could rely. They were the first who met face to face with fixed bayonets, the veteran legions of British regulars; and no troops poured out their blood more freely for the common cause than those of Maryland. No troops behaved more steadily.
>
> They were Washington's favorite troops and the heroes of his first campaign. And we can safely assert that if the rest of the army had displayed half the gallantry of Smallwood's "scarlets and buffs," many hard fought engagements would have ended in victories instead of defeats.[1]

On September 15, 1776 the British again attempted to surround the American army in the city of New York.

> Washington says that as soon as he heard the firing he rode with all possible despatch towards the place of landing, when, to "my great surprise and mortification, I found the troops that had been posted in the lines retreating with the utmost precipitation, and those ordered to support them, (Parson's and Fellow's Connecticut brigades,) flying in every direction, and in the greatest confusion, notwithstanding the exertions of their generals to form them. I used every means of my power to rally and get them into some order, but my attempts were fruitless and ineffectual; and on the appearance of a small party of the enemy, not more than sixty or seventy, their disorder increased, and they ran away in the greatest confusion, without firing a single shot."
>
> Under the disheartening revelations which this incident afforded of the unfitness of the material with which he had undertaken the task of securing American liberties, the firmness of Washington gave way, and flinging his hat upon the ground, in a transport of indignation and despair, he exclaimed: "Are these the men with whom I am to defend America?" At the moment General Greene says he sought death rather than life; and, bare-headed and alone, Washington would have remained to meet his fate at the hands of the advancing enemy, had not his bridle been seized

by an aid-de-camp [sic], who preserved the life of the commander-in-chief in spite of the despair which made him, for the time, indifferent to it.

Disgusted with such cowardice, Washington immediately sent a courier to General McDougall to send from his brigade Smallwood's battalion, knowing that he could depend upon its maintaining its position against all odds. It promptly came upon the ground and was ordered by Washington to take possession of an advantageous position near the enemy, on the main road, cover the retreat and defend the baggage of his flying army. They remained under arms at this post nearly all day, or until Sergeant's brigade passed (who were the last troops coming in), when the enemy, dividing their main body into two columns, endeavored to flank and surround them. Having accomplished the purpose of the commanding general, they now received orders to retreat, which they did in good order, and reached the lines about dusk.[2]

Colonel Tench Tilghman, one of Washington's staff, in a letter from Harlem Heights, dated September 16th, 1776 says: "I don't know whether the New England troops will stand there, [Harlen Heights,] but I am sure they will not upon open ground. I had a specimen of that yesterday. Her two brigades ran away from a small advanced party of the regulars, though the general did all in his power to convince them they were in no danger. He laid his cane over many of the officers who shewed their men the example of running."[3]

On October 28, 1776, at the Battle of White Plains Smallwood's regiment was called upon yet again to take the lead. General Washington initially sent three Virginia companies, with a body of Connecticut Rangers to attempt to get to the rear of the British. Unfortunately, they began their attack too soon and two of the commanding officers of the Virginia companies were killed.

> Finding that the enemy were receiving reinforcements, and that the Americans needed support, Washington advanced Griffith's and Richardson's Maryland regiments, of General Beale's brigade of the Maryland Flying Camp, with Major Price's three independent companies, and a detachment from a Rhode Island regiment. A letter from head-quarters, dated September 17th, says: "Never did troops go to the field with more cheerfulness and alacrity; when there began a heavy fire on both sides. It continued about one hour, when our brave southern troops dislodged them from their posts; the enemy rallied, and our men beat them the second time. They rallied again, our troops drove them the third time, and were rushing on them, but the enemy got on an eminence, and our troops were ordered to retreat, the general considering there might be a large number of the enemy behind the hill, concealed, which was the case."[4]

> Smallwood's regiment, which since the bravery exhibited on Long Island on the 27th of August, seems to have been chosen for all feats of peculiar danger, was ordered to march down the hill and attack the enemy. A long and severe contest ensued, in which the enemy gave way. They rallied again, however, and being supported by fifteen pieces of artillery, got the advantage. In the midst of this cannonade, Brook's Massachusetts regiment, which was stationed on the extreme right of the American line behind a stone fence, "fled in confusion, without more than a random scattering fire." The artillery, in great haste, then followed with the rest of

McDougall's brigade, excepting Smallwood's regulars and Reitzman's New York regiment. For about half an hour these troops, thus deserted on all hands, sustained themselves with the greatest gallantry under the heavy fire of the enemy's artillery and musketry. Twice they repulsed horse and foot, British and Hessians, until, cramped for room and greatly outnumbered, they slowly and sullenly retreated down the north side of the hill, where there was a bridge across the Bronx. Smallwood remained upon the ground for some time after the retreat had begun, and received two flesh wounds, one in the hip, the other through the arm. At the bridge over the Bronx, the retreating troops were met by General Putnam, who was coming to their assistance with General Beall's Maryland brigade, and in the rear of this force they marched back to camp.[5]

In consequence of Smallwood's wounds, the command of his regiment devolved upon Major Gist.[6]

Dr. John Pine, in a letter from White Plains dated November 7, 1776, to James Tilghman, writes: "On the 28th of October, in the afternoon, while our people were engaged in a very hot battle.... Colonel Smallwood's battalion suffered a great deal. The Colonel himself was wounded in two places; the number of killed and wounded, as the report is, in the camp amounts only to about ninety, but from the wounded I saw myself in our hospitals and adjacent houses, there must at least be one hundred and twenty or thirty wounded. The number killed I do not know."[7]

Maryland soldiers took the lead in the Southern campaign of the war as well. "Maryland quotas formed the real nucleus, and, indeed, constituted two-thirds of the southern army in the field."[8]

Ever since General Greene had taken command of the army, Maryland, according to her population, had furnished more troops than any other State in the confederacy. After the fearful reduction of her line at the defeat of Gates, we have seen that a large number of recruits were gathered and sent forward to fill the shattered ranks. At a very early period she had adopted the wise policy of enlisting men for the war, and the result of it was felt at the battle of Cowpens, Guilford, and the Eutaws. On the 17th of February, the Maryland troops in the field "to whose gallantry the country was so much indebted, and whose fidelity had risen superior to suffering and temptation, exhibited eight hundred and sixty-one fit for duty, two hundred and seventy-four in the hospitals." And on this day, the whole number of men in camp fit for duty is stated at, infantry and artillery, one thousand and seventy-eight; cavalry, sixty-four; legionary infantry, one hundred and twelve — Georgia, South Carolina and North Carolina, had not a single regular in the field, and the militia had all departed with the exception of Pickens' small force of about one hundred and fifty men. The Delaware battalion under Kirkwood, was now reduced to about sixty or eighty effectives, and like the Marylanders, was the admiration of the army.[9]

Epilogue

Myth and lore surround the story of The Maryland 400, even as to how they got their name. "The Maryland 400 name came from the fact that each company had 100 men and thus 4 MD companies were included in the last defense; however none of the companies ever had 100 men total at any one time that I can tell.... What is curious to me is the term MD 400. I don't see this in the early records and wonder if it was a term added much later apocryphally."[1]

Then we have the issue of the numbers. Throughout the years, it has been stated that there were 400 men sent forward under Lord Stirling of whom 256 were killed,

Old Stone House. Known also as the Cortelyou House, this is where The Maryland 400 held back overwhelming numbers of British soldiers to allow the defeated Americans to escape to safety, with many of them sacrificing their lives (courtesy Old Stone House).

but that figure has been taken out of context. General Smallwood reported that a total of 256 of his men were killed at the battle, but he did not specify that they were a part of the 400. It would be folly to believe that the only Marylanders killed that day were those at the Old Stone House.

Further, if the companies reported to have been part of The Maryland 400 are correct, there were 357 men (including Major Gist) who were members of this group. Of these, we know that 213 survived. This figure is out of line with the reported numbers.

Much work remains to be done. Some of the answers may lie in the mass grave in Brooklyn. With the advent of DNA technology, it may be possible to positively identify some of these men. The staff of the Old Stone House is currently pursuing the exact place where the bodies lie using the latest technology. Hopefully, they will be successful.

What has not changed in the pursuit of this story is that there were a group of young Marylanders who, under the leadership of Lord Stirling, willingly sacrificed themselves to hold off thousands of British and Hessian soldiers long enough for their fellow Americans to escape and that many of them lost their lives. And yes, they were heroes.

Chapter Notes

Preface

1. Ryan Polk, "Holding the Line: The Origin of 'the Old Line State,'" Maryland Archives Online, http://www.aomol.net/html/oldline.html.

Introduction

1. George Washington Parke Custis, *Recollections and Private Memoirs of Washington* (New York: Derby & Jackson, 1860), 269.
2. John J. Gallagher, *Battle of Brooklyn, 1776* (New York: Castle Books, 2002), 130.
3. From Walt Whitman's 1861–62 poem "The Centenarian's Story," in Walt Whitman, *Leaves of Grass* (New York: The Modern Library, 1921).
4. Gallagher, *Battle of Brooklyn,* 130.
5. Ibid., 168.

Storm Clouds Brew

1. Henry P. Johnson, *The Campaign of 1776 around New York and Brooklyn: Including an Account of the Battle of Long Island and the Loss of New York* (New York: The Long Island Historical Society, 1878), 115.
2. J. Thomas Scharf, *History of Maryland from the Earliest Period to the Present Day*, vol. 2, reprint (Hatsboro, PA: Tradition Press, 1967), 235.
3. Archives of Maryland, Annapolis, Maryland, vol. 11, 15–37. Most references to the Archives of Maryland are cited in the remainder of the text parenthetically with the abbreviation "MSA," followed by the volume and page numbers (e.g., MSA: 11, 15–37). The Archives of Maryland Online: http://aomol.net/html/index.html.
4. John C. Fitzpatrick, ed., *The Writings of George Washington from the Original Manuscript Sources*, vol. 3 (Charlottesville: University of Virginia, Electronic Text Center), 432–433, http://www.etext.virginia.edu/toc/modeng/public/WasFi03.html.
5. Joseph M. Balkoski, *The Maryland National Guard: A History of Maryland's Military Forces 1634–1991* (Baltimore: Maryland National Guard, 1991), 13.
6. Ann Jensen, "What Brave Fellows," *Annapolitan Magazine,* August 1991, 39.
7. Scharf, *History of Maryland,* 235.
8. Barnet Schecter, "Prologue," in *The Battle for New York: The City at the Heart of the American Revolution* (New York: Walker & Co., 2002), http:// www.thebattlefornewyork.com/prologue.php.

The Marylanders March

1. J. Thomas Scharf, *The Chronicles of Baltimore; Being a Complete History of "Baltimore Town" and Baltimore City from the Earliest Period to the Present Time* (Baltimore: Turnbull Bros., 1874), 265.

2. Custis, *Recollections*, 256–266.
3. Edmund Clarence, ed., *An American Anthology, 1787–1900* (Boston: Houghton Mifflin, 1900); Bartleby.com, 2001, 466, http://www.bartleby.com/248/.
4. Original letters of Williams Sands in the possession of Ann Jensen, Annapolis, Maryland.
5. "The Men of Old: How They Fought the Battle of Brooklyn," *Brooklyn Daily Eagle*, vol. 37, no. 203, August 26, 1876.
6. Ibid.
7. "Stand at Cortelyou House," *Brooklyn Daily Eagle*, August 10, 1902.
8. Ann Jensen, "What Brave Fellows," *Annapolitan Magazine,* August 1991, 57.

Lapse of Leadership

1. "Letter from Joseph Reed to William Livingston, August 30, 1776," American Archives, series 5, vol. 2, Northern Illinois University Libraries, Chicago, 1232, http://dig.lib.niu.edu/amarch.
2. Ibid.
3. Benson J. Lossing, "The Battle of Long Island, New York, 1776," *Our Country*, vol. 2, 1877, http://www.publicbookshelf.com/public_html/Our_Country_vol_2/index.html.

The Battle

1. "How the Continentals Met Defeat Bravely in Brooklyn," *Brooklyn Daily Eagle,* February 22, 1902.
2. "The Men of Old," *Brooklyn Daily Eagle*, August 26, 1876.
3. Scharf, *History of Maryland*, 242.
4. "Extract of a Letter from an Officer in General Fraser's Battalion, September 3, 1776," American Archives, series 5, vol. 1, 1259.
5. Gallagher, *Battle of Brooklyn*, 119.
6. "Old Brooklyn: The Services of the Maryland Battalion," *Brooklyn Daily Eagle*, December 1, 1870.
7. Henry Whittemore, *The Heroes of the American Revolution and their Descendants: Battle of Long Island* (Brooklyn: Heroes of the Revolution Publishing Co., 1897–1899), preface, vii and viii.
8. Gallagher, *Battle of Brooklyn*, 133.
9. "A Reminiscence," *Brooklyn Daily Eagle*, August 27, 1846.
10. Thomas W. Field, *Thomas W. Field's Battle of Long Island* (New York: Long Island Historical Society), 199.
11. Scharf, *The History of Maryland,* 248.
12. Ibid., 248.
13. Whittemore, *Heroes*, 24.
14. Rieman Steuart, *A History of the Maryland Line in the Revolutionary War, 1775–1783* (NSociety of the Cincinnati of Maryland,: n pl., 1969), 155.
15. Thomas W. Field, *The Battle of Long Island, with Connected Preceding Events, and the Subsequent American Retreat* (Brooklyn: Long Island Historical Society), 228.
16. Joseph Plumb Martin, *A Narrative of a Revolutionary Soldier: Some of the Adventures, Dangers, and Sufferings of Joseph Plumb Martin* (New York: Signet Classics, 2001), 24–25.
17. Gallagher, *Battle of Brooklyn*, 129.
18. Gallagher, *Battle of Brooklyn*, 129–130.
19. "Old Brooklyn," *Brooklyn Daily Eagle*, December 1, 1870.
20. Revolutionary War pension papers of Bryan Philpot, The National Archives, available online in partnership with Footnote.com, http://www.footnote.com/documents/10936943/revolutionary-war-pensions.
21. "Extract of a letter from New York, dated Aug. 28, 1776," *Maryland Gazette*, September 5, 1776.
22. Scharf, *History of Maryland*, 248–249.
23. "Old Brooklyn," *Brooklyn Daily Eagle*, December 1, 1870.
24. "Days of Defeat, Crushed in Battle, Nervous Patriot Troops Await a Knockout Punch," George

DeWan, staff writer, Newsday.com, http:// www.newsday.com/community/guide/lihistory/ny-history-hs404a,0,6174654.story?coll=ny-lihistory-navigation.

25. Edward J. Lowell, *The Hessians and the Other German Auxiliaries of Great Britain in the Revolutionary War* (Baltimore, MD: Clearfield Company, March 2003), 67.

Aftermath of the Battle

1. "Extract of a Letter from an Officer in General Frazier's Battalion, Dated Sept. 3, 1776," *Maryland Gazette*, May 1, 1777.
2. "Return of Prisoners Taken during the Campaign, 1776," *Maryland Gazette*, May 1, 1777.
3. "Extract of a Letter from Dr. Silas Holmes," *Maryland Gazette*, August 7, 1777.
4. Danske Dandridge, *American Prisoners of the Revolution* (Charlottesville, VA: The Michie Company Printers, 1911), 102–103.
5. Ibid., 104–105.
6. "Fort Greene Prison Ships in Wallabout Bay Witnessed Greatest Suffering for American Liberty," http://www.nyfreedom.com/fortgreene.htm.
7. Hamilton Fish, LL.D., *New York State: The Battleground of the Revolutionary War*. (New York, NY: Vantage Press, 1976). Accessed as "Martyrdom of thirteen thousand American Patriots aboard the monstrous Jersey and other British prison ships in New York Harbor," at http://longislandgenealogy.com/prison.html.
8. Ibid.
9. Ibid.
10. Hezekiah Niles, *Centennial Offering: Republication of Principles and Acts of the Revolution* (New York: A.S. Barnes & Co., 1876), 510–511.
11. Mary C. Gillett, *The Army Medical Department, 1775–1818* (Washington, DC: U.S. Government Printing Office, 1981), 69.

Colonel William Smallwood

1. *Loudon's Register*, February 25, 1792.
2. Joan M. Dixon, *National Intelligencer Newspaper Abstracts*, vol. 15, June 12, 1841 (Bowie, MD: Heritage Books, 2003), 191.

Lord Stirling

1. Gallagher, *Battle of Brooklyn*, 129.
2. "Letter from Lord Stirling to General Washington: His Account of the Engagement on the 27th," American Archives, series 5, vol. 1, 1246.
3. *Providence Gazette and Country Journal*, February 8, 1783.

The Men of The Maryland 400

1. Laura C. Cochrane, *The History of Caroline County, Maryland, from Its Beginning* Baltimore: Regional Publishing Company, 1971), 63.
2. Custis, *Recollections*, 266.
3. Ibid., 267–268.
4. Ibid., 269.

Mordecai Gist

1. Joseph M. Balkoski, "Mordecai Gist's Account of the Battle of Long Island," *The Maryland National Guard: A History of Maryland's Military Forces, 1634–1991* (Baltimore: Maryland National Guard, State of Maryland Military Department), 8.
2. *New York Journal & Patriotic Register*, September 26, 1792.

First Company

1. "Letter from Samuel Chase to Governor Thomas Johnson Dated October 7, 1777," Archives of Maryland, vol. 16, 396.
2. "John H. Stone to George Washington, March 21, 1778, *George Washington Papers*, Library of Congress, 1741–1799, Series 4. General Correspondence, 1697–1799. Image #125, http://www.snake.ne.jp/~yama/nph-docomo.cgi/010000A/http/memory.loc.gov/cgi-bin/query/P?mgw:10:./temp/~ammem_ezu0::.
3. "George Washington to John H. Stone, April 4, 1778," *George Washington Papers*, Library of Congress, 1741–1799, Series 4. General Correspondence, 1697–1799. Image #494, http://www.snake.ne.jp/~yama/nph-docomo.cgi/010000A/http/memory.loc.gov/cgi-bin/query/P?mgw:9:./temp/~ammem_ezu0::.
4. *Maryland Gazette*, October 11, 1804.
5. Custis, *Recollections*, 205.
6. Francis B. Heitman, *Historical Register of Officers of the Continental Army during the War of the Revolution*, rev. ed. (Washington, D.C.: The Rare Book Shop Pub. Co., 1914), 110.
7. Edward D. Boone, S.J., *The Genealogy of the Boone Family of Maryland* (Baltimore: Privately Published, n.d.).
8. *National Intelligencer*, February 13, 1837.
9. F. Edward Wright, *Maryland Calendar of Wills, 1774–1777*, vol. 16 (Westminster, MD: Family Lines Publications, 1995), 187.
10. Colonial Dames of America, *Ancestral Records and Portraits*, vol. 2 (New York: Grafton Press, 1910), 455.
11. American Archives, series 5, vol. 1, 1232–1233.
12. American Archives, series 5, vol. 3, 2260.
13. Heitman, *Historical Register of Officers*, 225.
14. Votes and Proceedings of the House of Delegates, State of Maryland, April 25, 1782–June 15, 1782, Archives of Maryland, Session 187, 95.
15. George D. Riley, *Tidewater Maryland Ancestors: Baldwin, Blakistone, Brewer, Chesdeldyne, Davis, Goldsmith, Keech, Lancaster, Maddox, Ridgely, Riley, Sothoron, Stockette, Tucker, Williams and Related Families* (Baltimore: Gateway Press, 1999), 57.
16. *Poulson's American Daily*, March 10, 1807.
17. *Writings of George Washington*, vol. 6, 180.
18. American Archives, series 5, vol. 2, 1139–1140.
19. Revolutionary War pension papers of Samuel Luckett, The National Archives, available online in partnership with Footnote.com, http://www.footnote.com/documents/10936943/revolutionary-war-pensions.
20. Lincoln County, Kentucky. Marriage Records, 1793–1800, will records 1801–1807, vol. 2.
21. Revolutionary War pension papers of Mark McPherson, The National Archives, available online in partnership with Footnote.com, http://www.footnote.com/documents/10936943/revolutionary-war-pensions.
22. Heitman, *Historical Register*, 375.
23. Revolutionary War pension papers of Josias Miller, The National Archives, available online in partnership with Footnote.com, http://www.footnote.com/documents/10936943/revolutionary-war-pensions.
24. Heitman, *Historical Register*, 395.
25. Swepson Earle, *The Chesapeake Bay Country* (Baltimore: Thomsen-Ellis Co., 1923), 116.
26. *Maryland Gazette*, October 29, 1812.
27. Revolutionary War pension papers of John Neale, The National Archives, available online in partnership with Footnote.com, http://www.footnote.com/documents/10936943/revolutionary-war-pensions.
28. Ibid.
29. Ibid.

30. Earle, *The Chesapeake Bay Country*, 99.
31. Brice McAdoo Clagett, MD, "The Ancestry of Capt. James Neale," *Maryland Genealogical Society Bulletin* 31, no. 2 (Spring 1990): 137.
32. Revolutionary War pension papers of John Plant, The National Archives, available online in partnership with Footnote.com, http://www.footnote.com/documents/10936943/revolutionary-war-pensions.
33. Revolutionary War pension papers of John Shaw, The National Archives, available online in partnership with Footnote.com, http://www.footnote.com/documents/10936943/revolutionary-war-pensions.
34. Charles County, Maryland Probate Records, 1777–1780.
35. "Proceedings and Acts of the General Assembly, Votes and Proceedings, November, 1796," Archives of Maryland, vol. 105, 143.
36. Charles Co. Deed Book K#4, Charles County, Maryland Land Records, 1791–1796 (Miami Beach: TLC Genealogy, 1994), 24.
37. Heitman, *Historical Register*, 497.
38. Ibid., 501.
39. Revolutionary War pension papers of Charles Smith, The National Archives, available online in partnership with Footnote.com, http://www.footnote.com/documents/10936943/revolutionary-war-pensions.
40. Ibid.
41. Revolutionary War pension papers of Richard Smith, The National Archives, available online in partnership with Footnote.com, http://www.footnote.com/documents/10936943/revolutionary-war-pensions.
42. Revolutionary War pension papers of Samuel Vermillion, The National Archives, available online in partnership with Footnote.com, http://www.footnote.com/documents/10936943/revolutionary-war-pensions.
43. Clarence S. Peterson, *Known Military Dead during the American Revolutionary War* (Baltimore: Genealogical Publishing Co., 1967), 177. Note that the Battle of Monmouth occurred on June 28, 1778, where Private Wheatley may have met his fate.

Second Company

1. Effie Gwynn Bowie, *Across the Years in Prince George's County* (Baltimore: Genealogical Publishing Co., 1975), 298.
2. Revolutionary War pension papers of Patrick Sim, The National Archives, available online in partnership with Footnote.com, http://www.footnote.com/documents/10936943/revolutionary-war-pensions.
3. Jean A. Sargent, *Stones and Bones, Cemetery Records of Prince George's Co., Maryland* (Bowie, MD: Prince George County Genealogical Society, 1984).
4. Tom Cavanaugh, *The Writing of the Star Spangled Banner*, http://www.tc-solutions.com/croom/ssb.html.
5. Heitman, *Historical Register*, 134.
6. Ibid., 157.
7. "The Official Roster of the Soldiers of the American Revolution Buried in the State of Ohio" (Columbus: Ohio Adjutant General's Dept., 1929–1959), 59.
8. Earle, *The Chesapeake Bay Country*, 157.
9. Maryland State Archives, Chancery Court Papers: Date: 1799, 998, Walter B. Cox. PG. Insolvent estate of Cox. Accession No.: 17,898–998 MSA S512-2-1041 Location: 1/36/1/.
10. Index to the Probate Records of Prince George's County, Maryland (1696–1900). Compiled by the Records Committee of the Prince George's County Genealogical Society, Inc. Prince George's County Genealogical Society, Bowie, Maryland, 1989.
11. Revolutionary War pension papers of William Evans, The National Archives, available online in partnership with Footnote.com, http://www.footnote.com/documents/10936943/revolutionary-war-pensions.
12. John Allen Miller, "How Whiskey Almost Started a War," Emmitsburg Area Historical Society, http://www.emmitsburg.net/archive_list/articles/history/rev_war/whiskey.htm.
13. Ibid.
14. Ibid.
15. Louis B. Wright, Julia H. Macleod, "William Eaton's Relations with Aaron Burr," *Mississippi Valley Historical Review* 31, no. 4 (March 1945): 523–536.

16. *National Intelligencer and Washington Advertiser*, June 29, 1811.
17. J. Thomas Scharf, *History of Western Maryland, being a History of Frederick, Montgomery, Carroll, Washington, Allegany, and Garrett Counties from the Earliest Period to the Present Day, Including Biographical Sketches of Their Representative Men*, vol. 1 (Baltimore: Regional Publishing Company, 1968), 475–476.
18. Henry C. Peden, Jr., *Revolutionary Patriots of Frederick County, Maryland, 1775–1783* (Westminster, MD: Family Line Publications, 1995), 155.
19. Revolutionary War pension papers of Jacob Holland, The National Archives, available online in partnership with Footnote.com, http://www.footnote.com/documents/10936943/revolutionary-war-pensions.
20. *A Roster of Revolutionary Ancestors of the Indiana Daughters of the American Revolution: Commemoration of the United States of America Bicentennial, July 4, 1976* (Evansville, IN: Unigraphic, 1976), 372.
21. Revolutionary War pension papers of John D. Latham, The National Archives, available online in partnership with Footnote.com, http://www.footnote.com/documents/10936943/revolutionary-war-pensions.
22. Votes and Proceedings of the House of Delegates of the State of Maryland, December Session 1820, 461.
23. Lineage Book of the National Society of the Daughters of the American Revolution, vols. 107 and 108 (Washington, DC: NSDAR, 1908), 125.
24. Prince George's County, Maryland Index to Wills, Administrations, and Inventories, 1696–1900, compiled by the Records Committee of the Prince George's County Genealogical Society, 1988.
25. Henry C. Peden, Jr., *Revolutionary Patriots of Prince George's County, 1775–1783* (Westminster, MD: Family Line Publications, 1997), 216.
26. Harry Wright Newman, *Anne Arundel Gentry*, vol. 3 (Westminster, MD: Family Line Publications, 1979).
27. Jordan Dodd, Liahona Research, comp., *Maryland Marriages, 1655–1850* [database on-line] (Provo, UT: The Generations Network, 2004), http://www.ancestry.com/search/db.aspx?dbid=7846.
28. Peden, *Revolutionary Patriots of Prince George's County*, 308.
29. Revolutionary War pension papers of Michael Waltz, The National Archives, available online in partnership with Footnote.com, http://www.footnote.com/documents/10936943/revolutionary-war-pensions.
30. Revolutionary War pension papers of Michael Waltz, The National Archives, available online in partnership with Footnote.com, http://www.footnote.com/documents/10936943/revolutionary-war-pensions.
31. Heitman, *Historical Register*, 575.
32. Whittemore, *The Heroes of the American Revolution and Their Descendants*, 62.
33. Revolutionary War pension papers of Gassaway Watkins, The National Archives, available online in partnership with Footnote.com, http://www.footnote.com/documents/10936943/revolutionary-war-pensions.
34. Whittemore, *The Heroes of the American Revolution*, 62.
35. J.D. Warfield, *The Founders of Anne Arundel and Howard Counties, Maryland: A Genealogical and Biographical Review from Wills, Deeds and Church Records* (Baltimore: Kohn & Pollock, 1905), 413–414.
36. Heitman, *Historical Register*, 133.
37. Ibid., 134.
38. Ibid., 232.

Third Company

1. AnnaBelle Kemp, *Lucas Genealog* (Hollywood, CA: A. Kemp, 1964), Heritage Quest, http://www.heritagequestonline.com/index.
2. Henry Steele Commager and Richard B. Morris, eds., *Revolutionary Incidents from the Spirit of 'Seventy-Six': The Story of the American Revolution as Told by Participants* (New York: Da Capo Press, 1995), 147–148.
3. Heitman, *Historical Register*, 359.
4. Revolutionary War pension papers of Alexander Allen, The National Archives, available online in partnership with Footnote.com, http://www.footnote.com/documents/10936943/revolutionary-war-pensions.

5. Ibid.
6. "Maryland Prisoners on Long Island," from an undated edition of the *Baltimore Sun*, reprinted in the *New York Times*, August 18, 1895.
7. Ibid.
8. Ibid.
9. Ibid.
10. Lieut. Fielder M.M. Beall, *Colonial Families of the United States Descended from the Immigrants: Bell, Beal, Bale, Beale, Beall Family* (Westminster, MD: Heritage Books, 2002), 175.
11. Helen White Brown, *Index of Marriage Licenses, Prince George's County, Maryland, 1777–1886* (Baltimore: Genealogical Publishing Co., 1973).
12. Revolutionary War pension papers of Christopher Beall, The National Archives, available online in partnership with Footnote.com, http://www.footnote.com/documents/10936943/revolutionary-war-pensions.
13. Ibid.
14. Ibid.
15. Ruth Beall Gelders, "Ninian Beall" (Atlanta: Daughters of the American Revolution, Joseph Habersham Chapter, 1976).
16. Ibid.
17. Sir Archibald Edmonstone, 3rd Bt., *American Descendants of the Edmonstones of Duntreath and Australians with Edmonstone Connections from the Family Edmonstone of Duntreath*, published 1875, appendix 3. Edited and with additions by Mary McGrigor, F.S.A. Scot. Published in 1996, http://www.edmonstone.com/Pages/ap3.htm.
18. Revolutionary War pension papers of John Brown, The National Archives, available online in partnership with Footnote.com, http://www.footnote.com/documents/10936943/revolutionary-war-pensions.
19. "Maryland Prisoners on Long Island," reprinted in the *New York Times*, August 18, 1895.
20. Peden, *Revolutionary Patriots of Prince George's County*, 308.
21. Revolutionary War pension papers of Abijah Buxton, The National Archives, available online in partnership with Footnote.com, http://www.footnote.com/documents/10936943/revolutionary-war-pensions.
22. "Oregon State Roster of Ancesters [sic]." Daughters of the American Revolution (Tillamook: Oregon Society, D.A.R., 1963).
23. Revolutionary War pension papers of John Flint, The National Archives, available online in partnership with Footnote.com, http://www.footnote.com/documents/10936943/revolutionary-war-pensions.
24. Peden, *Revolutionary Patriots of Prince George's County*, 308.
25. "Maryland Prisoners on Long Island," reprinted in the *New York Times*, August 18, 1895.
26. Revolutionary War pension papers of John Hughes, The National Archives, available online in partnership with Footnote.com, http://www.footnote.com/documents/10936943/revolutionary-war-pensions.
27. U.S. Federal Census, Mortality Schedule, 1850.
28. The Library of Virginia, Bible Records Collection, http://lvaimage.lib.va.us/Bible/33365/n/0011.tif.
29. "Maryland Prisoners on Long Island," reprinted in the *New York Times*, August 18, 1895.
30. Ibid.
31. Revolutionary War pension papers of James Murphy, The National Archives, available online in partnership with Footnote.com, http://www.footnote.com/documents/10936943/revolutionary-war-pensions.
32. Ibid.
33. Ibid.
34. Dodd, *Maryland Marriages, 1655–1850*.
35. Revolutionary War pension papers of James Murphy, The National Archives, available online in partnership with Footnote.com, http://www.footnote.com/documents/10936943/revolutionary-war-pensions.
36. Heitman, *Historical Register*, 467.
37. American Archives, series 5, vol. 1, 1232–1233.
38. *Maryland Historical Magazine*, vol. 14 (Baltimore: The Maryland Historical Society, 1919), 113.
39. Revolutionary War pension papers of Alexander Roxburgh, The National Archives, available online in partnership with Footnote.com, http://www.footnote.com/documents/10936943/revolutionary-war-pensions.
40. Earl Arnett, Robert J. Brugger, and Edward C. Papenfuse, *Maryland, A New Guide to the Old Line State*, 2nd ed. (Baltimore: Johns Hopkins University Press, 1999), 209.

41. Will of Alexander Roxburgh, Somerset County, Maryland, EB#23, folio 113.
42. Dodd, *Maryland Marriages.*
43. Will of Verlinda Saffel, Iredell County, North Carolina, dated July 22, 1812.
44. *Maryland Historical Magazine,* vol. 14 (Baltimore: The Maryland Historical Society, 1919), 113.
45. *Pennsylvania Packet,* August 20, 1782.
46. James B. Tannehill, *Genealogical History of the Tannahills, Tannehills and Taneyhills* (Rutland, VT: Tuttle Antiquarian Books, 1939), 29.
47. Revolutionary War pension papers of Leonard Watkins, The National Archives, available online in partnership with Footnote.com, http://www.footnote.com/documents/10936943/revolutionary-war-pensions.
48. Ibid.
49. "Maryland Prisoners on Long Island," reprinted in the *New York Times,* August 18, 1895.
50. Calvin E. Schildknecht and Thomas J.C. Williams, *Monocacy and Catoctin,* vol. 2, *Weller and Related Families* (Shippensburg, PA: Beidel Printing House, 1985–1994), 308.
51. Brown, *Index of Marriage Licenses, Prince George's County, Maryland.*
52. From an original petition for a new state located in the Library of Congress, no date on document, Papers of the Continental Congress 1774–1789, no. 48, folios 251–256, 89–96.
53. "Maryland Prisoners on Long Island," reprinted in the *New York Times,* August 18, 1895.
54. Revolutionary War pension papers of Thomas Windham, The National Archives, available online in partnership with Footnote.com, http://www.footnote.com/documents/10936943/revolutionary-war-pensions.
55. Revolutionary War pension papers of Joshua Lamb, The National Archives, available online in partnership with Footnote.com, http://www.footnote.com/documents/10936943/revolutionary-war-pensions.

Sixth Company

1. Commager and Morris, *The Spirit of 'Seventy-Six': The Story of the American Revolution,* 147–148.
2. Heitman, *Historical Register,* 31.
3. Edward C. Papenfuse, Alan F. Day, David W. Jordan, and Gregory A. Stiverson, *A Biographical Dictionary of the Maryland Legislature, 1635–1789,* vol. 1: A–H (Baltimore: The Johns Hopkins University Press, 1985), 98.
4. "W. Smallwood, George Town, to Gov. Lee (Favor of Mr. Denny)," letter dated September 12, 1781, *Journal of Correspondence of the Council of Maryland,* MSA: 47, 490.
5. Dixon, *National Intelligencer Newspaper Abstracts,* 247.
6. Clarence S. Peterson, *Known Military Dead during the American Revolutionary War,* (Baltimore: Genealogical Publishing Co., 1967, Genealogy.com), 27.
7. Ibid.
8. Dodd, *Maryland Marriages.*
9. Murtie June Clark, *Loyalists in the Southern Campaign of the Revolutionary War,* vol. 2 (Baltimore: Genealogical Publishing Co., 1981), 563, 570, 572, 574, 576.
10. "Maryland Prisoners on Long Island," reprinted in the *New York Times,* August 18, 1895.
11. Ibid.
12. Ibid.
13. Ibid.
14. Heitman, *Historical Register,* 211.
15. Votes and proceedings of the House of Delegates, State of Maryland, April 25, 1782–June 15, 1782, Archives of Maryland, session 187, 112.
16. Ibid., 118.
17. Peterson, *Known Military Dead,* 64.
18. Margaret K. Fresco, *Marriages and Deaths, St. Mary's County, Maryland 1634–1900* (Ridge, MD: Self-Published, 1982). Fresco's book contains several references to Nathanial Ewing, including the dates of his marriages and the following references to administrative accounts and Orphans Court records:

> 3/21/1794: Admin. accts. of Col. John Reeder. Widow, 1/3. Daughter: Mrs. Gustavus Brown, wife of Dr. Gustavus Brown. Nathaniel Ewing and Catherine, his wife, surviving administrators. (SMC Balances and Distributions).

1/1801: The court appointed Nathaniel Ewing guardian to Julian Cartwright, orphan of John Cartwright. Securities: Samuel Morton and James Cooke. Ewing stated that the orphan is entitled to a negro man who is now in Georgetown or the neighborhood thereof and refuses to return to this county; the court ordered that the orphan be allowed to sell the negro [Orphan Ct. Rec., Fenwick].

19. *Mercantile Adviser,* New York, February 26, 1818.
20. "Maryland Prisoners on Long Island," reprinted in the *New York Times,* August 18, 1895.
21. Henry Downes Cranor, *Marriage Licenses of Caroline County, Maryland, 1774–1815* (Kokomo, IN: Selby Publishing, 1904, Repr.), 6.
22. "Maryland Prisoners on Long Island," reprinted in the *New York Times,* August 18, 1895.
23. Mary Donaldson Sinclair, *Pioneer Days: Early History of Jefferson County, Ohio* (Steubenville, OH: n. pl., 1962) 102–103.
24. Ibid.
25. *News Leader,* Laurel, Maryland, July 23, 1790.
26. Revolutionary War pension papers of William H. Layton, The National Archives, available online in partnership with Footnote.com, http://www.footnote.com/documents/10936943/revolutionary-war-pensions.
27. "Maryland Prisoners on Long Island," reprinted in the *New York Times,* August 18, 1895.
28. Ibid.
29. Journal of the House of Representatives of the United States, 1804–1807.
30. Research of John Willis Barlow.
31. Will of Manassah Finney, Harford Co. Wills, Liber 2, folio 206, Hall of Records, Annapolis, Maryland, on microfilm.
32. Research of John Willis Barlow.
33. "Maryland Prisoners on Long Island," reprinted in the *New York Times,* August 18, 1895.
34. Ibid.
35. Heitman, *Historical Register,* 467.
36. Biographical notice from the *National Gazette,* October 25, 1821.
37. Henry C. Peden, Jr., *Revolutionary Patriots of Kent and Queen Anne's Counties, Maryland* (Westminster, MD: Family Line Publications, 1995), 192.
38. Biographical notice from the *National Gazette,* October 25, 1821.
39. William S. Lind, "Military Matters: Lessons from Decatur," *United Press International,* August 3, 2007, http://www.upi.com/International_Security/Industry/Analysis/2007/08/03/military_matters_lessons_from_decatur/7978/.
40. Biographical notice from the *National Gazette,* October 25, 1821.
41. Ibid.
42. David Edwin, *Dictionary of American Naval Fighting Ships,* Philadelphia, May 1814, http://www.history.navy.mil/danfs/index.html.
43. Revolutionary War pension papers of John McFadden, The National Archives, available online in partnership with Footnote.com, http://www.footnote.com/documents/10936943/revolutionary-war-pensions.

Ninth Company

1. Daniel Wunderlich Nead, *The Pennsylvania-German in the Settlement of Maryland* (Whitefish, MT: Kessinger Publishing, LLC, June 25, 2007), 268–270.
2. Peden, Jr., *Revolutionary Patriots of Frederick County,* 356.
3. Peden, Jr., *Revolutionary Patriots of Frederick County,* 356.
4. Heitman, *Historical Register,* 467.
5. "Maryland Prisoners on Long Island," reprinted in the *New York Times,* August 18, 1895.
6. Heitman, *Historical Register,* 323.
7. Letter dated June 23, 1781, from [Holland WILLIAMS], Bush river, S.C. To Elie WILLIAMS, Washington County, Md. Otho Holland Williams Papers, Maryland Historical Society, http://www.mdhs.org/library/Mss/ms000908.html.
8. Ibid.

9. Benson J. Lossing, *The Pictorial Field Book of the Revolution or Illustrations, by Pen and Pencil, of the History, Scenery, Relics and Traditions of the War for Independence*, vol. 2 (New York: Harper and Brothers Publishers, 1852), 679.

10. Revolutionary War pension papers of Benjamin Ford, The National Archives, available online in partnership with Footnote.com, http://www.footnote.com/documents/10936943/revolutionary-war-pensions.

11. J. Thomas Scharf, History of Western Maryland, being a History of Frederick, Montgomery, Carroll, Washington, Allegany, and Garrett Counties from the Earliest Period to the Present Day, Including Biographical Sketches of Their Representative Men, vol. 1 (Philadelphia: L.H. Everts, 1882), 574.

12. Heitman, *Historical Register*, 128.

13. *Charles County, Maryland Land Records, 1775–1782* (Miami Beach, FL: TLC Genealogy, 1997), 91.

14. Journal of the House of Delegates, 1812, Archives of Maryland, Session 224, 532.

15. Revolutionary War pension papers of William Bruce, The National Archives, available online in partnership with Footnote.com, http://www.footnote.com/documents/10936943/revolutionary-war-pensions.

16. Ibid.

17. *Maryland Gazette*, November 10, 1825.

18. Revolutionary War pension papers of Solomon Crutsinger, The National Archives, available online in partnership with Footnote.com, http://www.footnote.com/documents/10936943/revolutionary-war-pensions.

19. Henry C. Peden, Jr., *Quaker Records of Northern Maryland, 1716–1800* (Westminster, MD: Family Line Publications, 1993).

20. Revolutionary War pension papers of Miseal Deaver, The National Archives, available online in partnership with Footnote.com, http://www.footnote.com/documents/10936943/revolutionary-war-pensions.

21. Ibid.

22. "Maryland Prisoners on Long Island," reprinted in the *New York Times*, August 18, 1895.

23. Scharf, *History of Western Maryland*, 150.

24. Heitman, *Historical Register*, 177.

25. Note to the author from Joe Balkoski, command historian, Maryland National Guard, May 16, 2007.

26. Jethro Rumple, *A History of Rowan County, North Carolina; Containing Sketches of Prominent Families and Distinguished Men; With an Appendix* (Salisbury, NC: J. J. Brunner, 1881), 314.

27. J. Roy Guyther MD, *Charlotte Hall, The Village, 1797–1997* (Mechanicsville, MD: Self-Published, 1997), 46.

28. Historical marker erected by the Maryland Historical Trust located on Old Route 5, Charlotte Hall, Maryland, at the site of the springs.

29. Scharf, *History of Western Maryland*, 152.

30. Revolutionary War pension papers of Stephen Fluharty, The National Archives, available online in partnership with Footnote.com, http://www.footnote.com/documents/10936943/revolutionary-war-pensions.

31. Ibid.

32. Note to the author from Roy C. Fluharty, May 15, 2007.

33. "Maryland Prisoners on Long Island," reprinted in the *New York Times*, August 18, 1895.

34. Ibid.

35. Ibid.

36. Revolutionary War pension papers of Michael Hahn, The National Archives, available online in partnership with Footnote.com, http://www.footnote.com/documents/10936943/revolutionary-war-pensions.

37. Ibid.

38. "Maryland Prisoners on Long Island," reprinted in the *New York Times*, August 18, 1895.

39. Ibid.

40. Ibid.

41. Maryland State Archives, Maryland Indexes, Assessment of 1783, MSA S 1437.

42. Revolutionary War pension papers of George Kephart, The National Archives, available online in partnership with Footnote.com, http://www.footnote.com/documents/10936943/revolutionary-war-pensions.

43. Ibid.

44. Revolutionary War pension papers of Martin Kephart, The National Archives, available online in

partnership with Footnote.com, http://www.footnote.com/documents/10936943/revolutionary-war-pensions.

45. "Maryland Prisoners on Long Island," reprinted in the *New York Times*, August 18, 1895.

46. Peden, Jr., *Prince George's County, Maryland, Revolutionary Patriots,* 199.

47. Brown, *Index of Marriage Licenses, Prince George's County.*

48. Ibid.

49. William E Hunt, *Historical Collections of Coshocton County Ohio: A Complete Panorama of the County, from the Time of the Earliest Known Occupants of the Territory unto the Present Time, 1764–1876* (Cincinnati: Clarke & Co., 1876), 24.

50. Revolutionary War pension papers of Michael Miller, The National Archives, available online in partnership with Footnote.com, http://www.footnote.com/documents/10936943/revolutionary-war-pensions.

51. "Maryland Prisoners on Long Island," reprinted in the *New York Times*, August 18, 1895.

52. Ibid.

53. Research of Joseph M. Doyle whose source is the National Archives, M881, Company Muster Roll for the 1st Maryland Regiment of Foot.

54. Parker B. Brown, "Reconstructing Crawford's Army of 1782," *Western Pennsylvania Historical Magazine* 65 (1982): 31–32. Also see Pennsylvania Archives, 6th series, 2:228.

55. Genealogy Trails Military Data Sandusky Expedition, http://genealogytrails.com/main/sanduskyexpedition.html.

56. Research of Father Joseph M. Doyle, unpublished.

57. Letter to the author from Father Joseph M. Doyle, dated January 6, 2008.

58. Frederick County, Maryland Wills, Book GM#2, Register of Wills, Frederick County, Maryland, 304–306.

59. "Maryland Prisoners on Long Island," reprinted in the *New York Times*, August 18, 1895.

60. Revolutionary War pension papers of William Smith, The National Archives, available online in partnership with Footnote.com, http://www.footnote.com/documents/10936943/revolutionary-war-pensions.

61. Revolutionary War pension papers of Winfield Scott, The National Archives, available online in partnership with Footnote.com, http://www.footnote.com/documents/10936943/revolutionary-war-pensions.

62. Revolutionary War pension papers of Henry Young, The National Archives, available online in partnership with Footnote.com, http://www.footnote.com/documents/10936943/revolutionary-war-pensions.

63. Heitman, *Historical Register,* 177.

64. Ibid.

Unsung Heroes

1. Steuart, *A History of the Maryland Line,* 155.

2. Henry C. Peden, Jr., *Revolutionary Patriots of Calvert & St. Mary's Counties, Maryland 1775–1783* (Westminster, MD: Family Line Publications, 1996), 24.

3. Letter dated April 28, 1784, from O[tho] H[olland] WILLIAMS], Baltimore. To [Uhiah] FORREST, Otho Holland Williams Papers 1744–1839 (Part 3/8), Maryland Historical Society, http://www.mdhs.org/library/Mss/ms000908.html.

4. Maryland Archives Online, http://www.mdarchives.state.md.us/msa/speccol/sc2600/sc2685/html/adjgen.html.

5. Regina Combs Hammett, *History of St. Mary's County, Maryland* (Ridge, MD: privately published, 1977), 150.

6. *The Frantic Night of Frustration and Foolishness,* http://www.angelfire.com/fl2/htf/1812historydir/EnterBladensburg.html.

7. Dixon, *National Intelligencer Newspaper Abstracts,* 199.

8. Peden, *Revolutionary Patriots of Calvert & St. Mary's Counties,* 52.

9. *Baltimore Patriot,* April 23, 1824.

10. Revolutionary War pension papers of William Coe, The National Archives, available online in partnership with Footnote.com, http://www.footnote.com/documents/10936943/revolutionary-war-pensions.

11. Carl Robert Coe, "William Coe of Calvert County," *Maryland Genealogical Society Bulletin* 33, no.3 (Summer 1992): 577–585.

12. Ibid.
13. Peden, *Revolutionary Patriots of Calvert & St. Mary's Counties*, 70.
14. Revolutionary War pension papers of Anthony Davis, The National Archives, available online in partnership with Footnote.com, http://www.footnote.com/documents/10936943/revolutionary-war-pensions.
15. Edwin Beitzell, *St. Mary's County in the American Revolution*, St. Mary's County Bicentennial Commission, 1975, 29.
16. St. Mary's County Historical Society, *Chronicles of St. Mary's* 24, no. 1 (January 1976).
17. Revolutionary War pension papers of Thomas Lynch, The National Archives, available online in partnership with Footnote.com, http://www.footnote.com/documents/10936943/revolutionary-war-pensions.
18. Peden, *Revolutionary Patriots of Calvert & St. Mary's Counties*, 201.
19. Heitman, *Historical Register*, 410.
20. Wesley Pippenger, Georgetown, DC, Marriages and Death Notices, 1801–1838.
21. Proceedings of the Orphan's Court of St. Mary's County, Maryland Book I, 1777–1801, transcribed and compiled by Charles E. Fenwick, Sr., indexed by Claude G. Blackwell. St. Mary's County Historical Society, Leonardtown, Maryland, 1996.
22. Revolutionary War pension papers of Aaron Spalding, The National Archives, available online in partnership with Footnote.com, http://www.footnote.com/documents/10936943/revolutionary-war-pensions.
23. Revolutionary War pension papers of Edmund Howard Compton, The National Archives, available online in partnership with Footnote.com, http://www.footnote.com/documents/10936943/revolutionary-war-pensions.
24. Revolutionary War pension papers of Henry Spalding, The National Archives, available online in partnership with Footnote.com, http://www.footnote.com/documents/10936943/revolutionary-war-pensions.
25. Ibid.
26. *Final Pension Payment Vouchers 1818–1864, Maryland, Baltimore*. Abstracted by Alycon Trubey Pierce, C.G. (Lovettsville, VA: Willow Bend Books, 1997), 173.
27. Heitman, *Historical Register*, 520.
28. American Archives, series 5, vol. 2, 467–469.
29. Revolutionary War pension papers of Jeremiah Tarlton, The National Archives, available online in partnership with Footnote.com, http://www.footnote.com/documents/10936943/revolutionary-war-pensions.
30. Peden, *Revolutionary Patriots of Calvert & St. Mary's Counties*, 269.
31. Revolutionary War pension papers of Nathan Thomas, The National Archives, available online in partnership with Footnote.com, http://www.footnote.com/documents/10936943/revolutionary-war-pensions.
32. Ibid.
33. Ibid.
34. Revolutionary War pension papers of Electious Thompson, The National Archives, available online in partnership with Footnote.com, http://www.footnote.com/documents/10936943/revolutionary-war-pensions.
35. Revolutionary War pension papers of Jesse Thompson, The National Archives, available online in partnership with Footnote.com, http://www.footnote.com/documents/10936943/revolutionary-war-pensions.
36. Ibid.
37. Peden, *Revolutionary Patriots of Calvert & St. Mary's Counties*, 278.
38. Research of Linda Reno, unpublished.

The Marylanders Fight On

1. Scharf, *History of Maryland*, 260.
2. Ibid., 252.
3. Ibid., 370.
4. Ibid., 370.
5. Ibid., 283.
6. Ibid., 262.

7. Ibid., 262.
8. Ibid., 382.
9. Ibid., 434–443.

Epilogue

1. Letter to the author from Rev. Christos Christou, Jr., then president of the Maryland Society, Sons of the American Revolution, dated April 5, 2005.

Bibliography

American Archives. Northern Illinois University Libraries, Chicago. http://dig.lib.niu.edu/amarch/.
Archives of Maryland, Annapolis, Maryland. The Archives of Maryland Online: http://www.aomol.net/html/index.html.
Arnett, Earl, Robert J. Brugger, and Edward C. Papenfuse. *Maryland: A New Guide to the Old Line State*. 2nd ed. Baltimore: Johns Hopkins University Press, 1999.
Balkoski, Joseph M. *The Maryland National Guard: A History of Maryland's Military Forces, 1634–1991*. Baltimore: Maryland National Guard, 1991.
Baltimore Patriot, April 23, 1824.
Beall, Lieut. Fielder M. M. *Colonial Families of the United States Descended from the Immigrants: Bell, Beal, Bale, Beale, Beall Families*. Westminster, MD: Heritage Books, 2002.
Beitzell, Edwin. *St. Mary's County in the American Revolution*. St. Mary's County Bicentennial Commission, 1975.
Boone, Edward D., S.J. *The Genealogy of the Boone Family of Maryland*. Privately Published.
Bowie, Effie Gwynn, *Across the Years in Prince George's County*. Baltimore: Genealogical Publishing Co., 1975.
Brown, Helen White. *Index of Marriage Licenses, Prince George's County, Maryland, 1777–1886*. Baltimore: Genealogical Publishing Co., 1973.
Calendar of Maryland State Papers. Vol. 4, Part 1.
Cavanaugh, Tom. *The Writing of the Star Spangled Banner*. http://www.tc-solutions.com/croom/ssb.html.
Chadwick, John W. "The Battle of Long Island." *Harper's Magazine*, August 1876.
Charles Co. Deed Book K#4. Charles County, Maryland Land Records, 1791–1796. Miami Beach, FL: TLC Genealogy, 1994.
Charles County, Maryland Land Records, 1775–1782. Miami Beach, FL: TLC Genealogy, 1997.
Charles County, Maryland Probate Records, 1777–1780.
Chestnut, Mary Boykin (Miller). *A Diary from Dixie*. New York: D. Appleton and Company, 1905.
Clagett, Brice McAdoo, MD. "The Ancestry of Capt. James Neale," *Maryland Genealogical Society Bulletin* 31, no. 2 (Spring 1990).
Clarence, Edmund, ed. *An American Anthology, 1787–1900*. Boston: Houghton Mifflin, 1900, Bartleby.com, 2001. www.bartleby.com/248/.
Clark, Murtie June. *Loyalists in the Southern Campaign of the Revolutionary War*. Vol. 2. Baltimore: Genealogical Publishing Co., 1981.
Cochrane, Laura C. *The History of Caroline County, Maryland, From Its Beginning*. Baltimore: Regional Publishing Company, 1971.
Coe, Carl Robert. "William Coe of Calvert County." *Maryland Genealogical Society Bulletin* 33, no. 3 (Summer 1992).
Colonial Dames of America. *Ancestral Records and Portraits*. Vol. 2. New York: Grafton Press, 1910.
Commager, Henry Steele, and Richard B. Morris, eds. *Revolutionary Incidents from the Spirit of 'Seventy-Six': The Story of the American Revolution as Told by Participants*. New York: Da Capo Press, 1995.

Cranor, Henry Downes. *Marriage Licenses of Caroline County, Maryland, 1774–1815*. Kokomo, IN: Selby Publishing, 1904 Repr.

Custis, George Washington Parke. *Recollections and Private Memoirs of Washington*. New York: Derby & Jackson, 1860.

Dandridge, Danske. *American Prisoners of the Revolution*. Charlottesville, VA: The Michie Company Printers, 1911.

"Days of Defeat, Crushed in Battle, Nervous Patriot Troops Await a Knockout Punch." George DeWan, Staff Writer, Newsday.com. http://www.newsday.com/community/guide/lihistory/ny-history-hs404a,0,6174654.story?coll=ny-lihistory-navigation.

Dixon, Joan M. *National Intelligencer Newspaper Abstracts*. Vol. 15, June 12, 1841. Bowie, MD: Heritage Books, 2003.

Dodd, Jordan. Liahona Research, comp. *Maryland Marriages, 1655–1850* [database on-line]. Provo, UT: The Generations Network, 2004. http://www.ancestry.com/search/db.aspx?dbid=7846.

Earle, Swepson. *The Chesapeake Bay Country*. Baltimore: Thomsen-Ellis Co., 1923.

Edmonstone, Sir Archibald, 3rd Bt. *American Descendants of the Edmonstones of Duntreath and Australians with Edmonstone Connections from The Family Edmonstone of Duntreath*. Published 1875. Appendix 3. Edited and with additions by Mary McGrigor, F.S.A. Scot. Published in 1996. http://www.edmonstone.com/Pages/ap3.htm.

Edwin, David. *Dictionary of American Naval Fighting Ships*. Philadelphia, May, 1814. http://www.history.navy.mil/danfs/index.html.

"Extract of a Letter from New York, dated Aug. 28, 1776." *Maryland Gazette*, September 5, 1776.

"Extract of a Letter from an Officer in General Frazier's Battalion, Dated Sept. 3, 1776." *Maryland Gazette*, May 1, 1777.

Fenwick, Sr., Charles E. "Proceedings of the Orphan's Court of St. Mary's County, Maryland, Book I, 1777–1801. Transcribed by Charles E. Fenwick, Sr. Indexed by Claude G. Blackwell. St. Mary's County Historical Society, Leonardtown, Maryland, 1996.

Field, Thomas W. *The Battle of Long Island, with Connected Preceding Events, and the Subsequent American Retreat*. Brooklyn: Long Island Historical Society, 1869.

_____. *Thomas W. Field's Battle of Long Island*. New York: Long Island Historical Society.

Fish, Hamilton, LL.D. *New York State: The Battleground of the Revolutionary War*. New York, NY: Vantage Press, 1976. http://longislandgenealogy.com/prison.html.

Fitzpatrick, John C., ed. *The Writings of George Washington from the Original Manuscript Sources*. Electronic Text Center, University of Virginia Library, Charlottesville, Virginia. http://etext.virginia.edu/toc/modeng/public/WasFi03.html.

"Fort Greene Prison Ships in Wallabout Bay Witnessed Greatest Suffering for American Liberty." http://www.nyfreedom.com/fortgreene.htm.

Frederick County, Maryland Wills, Book GM#2, Register of Wills, Frederick County, Maryland.

Fresco, Margaret K. *Marriages and Deaths, St. Mary's County, Maryland 1634–1900*. Ridge, MD: Self-Published, 1982.

From an Original Petition for a New State Located in the Library of Congress, No date on document. Papers of the Continental Congress 1774–1789, no. 48, folios 251–256.

Gallagher, John J. *Battle of Brooklyn, 1776*. New York: Castle Books, 2002.

Gelders, Ruth Beall. "Ninian Beall." Atlanta: Daughters of the American Revolution, Joseph Habersham Chapter, 1976.

George Washington Papers. Library of Congress, 1741–1799: Series 4. General Correspondence, 1697–1799. Image no. 125. http://www.snake.ne.jp/~yama/nph-docomo.cgi/010000A/http/memory.loc.gov/cgi-bin/query/P?mgw:10:./temp/~ammem_ezu0::.

Gillett, Mary C. *The Army Medical Department, 1775–1818*. Washington, DC: U.S. Government Printing Office, 1981.

Guyther, J. Roy, MD. *Charlotte Hall: The Village, 1797–1997*. Mechanicsville, MD: Self-Published, 1997.

Hammett, Regina Combs. *History of St. Mary's County, Maryland*. Ridge, MD: Privately Published, 1977.
Heitman, Francis B. *Historical Register of Officers of the Continental Army during the War of the Revolution*. Rev. ed. Washington, DC: The Rare Book Shop Pub. Co., 1914.
"How the Continentals Met Defeat Bravely in Brooklyn." *Brooklyn Daily Eagle*, February 22, 1902.
Hunt, William E. *Historical Collections of Coshocton County Ohio: A Complete Panorama of the County, from the Time of the Earliest Known Occupants of the Territory unto the Present Time, 1764–1876*. Cincinnati: Clarke & Co., 1876.
Index to the Probate Records of Prince George's County, Maryland (1696–1900). Compiled by The Records committee of the Prince George's County Genealogical Society, Inc. Prince George's County Genealogical Society. Bowie, MD: 1989.
Jensen, Ann. "What Brave Fellows." *Annapolitan Magazine*, August 1991.
Johnson, Henry P. *The Campaign of 1776 around New York and Brooklyn: Including an Account of the Battle of Long Island and the Loss of New York*. New York: Long Island Historical Society, 1878.
Journal of the House of Representatives of the United States, 1804–1807.
Kemp, AnnaBelle. *Lucas Genealogy*. Hollywood, CA: A. Kemp, 1964, Heritage Quest. http://www.heritagequestonline.com/index.
The Library of Virginia, Bible Records Collection. http://lvaimage.lib.va.us/Bible/33365/n/0011.tif.
Lincoln County, Kentucky. Marriage Records, 1793–1800, Will Records 1801–1807. Vol. 2.
Lind, William S. "Military Matters: Lessons from Decatur." *United Press International*, August 3, 2007. http://www.upi.com/International_Security/Industry/Analysis/2007/08/03/military_matters_lessons_from_decatur/7978/.
Lineage Book: National Society of the Daughters of the American Revolution. Vols. 107 and 108. Washington, DC: NSDAR, 1908.
Lossing, Benson J. "The Battle of Long Island, New York, 1776," *Our Country*. Vol. 2, 1877. http://www.publicbookshelf.com/public_html/Our_Country_vol_2/index.html.
———. *The Pictorial Field Book of the Revolution or Illustrations, by Pen and Pencil, of the History, Scenery, Relics and Traditions of the War for Independence*. Vol. 2. New York: Harper and Brothers Publishers, 1852.
Loudon's Register, February 25, 1792.
Lowell, Edward J. *The Hessians and the Other German Auxiliaries of Great Britain in the Revolutionary War*. Baltimore, MD: Clearfield Company, March 2003.
Martin, Joseph Plumb. *A Narrative of a Revolutionary Soldier: Some of the Adventures, Dangers, and Sufferings of Joseph Plumb Martin*. New York: Signet Classics, 2001.
Maryland Gazette, November 10, 1825.
Maryland Gazette, October 11, 1804.
Maryland Gazette, October 29, 1812.
Maryland Historical Magazine. Vol. 14. Baltimore: Maryland Historical Society, 1919.
Maryland Historical Society. http://www.mdhs.org/library/Mss/ms000908.html.
"Maryland Prisoners on Long Island." From an undated edition of the *Baltimore Sun*, reprinted in the *New York Times*, August 18, 1895.
Maryland State Archives, Chancery Court Papers: Date: 1799. 998: Walter B. Cox. PG. Insolvent estate of Cox. Accession No.: 17,898–998 MSA S512-2-1041 Location: 1/36/1/.
Maryland State Archives, Maryland Indexes, Assessment of 1783, MSA S 1437.
The Masonic Correspondence of George Washington. Compiled by Julius F. Sachse, Philadelphia, PA: Press of the New Era, 1915.
"The Men of Old: How They Fought the Battle of Brooklyn." *Brooklyn Daily Eagle*, August 26, 1876.
Mercantile Adviser, New York, February 26, 1818.
Miller, John Allen. "How Whiskey Almost Started a War." Emmitsburg Area Historical Society.

http://www.emmitsburg.net/archive_list/articles/history/rev_war/whiskey.htm.

National Gazette, October 25, 1821.

National Intelligencer, February 13, 1837.

Nead, Daniel Wunderlich. *The Pennsylvania-German in the Settlement of Maryland.* AU: Whitefish, MT: Kessinger Publishing, LLC, June 25, 2007.

Newman, Harry Wright. *Anne Arundel Gentry.* Vol. 3. Westminster, MD: Family Line Publications, 1979.

Niles, Hezekiah. *Centennial Offering: Republication of Principles and Acts of the Revolution.* New York: A.S. Barnes & Co., 1876.

"Old Brooklyn: The Services of the Maryland Battalion." *Brooklyn Daily Eagle*, December 1, 1870.

"Oregon State Roster of Ancesters [*sic*]." Daughters of the American Revolution. Tillamook: Oregon Society, D.A.R., 1963.

Otho Holland Williams papers, Maryland Historical Society. http://www.mdhs.org/library/Mss/ms000908.html.

Papenfuse, Edward C., Alan F. Day, David W. Jordan, and Gregory A. Stiverson. *A Biographical Dictionary of the Maryland Legislature, 1635–1789.* Vol. 1: A–H. Baltimore: The Johns Hopkins University Press, 1985.

Peden, Jr., Henry C. *Quaker Records of Northern Maryland, 1716–1800.* Westminster, MD: Family Line Publications, 1993.

_____. *Revolutionary Patriots of Calvert & St. Mary's Counties, Maryland 1775–1783.* Westminster, MD: Family Line Publications, 1996.

_____. *Revolutionary Patriots of Frederick County, Maryland, 1775–1783.* Westminster, MD: Family Line Publications, 1995.

_____. *Revolutionary Patriots of Kent and Queen Anne's Counties, Maryland.* Westminster, MD: Family Line Publications, 1995.

_____. *Revolutionary Patriots of Prince George's County, 1775–1783.* Westminster, MD: Family Line Publications, 1997.

Peterson, Clarence S. *Known Military Dead during the American Revolutionary War.* Baltimore: Genealogical Publishing Co., 1967, Genealogy.com.

Pippenger, Wesley. *Georgetown, D.C., Marriages and Death Notices, 1801–1838.*

Polk, Ryan, "Holding the Line: The Origin of 'the Old Line State.'" Maryland Archives Online. http://www.aomol.net/html/oldline.html.

Poulson's American Daily, March 10, 1807.

Prince George's County, Maryland Index to Wills, Administrations, and Inventories, 1696–1900. Compiled by the Records Committee of the Prince George's County Genealogical Society, Inc., 1988.

"A Reminiscence." *Brooklyn Daily Eagle*, August 27, 1846.

"Return of Prisoners Taken during the Campaign, 1776." *Maryland Gazette*, May 1, 1777.

Revolutionary War Pension Papers. The National Archives. Available online at Footnote.com. http://www.footnote.com/documents/10936943/revolutionary-war-pensions.

Riley, George D. *Tidewater Maryland Ancestors: Baldwin, Blakistone, Brewer, Chesdeldyne, Davis, Goldsmith, Keech, Lancaster, Maddox, Ridgely, Riley, Sothoron, Stockette, Tucker, Williams and Related Families.* Baltimore: Gateway Press, 1999.

A Roster of Revolutionary Ancestors of the Indiana Daughters of the American Revolution: Commemoration of the United States of America Bicentennial, July 4, 1976. Evansville, IN: Unigraphic, 1976.

Rumple, Jethro. *A History of Rowan County, North Carolina; Containing Sketches of Prominent Families and Distinguished Men; With an Appendix.* Salisbury, NC: J.J. Brunner, 1881.

St. Mary's County Historical Society. *Chronicles of St. Mary's* 24, no. 1 (January 1976).

Sargent, Jean A. *Stones and Bones, Cemetery Records of Prince George's Co., Maryland.* Bowie, MD: Prince George County Genealogical Society, 1984.

Scharf, J. Thomas. *The Chronicles of Baltimore; Being a Complete History of "Baltimore Town" and Baltimore City from the Earliest Period to the Present Time.* Baltimore: Turnbull Bros., 1874.

———. *History of Maryland from the Earliest Period to the Present Day.* Hatsboro, PA: Tradition Press, 1967.

———. *History of Western Maryland, being a History of Frederick, Montgomery, Carroll, Washington, Allegany, and Garrett Counties from the Earliest Period to the Present Day, Including Biographical Sketches of Their Representative Men.* Vol. I. Baltimore: Regional Publishing Company, 1968.

———. *History of Western Maryland, being a History of Frederick, Montgomery, Carroll, Washington, Allegany, and Garrett Counties from the Earliest Period to the Present Day, Including Biographical Sketches of Their Representative Men.* Vol. 1. Philadelphia: L.H. Everts, 1882.

Schecter, Barnet. *The Battle for New York: The City at the Heart of the American Revolution.* New York: Walker & Co., 2002. http://www.thebattlefornewyork.com/prologue.php.

Schildknecht, Calvin E., and Thomas J.C. Williams. *Monocacy and Catoctin, Weller and Related Families.* Vol. 2. Shippensburg, PA: Beidel Printing House, 1985–1994.

Selected Final Pension Payment Vouchers 1818–1864, Maryland, Baltimore. Lovettsville, VA: Willow Bend Books, 1997.

Sinclair, Mary Donaldson. *Pioneer Days: Early History of Jefferson County, Ohio.* Steubenville, OH: n. pl., 1962.

"Stand at Cortelyou House." *Brooklyn Daily Eagle,* August 10, 1902.

Steuart, Rieman. *A History of the Maryland Line in the Revolutionary War, 1775–1783.* Society of the Cincinnati of Maryland: n. pl., 1969.

Tannehill, James B. *Genealogical History of the Tannahills, Tannehills and Taneyhills.* Privately published about 1940.

National Intelligencer and Washington Advertiser, June 29, 1811.

New York Journal & Patriotic Register, September 26, 1792.

News Leader, Laurel, Maryland, July 23, 1790.

"The Official Roster of the Soldiers of the American Revolution Buried in the State of Ohio." Columbus: Ohio Adjutant General's Dept., 1929–1959.

Pennsylvania Packet, August 20, 1782.

Port Folio Magazine, Philadelphia, PA, May 1814.

Providence Gazette and Country Journal, February 8, 1783.

U.S. Federal Census, Mortality Schedule, 1850.

Warfield, J.D. *The Founders of Anne Arundel and Howard Counties, Maryland : A Genealogical and Biographical Review from Wills, Deeds and Church Records.* Baltimore: Kohn & Pollock, 1905.

Whitman, Walt. *Leaves of Grass.* New York: The Modern Library Publishers, 1921.

Whittemore, Henry, *The Heroes of the American Revolution and Their Descendants: Battle of Long Island.* Brooklyn: Heroes of the Revolution Publishing Co., 1897–1899.

Will of Alexander Roxburgh. Somerset County, Maryland, EB#23, Folio 113.

Will of Manassah Finney. Harford Co. Wills, Liber 2, folio 206, Hall of Records, Annapolis, Maryland, on microfilm.

Will of Verlinda Saffel. Iredell County, North Carolina, dated July 22, 1812.

Wright, F. Edward. *Maryland Calendar of Wills, 1774–1777.* Vol. 16. Westminster, MD: Family Lines Publications, 1995.

Wright, Louis B, and Julia H. Macleod. "William Eaton's Relations with Aaron Burr." *Mississippi Valley Historical Review* 31, no. 4 (March 1945).

Index

Adams, Fort *see* Fort Adams
Adams, James, Pvt. 76
Adams, John, Pvt. 55
Adams, Nathan 115
Adams, Peter, Capt. 45, 55, 95; as commander of Sixth Company 115–129
Adams, William 115
Adlum, Ann Maria (Mrs. Henry Hatch Dent) 13
Adlum, John, Maj. 12–13
African-Americans, in the Revolutionary War 115–116
Aitken, William, Pvt. 116
Alexander, Jacob, Cpl. 133
Alexander, James 42
Alexander, Mary (Mrs. Jacob) 134
Alexander, William, Gen *see* Lord Stirling
Allanson, Elizabeth (Mrs. Edward Ford) 133
Allanson, Thomas 133
Allen, Alexander, Pvt. 95
Allen, Amos, Pvt. 96
Allen, Susanna (Mrs. John D. Latham) 86
Allen, Winifred (Mrs. Alexander) 95
Almeny, Ann (Mrs. John Johnston) 120
Ambrose, Catherine (Mrs. John Weller) 112
Annapolis, MD, role in pre-war preparations 7–11
Anne Arundel County, MD 74, 78, 79, 88, 89, 91, 92, 98, 111, 112, 138
Armstrong, John, Pvt. 96
Association of Freeman of Maryland 9
Atlee, Col. 21

Baggett, Francis Green, Pvt. 55
Baggett, John 55
Bailey, Dr. Richard 32
Baker, John, Pvt. 97
Baker (Backer), William 97
Balkoski, Joseph 140

Baltimore, Lord *see* Calvert, Charles
Baltimore County, MD 48, 97
Baltimore Independent Company *see* Ninth Company
Baltimore Patriot 79, 160
Barclay (Barkley), James 116
Barker, Mary (Mrs. Joseph Waters Davis) 138
Barlow, John Willis 123
Barnitt, Michael, Pvt. 77
Barry (Beary), Joseph, Pvt. 97
Bayer, Michael, Capt. 146, 147
Beale, James, Pvt. 134
Beall, Christopher, Pvt. 97–99
Beall, Hepzibah (Mrs. Allanson Ford) 133
Beall, James 98
Beall, Lloyd, Capt. 106, 120, 142
Beall, Ninian, Col. 98–99
Beanes, Christopher 77
Beanes, John Hancock, Lt. 77
Beanes, Dr. William 77
Bell, James, Pvt. 116
Bellefield, home of Capt. Patrick Sim 76
Blackistone, John, Sgt. 157
Blacklock, Edward, Pvt. 78
Blacklock, Thomas 78
Boarman, Eleanor (Mrs. Edward Edelin, Jr.) 58
Boarman, Mary Rose (Mrs. Horatio Dyer) 70
Boarman, Raphael H. 70
Boone, Daniel 48
Boone, Henry 55
Boone (Boen, Boon), John, Pvt. 55
Boone, John, of the Cliffs 55
Boone, Mary (Mrs. Henry Hardy) 55
Boone, Mary Jane 55
Bootman, Joseph, Pvt. 116
Bordley, Elizabeth 54
Boston, Alexander, Pvt. 134
Bowie, Daniel, Lt. 56, 74, 77
Bowie, John 77
Bowie, Mary (Mrs. William Beanes) 77

Bowie, Thomas 56
Bowling, Mary (Mrs. Charles Smith) 70
Brady, Patrick, Pvt. 56
Brandywine, Battle of 51, 54, 76, 83, 94, 98, 114, 148, 162, 164, 166
Brashears, Mary (Mrs. Levin Wilcoxon) 112
Brashears, Ruth (Mrs. Frederick Miles) 150
Breat, Peter, Pvt. 134
Brinkenhoof, Garret, Pvt. 99
British troop strength 3, 11, 14–15, 17
Brobeck, Meicher, Pvt. 134
Broderick, Dennis, Pvt. 57
Bromcord, Adam, Pvt. 134
Brooke, Ann (Mrs. Christopher Beall) 97
Brooke, Ann (Mrs. Christopher Beanes) 77
Brooke, Baker 81
Brooke, Henry 97
Brooke, John B. 71
Brooke, Robert 77, 81
Brooke, Sarah (Mrs. John Cox) 81
Brooke, Walter 81
Brookes, Richard, Pvt. 99
Brooklyn, Battle of *see* Long Island, Battle of
Brooklyn Daily Eagle 23, 29
Brooklyn, NY: as battle site 3–6, 15, 17, 28; as burial site 45, 171
Brown, John, Pvt. 99
Brown, Peter, Sgt. 97, 99–100, 106
Brown, Dr. Richard Gustavus 51, 121
Bruce, Charles 136
Bruce, John 134
Bruce, William, Sgt. 134–136
Brumbargher, Christopher, Pvt. 78
Brunswick, Battle of 75
Bryan, John, Pvt. 116
Buchanan, William 8
Bunker Hill, Battle of 164

Index

Burgess, John, Cdt. 94
Burgess, Joseph, Capt. 78
Burgess, Michael, Cpl. 94
Burgess, Vachel (Veach, Basil), Pvt. 69, 78–79, 150
Burn, Mary (Mrs. William Cox) 58
Burnes, James, Sgt. 100
Burns (Burn), Carberry (Carbry), Pvt. 116
Burr, Aaron 83
Burroughs, Benjamin, Pvt. 79
Burroughs, Charles, Pvt. 79
Burrows, Joshua 57
Burrows, Thomas, Pvt. 57
Buxton (Buxtone), Abijah, Pvt. 99, 100
Byzch, James, Pvt. 79

Calhoun, John C., Hon. 135
Calvert, Caroline (Mrs. Robert Eden) 8
Calvert, Charles 8
Calvert County, MD 55, 75, 99, 160
Camden, SC, Battle of 40, 50, 79, 92, 93, 116, 132, 135, 143, 154, 162, 166
Campbell, William, Capt. 132–133, 160, 161
Carberry (Carbery, Carbury), Henry, Cdt. 158–159
Carmichael, James, Pvt. 117
Carney, Thomas 115
Caroline County, MD 8, 115, 119
Carroll, Charles 11, 66
Carroll, Daniel 75
Carroll, Edmund, Pvt. 79
Carroll, Elizabeth (Mrs. John Bryan) 116
Carroll, Mary (Mrs. Patrick Sim) 75
Cartwright, Elizabeth (the second Mrs. Nathanial Ewing) 119
Cartwright, Judith (Mrs. Lancelot Chunn) 57
Casbear (Casser), William, Pvt. 136
Catons, Michael, Pvt. 100
Cavenaugh, Monica (Mrs. James Hilton) 61
Cecil County, MD 124, 129
Centinel of Liberty 162
Chandler, Robert, Cpl. 136
Chapman, Elizabeth (Mrs. Robert Hanson Harrison) 121
Charles County, MD: home of Captains Stone and Ford 45; home of First Company soldiers 51–75; of Ninth Company soldiers 133–141; home of Col. Smallwood 36, 41; of Second Company soldiers 86; of Sixth Company soldiers 121
Charlotte Hall School 141–142
Chase, Samuel 11
Chatham (Cheatham), Joseph, Pvt. 57
Chesapeake Bay 8, 113, 130, 165
Chesley, Robert, Cdt. 159
Chilton, Charles, Pvt. 160
Chunn, Jonathan, Pvt. 57
Chunn, Lancelot 57
Church, Elizabeth (Mrs. Richard Smith) 71
Cissell, John, Pvt. 100
Clagett, William 77
Clark, Howard 165
Clark, John, Pvt. 117
Clark, William, Pvt. (First Company) 57
Clark, William, Pvt. (Sixth Company) 117
Clarke, Peter, Sgt. 79–80
Clements, Henry 60
Clift (Cuff), Crisenberry (Christenburry) 117
Clift, Henry, Pvt. 117
Cobble Hill 4, 23, 27
Cobeth, John, Pvt. 136
Cockey, Susannah (Mrs. Mordecai Gist) 48
Coe, John 80
Coe (Cox), Milburn, Pvt. 80
Coe, Richard, Pvt. 63, 94
Coe, William, Pvt. 160
Coe, Dr. William Gwynn 160
Coghill, Lydia (Mrs. John Marlow) 87
Cole, Francis, Pvt. 100
Collins, Patrick, Pvt. 100
Collins, Timothy, Pvt. 113–114
Columbia University (formerly Kings College) 42
Conn, Hugh, Pvt. 114
Connally, Josias, Pvt. 100
Connecticut, Connecticut Regiment 24–25, 39, 85, 157, 163–164, 167, 168
Connell, Thomas Way, Pvt. 57
Conner, Alexius, Pvt. 80
Connor, Thomas, Pvt. 80
Conslean, Andrew, Pvt. 136
Contee, Thomas 81
Continental Army 7, 10, 51, 55, 106, 146, 158, 164
Continental Congress 3, 7, 11, 12, 14, 15, 42, 51, 61, 65, 75, 112
Coole Springs 142
Cooper, Thomas, Pvt. 117
Cornwallis, Lord, Gen.: in the battle 22–25, 38, 42; surrender 55, 122, 164; with the Tories 130
Cortelyou House *see* Old Stone House

Coudon, Mary (Mrs. John Hopkins Stone) 53
Courts, Elizabeth (Mrs. James Thomas) 57
Courts, William, Lt. 57, 74, 107, 108
Covington, Henry, Pvt. 117
cowardice 29, 39, 163, 168
Cowpens, Battle of: 92, 93, 132, 143, 162, 169
Cox, Edmund, Pvt. 58
Cox, John 81
Cox, Sarah Ann (Mrs. Lt. Richard Harwood) 81
Cox, Walter Brooke (Brook), Cdt. 81
Cox, William 58
Craddock, Mary (Mrs. James Murphy) 106
Craig, James, Pvt. 117
Craik, Adam 121
Craik, Dr. James 51, 54, 121
Crawford, William, Col. 152–153
Crawford expedition 152–153
Cresap, Michael 143
Cromwell, Oliver 98–99
Crutsinger, Elizabeth 136
Crutsinger, George 136
Crutsinger (Kretsinger, Krutsinger), George, Pvt. 136
Crutsinger, Katherine (Mrs. Solomon) 137
Crutsinger, Solomon, Pvt. 136–138
Cunningham, William 32, 34
Curtz, Michael, Pvt. 138
Custis, George Washington Parke 54

Dallam, Richard, Col. 121, 123
Darnell, Margaret (Mrs. Henry Brooke) 97
Dashiell (Dasheil), John, Capt. 101
Daughters of the American Revolution 101
Davidson, John, Lt. 161
Davidson, John, Maj. 118
Davis, Anthony, Pvt. 161
Davis, Joseph Waters 138
Davis, Mary Ann (Mrs. John Plant) 67
Davis, Notley, Pvt. 138
Daws Thomas, Pvt. 81
Deaver, Abraham 139
Deaver, Basil 138
Deaver, Henry 140
Deaver (Deavour), Miseal (Michael, Misail, Miscal, Misal) 138–140
Deaver, Sarah (Mrs. Miseal Deaver) 140
Decatur, Stephen 127

Index

Declaration of Independence 6, 8, 11, 25, 51, 75, 144
DeCourcy (deCoursey), Edward, Capt. 13, 27, 108
De Heister, Gen. 43
Delabrooke (De La Brooke) Manor 77, 81
Delaware, Delaware Line 4, 18, 21, 27, 37, 116, 122, 169
Denny, Robert, Capt. 81
Denny (Denney), Samuel, Pvt. 132, 140
Dent, Eleanor (Mrs. John Jordan) 121
Dent, Rev. Hatch, Jr., Ens. 58, 107, 108, 140–142
Dent, Henrietta (the first Mrs. John Hancock Beanes) 77
Dent, Henry Hatch 13
Dent, John, Capt. 142
Dick, Dr. Elisha Cullen 121
disease: among troops 15; in prison camps 33
Dorsey, Daniel, Capt. 114, 155
Dorsey, Elizabeth (Mrs. Joseph Burgess) 78
Dorsey, Larkin, Cdt. 155
Dorsey, Rebecca (Mrs. Vachel Burgess) 78
Dorsey, Richard, Cdt. 156
Dorsey, Ruth (Mrs. Gassaway Watkins) 96
Dorsey, Thomas 78
Douglass (Doyglass), Ignatius, Pvt. 58
Dowling, George, Pvt. 117
Downing, Nathaniel, Pvt. 58
Drafts, Robert Orme 97
Dunmore, Lord 9, 10, 11, 51, 143, 161
Dunn, John, Pvt. 100–101
Dwiggins (Dwigens), Daniel, Cpl. 117
Dwiggins (Dwigens), Samuel, Cpl. 117–118
Dwyer, Thomas, Sgt. 118
Dyer, Horatio 70
Dyer, John 77
Dyson, Thomas A., Capt. 57

Eastern Shore (of MD) 9, 107, 115, 122
Easton, David 121
Eberle, Johan 142
Edelen, Clement, Pvt. 73
Edelen, Edward 58
Edelen (Eadlin), Edward, Jr., Pvt. 58
Edelen (Edelin, Eadlin), John, Pvt., 81
Eden, Sir Anthony 8
Eden, Sir Robert, Gov. 7–8
Edgerly, Edward, Sgt. 118

Elkton, MD, Head of the Elk 12, 94, 129
Elliott, Joseph, Sgt. 118
Elson, John, Cpl. 81
Enright, John, Pvt. 101
Episcopal Church 8, 54, 98, 140–141, 160
Eutaw Springs, Battle of 55, 79, 92, 118, 143, 162, 166, 169
Evans, George, Pvt. 114
Evans, William, Pvt. 81
Everett (Everit), Elisha, Pvt. 82
Everly, Adam, Cpl. 142
Ewing, Nathaniel, Lt. 118–119

Ferguson, Thomas, Pvt. 101
Fernandis (Fernandes, Faarnandez), James, Cdt. 27, 52, 58–59, 64, 74, 107
Fernandis, Peter 59
Fifth Independent Company 34, 47, 157, 161, 166
Fifth Maryland Regiment 101, 118, 119, 132, 155
Filford, Capt. 166
Finney, Hannah (Mrs. John Lowery) 124
Finney, Manassah 124
Firor, Mary Magdalen (Mrs. John Weller) 112
First Company 44, 45, 51–74, 77
Fisher, Jacob, Pvt. 142
Fisher, Thomas, Pvt. 119
Flatbush NY 21, 32
Fleming, John, Pvt. 101
Flint, John, Pvt. 101
Floyd, Daniel, Cpl. 119
Floyd, Elijah, Pvt. 119
Floyd, John, Pvt. 119
Floyd, Moses, Pvt. 119
Floyd, William 163
Fluharty, Roy 143
Fluharty (Fleehearty, Fleeharty, Flaharty, Fluhart, Floharty), Stephen, Pvt. 142–143
Flying Camp, Maryland Companies of 14, 40, 94, 156, 168
Ford, Allanson 133
Ford (Floyd), Benjamin, Lt. 45, 49, 94, 131, 132, 133, 144, 145, 155, 156
Ford, Charles Allanson 133
Ford, Charles Allanson (Allison), Jr. 133
Ford, Edward 133
Ford, Robert 133
Ford, Susan 133
Forrest, Uriah 158–159
Fort Adams (Mississippi) 82
Fort McHenry 77
Fort Miamis 82
Fort Pitt 143
Fort Putnam 28, 39

Fort Washington 28, 39, 84, 110, 164
Frazier, General 30
Frederick (County), MD 61, 75, 84, 90, 100, 104, 111, 112, 116; as home to soldiers in Ninth Company 130–155
French and Indian War 15, 48, 95, 130
Fritchie, Barbara 131
Fulford, John, Capt. 114
Fulton, Alexander, Pvt. 119

Gadman, Sam 138
Gaither, Actions (Mrs. Basil Ridgley) 89
Gaither, Henry 82
Gaither, Henry, Ens. 82, 84
Gallagher, John J. 6
Gallworth, Peter, Pvt. 83
Galway (Galloway), Hugh, Pvt. 119
Galway, Jonathan, Pvt. 119
Gardiner (Gardner), James, Pvt. 101
Gardiner, John, Pvt. 161
Gardner, Jacob, Pvt. 143
Garland, Gilbert, Pvt. 59
Garner, Matthew, Pvt. 60
George, Edward, Fifer 10
German Regiment 131, 133, 146, 147, 156
Germans, as Tories 130
Germantown, Battle of 51, 54, 64, 71, 93, 94, 116, 143, 148, 164, 165
Gerrish, John, Pvt. 143
Gibony (Giveny, Gibeny), David, Sgt. 132, 143
Gibson, James, Pvt. 120
Giles, Edward 132
Gill, Ann (Mrs. James Neale) 66
Girish, Mary (Mrs. Henry Young) 155
Gist, Christopher 48
Gist, Mordecai, Maj.: aftermath of the battle 40; background 6, 8, 10, 44, 45, 48–50; in battle 18, 21, 22, 25, 27; epilogue 171; in individual soldiers' entries 80, 169
Gist, Nathanial 48
Gist, Thomas 48
Glatz, John, Pvt. 143
Glover, William, Pvt. 120
Good, John, Sgt. 132, 143
Gowanus Bridge 20, 22
Gowanus Swamp, Creek 4, 19, 22, 25, 28, 157
Granger, Samuel, Pvt. 60
Grant, John, Pvt. 83
grave site, the Maryland 400, 4, 25, 33, 171

Index

Gray, Benjamin, Pvt. 60
Gray, Comfort (Mrs. Zachariah Gray) 102
Gray, Zachariah, Pvt. 96, 101
Grayson, William, Col. 36
Green, Amos, Pvt. 83
Green, Ann (Mrs. Patrick Hamilton) 60
Green, Charles, Pvt. 60
Green, Edward, Pvt. 60
Greene, Nathanial, Gen. 18, 93, 122, 132, 133, 167, 169
Greenfield, Mary Ashcom (Mrs. Walter Brooke) 81
Greenwald, Jacob, Pvt. 132, 144
Griffin, Charles, Pvt. 60
Guilford Court House, Battle of 92, 116, 143, 162, 166, 169
Gunby, John, Capt. 114, 132–133

Hackethorn, Michael, Pvt. 144
Hagarty, John 84
Hagarty, Paul, Pvt. 83
Hahn (Haun), Michael, Pvt. 144–146
Hahn, Nancy (Mrs. Michael Hahn) 146
Hall, Richard 99
Halsey (Holsey), John, Pvt. 102
Hamilton (Hamiltone), George, Pvt. 102
Hamilton, Henrietta (Mrs. John Baggett) 55
Hamilton, Patrick 60
Hamilton (Hamiltone), Samuel, Cpl. 102
Hamilton, Samuel, Pvt. 60–61
Hancock, John 11
hand-to-hand combat, in battle 20–21
Handy, Ebenezer, Capt. 101
Handy, Frances (Mrs. Alexander Roxburgh) 107
Handy, Isaac, Col. 107
Handy, Robert, Capt. 101
Hanson, Ann (Mrs. Hugh Mitchell) 65
Hanson, John 51, 61, 65
Hanson, Samuel, Cpl. 60, 61
Hanson, Thomas, Capt. 74
Hanson, Walter 61
Hardy, Andrew, Pvt. 146
Hardy, Ann (Mrs. John Boone) 55
Hardy, Henry, Jr. 55
Harford County MD 56, 121, 123, 124, 125
Harlem, Battle of 84, 139, 168
Harman, Jacob, Pvt. 146
Harris, Robert 88
Harrison, Robert Hanson 121
Harrison, Sarah (Mrs. John Jordan, Mrs. James Craik) 121

Hartman, Henry, Maj. 111
Harwood, Richard, Lt. 81
Haslet, Col. 21, 28, 37
Hatton, John, Pvt. 120
Hatton (Hattou), Josias, Pvt. 102
Hatton, Margaret 102
Hatton, Thomas 102
Hatton, William 102
Heaberd, Priscilla (Mrs. Pryor Smallwood) 36
Head of the Elk *see* Elkton, MD
Heckendorn, Reinhard Jacob 144
Hellmold, George, Pvt. 146
Henderson, Arianna (Mrs. Patrick Sim) 75
Hessians: aftermath of the battle 30, 32; in battle 3, 14–25, 43; in the Battle of White Plains 169; in individual soldiers' entries 84, 91, 137, 148, 164
Heyder, William, Pvt. 84
Heywood, John, Pvt. 146
Highlanders 17, 20, 21, 30
Hill, Causamer (Casemar, Casimir, Cosomer), Pvt. 146
Hiller, A. D. 86, 104
Hilton, James 61
Hilton, Truman, Pvt. 61
Hite, John, Pvt. 146
Hobkirk's Hill, Battle of 116, 132
Hoffman, Mary 155
Hogg (Hoge), James, Pvt. 73
Holland, Abraham 146
Holland, Basil (Beall), Pvt. 146–147
Holland, Beall 132
Holland, Elizabeth (Mrs. Jacob Holland, Sr.) 85
Holland, Jacob, Pvt. 84–85
Holland, Jacob, Sr. 85
Hollyday, Ann (Mrs. Walter Brooke Cox) 81
Holmes, Dr. Silas 32
Holmes (Holms, Holme), William, Pvt. 120
Hoofman, John, Pvt. 147
Hopson, John, Pvt. 61
Horson, Thomas, Pvt. 85
Hoskins, Elizabeth (Mrs. Walter Hanson) 61
Hously, Rhody, Pvt. 102
Howard County MD 92
Howe, Gen. 24, 33
Hubbel, William, Capt. 163
Hudson River, importance to British 11
Hughes (Hughs), John, Pvt. 102–104
Hungerford, Ann (Mrs. Thomas Lucas) 95
hunting shirts *see* uniforms
Hurdle, James, Pvt. 104
Hurdle, Lawrence 104

Hurdle, Robert 104
Hutchins, Zachariah, Pvt. 104

Indiana 61, 86, 101, 147, 148, 153

Jackson, Alexander, Pvt. 104
Jackson, George, Pvt. 120
Jackson, John, Pvt. 105
Jackson, Stonewall 131
Jacobs, Ruth (Mrs. John Mills) 88
Jamaica Road 18, 20
Jefferson, Thomas 160
Jenifer, Dr. Daniel of St. Thomas 51
Jenifer, Elizabeth (Mrs. David Stone) 51
Jenkins, Basil (Bazel), Pvt. 105
Jenkins, Joseph Jason, Pvt. 61
Jenkins (Jinkins), Philip, Pvt. 85
Jenkins, Sarah (Mrs. Philip Jenkins) 85
Jennings, Charles 97
Johnson, Elizabeth (Mrs. John Flint) 101
Johnson, Elizabeth (Mrs. Valentine Lynn) 149
Johnson, Richard, Pvt. 85
Johnson, Thomas 7, 46
Johnston (Johnson), John, Pvt. 120
Jones, Charles, Pvt. 105
Jones, Edward, Pvt. 85
Jones, Samuel, Cdt. 74
Jordan, Jesse, Pvt. 161
Jordan, John 121
Jordan, John, Ens. 121
Jordan, Maria 121
Joy, Mary M. (Mrs. Stephen Joy) 155
Joy, Stephen 155

Kasler (Coater, Kesler), John, Pvt. 132, 147
Kay, Daniel M. 96
Keller, Frederick, Pvt. 147
Kelly, Benjamin, Pvt. 105
Kelly, James, Pvt. 121, 123
Kennedy, Clement 63
Kennedy, Monica (Mrs. Samuel Luckett) 63
Kent County, DE 115, 122
Kent County, MD 115, 124, 125
Kentucky 48, 63, 64, 112, 122, 147, 153, 162, 164, 165, 166
Kephart (Kepheard, Keephart, Kephard, Kepphard, Keiphart), George, Pvt. 147
Kephart, Margaret (Mrs. George Kephart) 147
Kephart, Martin, Pvt. 148
Kern (Hern), Philip, Pvt. 132, 147
Key, Francis Scott 66, 77
Kidd, John, Lt. 62

196

Index

King, Philip, Pvt. 85
Kingsbridge 129, 145, 164
Kirby (Kerby), John, Pvt. 121
Kirk, James, Pvt. 122
Kline, Peter, Pvt. 148
Knott, George, Pvt. 105
Kurk, Samuel, Pvt. 62

Laffy, Thomas, Pvt. 122
Lamar, W., Lt. 140, 142
Lamb, John 113
Lamb, Joshua 112, 113
Lamb, Sarah (Mrs. Joshua Lamb), (Mrs. Thomas Windham) 112
Lanham, Charity (Mrs. Thomas Blacklock) 78
Lanham, Elizabeth (Betsy) (Mrs. Robert Bier) 86
Lanham, Elizabeth (Mrs. Josias Lanham) 86
Lanham, Henry, Pvt. 86
Lanham, John 86
Lanham, John D., Pvt. 86
Lanham, Josias 86
Lansdale, Thomas, Maj. 135
Layton (Laighton), William, Pvt. 122
leadership, lack of 18–19
Ledburn, (Leadbarn) George, Pvt. 105
Lee, Hannah (Mrs. Thomas Bowie) 56
Lee, Richard Henry, Col., Esq. 36, 56
Lee, Thomas Sim, Gov. 80, 138
Leeke (Leek), Henry, Pvt. 86
Leeson (Leamon), William, Pvt. 123
Legion of the United States 82
Leonard, George Rex, Pvt. 105
Leonard, John Rex, Pvt. 105
Leonardtown 160, 161, 164, 165
Lesache, Robert, Pvt. 105
Lewis, Benjamin, Pvt. 87
Lexington and Concord 8
Lindsay, Andrew Ross, Pvt. 62
Lindsay, John, Pvt. 87
Locke (Lock), William, Pvt. 123
Logan, Margaret 98
Long Island, Battle of 20–29
Lord Baltimore *see* Calvert, Charles
Lord Dunmore *see* Dunmore, Lord
Lord Stirling *see* Stirling, Lord
Loring, Joshua, Commissioner 33, 34
Lowe, Henrietta (Mrs. Charles Allanson Ford, Jr.) 133
Lowe, Richard, Pvt. 87
Lowrey (Lowry), John, Pvt. 123
Lowrey, Margaretta (Mrs. Cornelius Willis) 124
Lowry, James 124

Lucas, Barton, Capt.: background 45, 95; in individuals soldiers' entries 97–114, 115
Lucas, Thomas 95
Luckett, Francis Ware, Pvt. 62
Luckett, Ignatius, Jr. 63
Luckett, Samuel, Pvt. 62
Luckett, William 62
Lynch, John, Pvt. 124
Lynch, Thomas, Pvt. 161
Lynn (Linn), Valentine (Valen), Pvt. 132, 148
Lynn, William, Pvt. 149

macaroni 12–14, 22
Mack, Silas W. 112
Magruder, Eleanor (Mrs. Paul Hagarty) 84
Mainwaring, Mary (Mrs. Robert Brooke) 77
Mamaroneck, Battle of 75
Man, Robert, Pvt. 125
Mankin, Elizabeth (Mrs. Wheedon Wallace) 59
march to New York, Marylanders 12–15
Marlow, John 87
Marlow, Ralph Middleton (Middlen), Pvt. 87
Marlow, Ruth 88
Martin, Ignatius 88
Martin, Joseph Plumb 25
Martin, Michael 88
Martin, Pacel, Pvt. 149
Maryland Council of Safety 8–9, 10, 31, 40, 51, 161
Maryland Gazette 27, 53, 108, 135
Maryland, prewar preparations 7–11
Maryland Society, Sons of the American Revolution 100
Marylanders, roles in other battles 32, 167–169
Massachusetts 8–9, 27; Marblehead regiment 27, 28
Mastin, Francis. Capt. 62
May, Dennis, Pvt. 149–150
McCabe, John, Pvt. 156
McClain (McLane, McClean), Hugh, Pvt. 125, 152
McClain (McLaine, McLane, McClaine), John, Pvt. 125
McClain, John (of Harford), Pvt. 125
McCoy, John, Lt. 152
McCubbin, Samuel, Pvt. 126
McDaniel, William, Pvt. 126
McDaniel, William, 2nd Pvt. 126
McDougall, Gen. 28, 169
McFadden (McFadon), John, Pvt. 129
McGregor (McGreger), William, Pvt. 126

McHenry, Fort *see* Fort McHenry
McKay (McCoy), Daniel, Pvt. 105
McKay, Eleanor (Mrs. Henry Lanham) 86
McKeel, Charles, Fifer 129
McKeel (McKee), Thomas, Sgt. 126
McLean, Margaret (Mrs. Ignatius Luckett, Jr.) 63
McNaughton (McNorton, McNaughtan), Peter, Sgt. 150
McNew, Moses, Pvt. 87–88
McPherson, Chloe (the second Mrs. James Fernandis) 59, 64
McPherson, John, Pvt. 63
McPherson, Mark, Pvt. 63–64
McPherson, Samuel, Ens. 64
McPherson, William, Cpl. 150
medical care, of troops 15, 32–35
Medley, Eleanor (Mrs. Jeremiah Tarlton) 164
Meek, John 10
Miami Indians 82
Miamis, Fort *see* Fort Miamis
Middle Green Enlarged 69
Middleton, Mary (Mrs. Mark McPherson) 63
Mifflin, Gen. 28
Milburn, Mary (Mrs. John Coe) 80
Miles, Frederick, Pvt. 150
Miles, Joshua, Capt. 111
militia formation, Maryland 9–10
Miller, Henry, Pvt. 150
Miller, James, Pvt. 150
Miller, Josias (Josiah), Pvt. 64
Miller, Margaret (Mrs. Michael Miller) 151
Miller, Michael, Pvt. 150–151
Mills, John, Pvt. 88
Mills, Mary (the second Mrs. Alexander Naylor) 153
Mingo, Chief Logan 143
Mitchell, Hugh 65
Mitchell, James, Pvt. 88
Mitchell, John, Cdt. 61, 65, 67, 152
Mitchell, Mary (Mrs. Josias Hatton) 102
Monmouth, Battle of 64, 66, 82, 83, 92, 93, 94, 98, 111, 143, 148, 162, 163
Monroe, James, president 36, 159, 160
Monroe, Susanna (Mrs. James Monroe) 36
Montgomery County, MD 60, 75, 82, 84, 85, 86, 87, 95, 104, 106, 108, 111, 146
Moore, James, Capt. 122
Morgan, Daniel, Capt. 16, 45, 46
Morriner, George, Pvt. 151

Index

Morrisania Heights, Battle of 75
Morrow, John, Pvt. 126
Mugg, John, Pvt. 151
Muir, John 127
Mullen, Michael, Pvt. 151
Murdock, Catherine (the first Mrs. Joseph Sim) 75
Murphy (Murphey), James, Pvt. 105–106
Murphy, John, Pvt. 106
Murphy, William 106
USS Murray 128
Murray, Alexander, Lt. 126–128
Murray, Alexander, Rear Adm. 128
Murray, James 126
Murray, Thomas, Pvt. 106
Murray, Dr. William 126
Myers (Myer, Myre, Mire, Moyer, Meyers, Myirs), Frederick (Pvt.) 125, 132, 151–152
Myers (Myre, Moire), Peter, Pvt. 152

Nagle (Neagle), William, Pvt. 128
Nash, Barnard, Pvt. 65
National Intelligencer 75, 159
Naylor (Nailor, Nailer), Alexander, Pvt. 152
Naylor, Magdalena (Mrs. Alexander Naylor) 153
Naylor, Nicholas, Pvt. 153
Naylor, Samuel 153
Neale, Bennet 66
Neale, Henry, Lt. 161
Neale, James, Capt. 59
Neale, James, Capt. (great-great-grandfather of John Neale) 66
Neale, John, Pvt. 65
Neary, John, Pvt. 67
Neill, Benjamin 66
Nelson, Robert, Pvt. 88
Neriah Baptist Church 103
New England 38, 40, 168
New Jersey (Jersey) 12, 23, 24, 28, 35, 45, 50, 52, 73, 75, 76, 86, 94, 95, 103, 108, 121, 139, 144, 158, 163, 170
New Utrecht 32
New York 3, 11, 13, 14, 15, 24, 30, 31, 33, 34, 37, 39, 42, 65, 75, 84, 85, 95, 103, 111, 123, 129, 133, 144, 145, 148, 153, 164, 165
New York City 18, 22, 42, 43, 48, 145, 167
Newton, Ann 106
Nicholson, Zachariah, Pvt. 128
Ninety-Six, Battle of 92, 99, 116, 166
Ninth Company 10, 44, 45, 48, 94, 130–156
Norris, John, Pvt. 67
Norris, Thomas, Pvt. 67

North Carolina 61, 71, 72, 73, 88, 89, 100, 108, 119, 127, 132, 140, 141, 166, 169
Nott, George 96
Nowlan, Patrick, Pvt. 88

Ohio 64, 68, 80, 91, 108, 113, 116, 120, 139, 143, 144, 145, 146, 148, 150, 151, 152
Old Stone House, Cortelyou House 4, 22, 24–26, 170, 171
Orme, Moses, Lt. 100
Osborn, Francis, Pvt. 89
Owings, Jeremiah, Pvt. 106
Owings, John, Pvt. 106
Owings, Roddey, Pvt. 106

Paca, William, Gov. 11, 66, 161
Palmer, John Williamson 14
Patrick, Christena (Mrs. Truman Hilton) 61
Paulus Hook, Battle of 114
Peake, Nathan, Pvt. 114
Peale, James, Capt. 64
Pearce, William, Pvt. 106
Peckinpaugh, Eva Maria (Mrs. Johan Eberle) 142
Peggy Stewart 7
Penn, Jacob, Pvt. 89
Pennsylvania 4, 15, 18, 27, 28, 29, 84, 91, 95, 111, 112, 119, 126, 129, 137, 142, 143, 145, 146, 152, 153, 158
Pennsylvania Evening Post 108
Pennsylvania Line 13, 21, 91, 134, 137, 142, 145, 153, 158
Perkins (Pirkens), Joseph, Pvt. 128
Perkins, Thomas, Pvt. 89
Perry, Elias, Pvt. 89
Perry, James, Pvt. 89
Perry, John, Lt. Col. 100
Peterson, Clarence S. 118
Phelps, John, Pvt. 128
Phelps, William, Sgt. 163
Philadelphia 6, 7, 11, 12, 13, 14, 25, 31, 35, 40, 73, 77, 80, 88, 120, 122, 126, 127, 129, 137, 144, 148, 154, 158, 165
Philips Heights, Battle of 69
Philpot, Bryan, Ens. 25
Philpot, John 25–26
Pierpoint, Chew (Mrs. Basil Deaver) 138
Pine, Dr. John 169
Pitt, Fort *see* Fort Pitt
Plant, John, Pvt. 67
Plater, John Rousby, Hon. 135
Pope, Charity (Mrs. Francis Osborn) 89
Port Tobacco (Parish), MD 60, 62, 63, 66, 121
Poston, Judith (Mrs. Hatch Dent) 140

Potomac River 8, 9, 51, 66, 157
Powell, John, Pvt. 128
Prall, Edward, Capt. 150
Prather, Verlinda (Mrs. Joshua Saffell) 108
Pratt, John Baptist, Pvt. 162
Pratt, Susanna (Mrs. John Baptist Pratt) 162
Pratt, Zepheniah 162
Price, Samuel, Pvt. 153
Price, Thomas, Maj. 10, 40, 129, 144, 145, 168
Prince George's County, MD 45, 56, 58, 61, 71, 75, 76, 77, 78, 80, 81, 84, 86, 87, 89, 90, 95, 97, 98, 101, 102, 105, 110, 112, 130, 149, 150, 163, 165
Princeton, Battle of 13, 51, 54, 71, 114, 148, 153
prisoners, treatment of, 23, 32–35
Prospect Park 25
Purviance, Samuel and Robert 127
Putnam, Fort *see* Fort Putnam
Putnam, Israel, Gen. 18–19, 20, 23, 39, 169

Quebec, Battle of 16, 45, 164
Queen Anne's County MD 115, 126
Querney (Quarney), Lawrence, Pvt. 89
Quigley, Patrick, Pvt. 128

Raisin, William, Lt. 150
Ramsburg (Remsburg), Henry, Pvt. 153
Ramsburg, Stephen 153
Rankins, Daniel, Pvt. 94
Ratcliff, Mary (Mrs. Clement Kennedy) 63
Ray, Samuel, Pvt. 107
Ray, William, Pvt. 128
Reed, Rev. Thomas 108
Reeder, Catherine (the first Mrs. Nathaniel Ewing) 119
Reid, Casper, Capt. 145
Rice (Rue), Isaac, Pvt. 154
Richmond, Christopher, Lt. 118
Ridgely, Margaret (Mrs. William Ridgely) 89
Ridgely, Martha (Mrs. Henry Gaither) 82
Ridgely, William 89
Ridgley (Ridgly), Basil, Pvt. 89
Ridgley, Henry, Cdt. 74
Ritchie, Robert, Pvt. 128
Robinson, Jonathan, Pvt. 89
Robinson, Zadock 56
Rock Creek Hundred 95
Rockhold Plantation 55
Rodery, John, Pvt. 89

Index

Rogan, James, Cpl. 128
Rogers, John 75
Rose Hill 121
Ross, John, Pvt. 154
Ross, Robert, Pvt. 128
Row, John, Pvt. 154
Roxburgh, Alexander, Lt. 107
Roxburgh, Elizabeth 108
Roxburgh, Matthew 108
Roxburgh, William 108
Rue, Isaac 132
Rumbley, Drucilla (Mrs. Moses Floyd) 119
Russell (Russel), John, Pvt. 89

Saffell, Joshua, Pvt. 108
St. Anne's Episcopal Church 8, 54
St. George's Island, MD 11
St. Mary's County, MD 11, 47, 57, 61, 77, 119, 121, 140, 155, 157, 159, 160, 161, 162, 164, 165, 166
Saltzgater, G. M. 76
Sands, William. Sgt. 14, 58
Sandusky Expedition 152
Sapp, Robert, Pvt. 90
scarlet and buff *see* uniforms
Scharf 27
Scotland 42, 53, 65, 75, 76, 77, 98, 120, 126
Scott, Thomas, Pvt. 108
Second Company 75–94
Selby, Mary (Mrs. Nicholas Naylor) 153
Shannen, Thomas, Pvt. 108
Shaw, John, Pvt. 67
Sheirburn, Charles 68
Sheirburn, Luke Matthews, Pvt. 68
Sheirburn, Mary (Mrs. Nicholas Sheirburn) 68
Sheirburn, Nicholas 68
Shepard (Sheppard, Sherrard), Francis, Pvt. 68–69, 99
Sim, Joseph, Col. 75
Sim, Dr. Patrick 75
Sim, Patrick, Capt. 45, 56, 75, 76, 84
Simms, Andrew Green, Pvt. 69
Simms, James, Jr., Pvt. 69
Simms (Semmes), James, Sr., Cpl. 69
Simpkins, Thomas, Pvt. 90
Simpson, Thomas, Pvt. 70
Sim's Delight 76
Sixth Company 44, 45, 115–129, 152, 155
Skinner, Truman 100
Skipper, John, Pvt. 70
Skipper, William, Pvt. 90
Slicer, Andrew 113
Slicer, Sarah (Mrs. Joshua Lamb) 113
Smallpox 11, 15, 33, 73

Smallwood, Heaberd, Capt. 36
Smallwood, Pryor 36
Smallwood, William, Col.: aftermath of the battle 31; background 36–41; in battle 22–30; before the war 6, 13–18
Smallwood Foundation 41
Smallwood State Park 41
Smallwood's battalion: creation 10; deployment to New York 11–12
Smith, Alban (Alvin), Pvt. 70
Smith, Ann (Mrs. William Murray) 126
Smith, Barbara (Mrs. Adam Everly) 142
Smith, Charles, Cdt. 70–71
Smith, Christina (Mrs. Samuel Hamilton) 60
Smith, Edward M., Lt. 142
Smith, Edward, Pvt. 71
Smith, James, Pvt. 108
Smith, John, Pvt. 71
Smith, John Baryann 66
Smith, Margaret (Mrs. John Neale) 66
Smith, Mary (Mrs. Jacob Holland) 85
Smith, Mary (Mrs. Raphael Boarman) 70
Smith, Nathaniel, Capt. 156
Smith, Richard, Pvt. 71
Smith, Thomas, Pvt. 71
Smith, William, Pvt. 154
Smoot, John, Pvt. 71
Smoot, William, Pvt. 71–72
Smyth, Thomas, Jr., Lt. 156
Society of the Cincinnati 54, 92, 127, 158
Somerset County, MD 107, 114
Sothoron, Harriett (the second Mrs. John Hancock Beanes) 77
Southern campaign, Marylanders in 169
Spalding, Aaron, Pvt. 162
Spalding, Henry (of Peter), Pvt. 162
Spalding, Jane (Mrs. Henry Boone) 55
Speake (Sheake), Richard, Pvt. 72
Spires, Asenath (Mrs. Abraham Holland) 146
Sprigg, Elizabeth (Mrs. Bennet Neale) 66
Sprigg, Thomas, Lt. 100
Star Spangled Banner 77
Staten Island 14, 15, 93, 162, 163
Stephenson, Francis, Capt. 116
Sterett (Steret, Sterrett), William, Lt. 108–110
Stevenson, Absalom (Absolarn), Pvt. 110
Steward, Joseph, Pvt. 90

Stewart, Anthony 7
Stewart, John, Lt. 163–164
Stirling, Lord (Gen. William Alexander) 4, 18, 21–30, 42–43, 157, 170, 171
Stoddert, William Truman 36
Stone, David 51
Stone, John Hoskins, Capt.: commander of First Company 51–54; in individual soldiers' entries 59, 64, 66, 68, 69, 75, 76, 82, 112, 129, 135, 152, 153; in Smallwood's battalion 40, 45
Stone, Richard. Pvt. 110
Stone, Thomas, Gov. 8, 11, 13, 14, 51
Stone, William, Gov. 51
Stony Point, Battle of 52, 59, 64, 71, 84, 98, 163, 164
Stottlemyer (Stottlemeir), Dewalt (Devall), Pvt. 156
Stricker, George, Capt. 10, 94, 131, 135, 139, 143, 144, 145, 147, 148, 154, 155, 156
Sullivan, John, Gen. 18, 19, 27, 137, 148
Summers (Sumers), Obediah, Pvt. 114

Talbot County, MD 157
Talbott, Coxon, Pvt. 90
Tannehill, Zachariah, Sgt. 110
Tarlton, Jeremiah, Pvt. 164
Tarrance, William, Pvt. 154
Taylor, James, Pvt. 154
Taylor, John, Pvt. 154
Temple, William, Pvt. 128
Tennessee 119, 136, 137
Third Company 44, 45, 95–114
Third Maryland Regiment 55, 79, 82, 91, 94, 113, 150
Thomas, Betsy (Mrs. William Courts) 57
Thomas, George, Pvt. 72
Thomas, Dr. James 57
Thomas, John Allen, Capt.: aftermath of battle 31, 34–35, 38–39; in battle 24–25; as commander of Fifth Independent Company 157–166
Thomas, Margaret (Mrs. Nathan Thomas) 164
Thomas, Nathan, Pvt. 164
Thompson, Ann (Mrs. John Thompson) 72
Thompson, Electious, Pvt. 165
Thompson, Florence M. 76
Thompson, Francis, Pvt. 90
Thompson, George 72
Thompson, James, Pvt. 72
Thompson, Jesse, Pvt. 161, 166
Thompson, John 72
Thompson, Samuel, Pvt. 72

Index

Thompson, Wordsworth 13
Tilghman, James 169
Tilghman, Tench, Col. 24, 168
Tilley, Zachary, Pvt. 110
Todd, Levean, Pvt. 154
Tomlin (Tomling), Hugh, Pvt. 90
Tongue, Mary (Mrs. Milburn Coe) 80
Tories 13, 14, 22, 130
Townshend Act 7
Trenton, Battle of 35, 54, 75, 84, 85, 91, 114, 122, 129, 143, 144, 145, 148, 153, 157, 164, 166
Troup, Robert, Lt. 32
Tune, Robert, Pvt. 155
Turner, Charles, Pvt. 166

uniforms: hunting shirts 5, 12, 16, 45–46, 157; importance of 10, 46; scarlet and buff 4–5, 8, 12, 14, 45, 167
United Colonies 3, 9
Upper Marlboro (Marlborough), MD 77, 99

Valley Forge 52, 112, 152, 153
Vansant, John 81
Veach, John, Pvt. 90
Veazey, Mary (Mrs. James Lowrey) 124
Veazy, Capt. 27, 40, 58
Vermillion, Benjamin, Pvt. 90
Vermillion, Samuel (Saul), Pvt. 72
Virginia 9, 11, 36, 40, 56, 84, 85, 86, 95, 103, 104, 112, 121, 133, 143, 154, 159, 166, 168
von Heerington, Heinrich, Col. 29

Wade, Richard, Pvt. 110
Wales, Benjamin, Capt. 100
Walker, John, Pvt. 90
Wallabout Bay 28, 33 140
Wallace, Charles 162
Wallace, Elizabeth (the first Mrs. James Fernandis) 59
Wallace, Hugh, Pvt. 128

Wallace, Wheedon 59
Walnut Grove 96
Walsh, Thomas, Pvt. 91
Waltz, Michael, Pvt. 91
Walworth, Henry, Pvt. 73
War of 1812 77, 92, 134, 159
Ward, John, Pvt. 73
Ware, Francis, Lt. Col. 10, 37, 40, 62
Ware, Susanna (Mrs. William Luckett) 62
Warfield, Mary (Mrs. Thomas Dorsey) 78
Warner, Benjamin, Cpl. 110
Washington, George: aftermath of the battle 31–35; in battle 20, 21, 23, 24, 28, 29; in individual soldiers' entries 36–39, 42, 43, 45, 46, 48, 49, 51, 52, 54, 62, 100, 121, 122, 129, 133, 135, 145, 148, 157, 158, 160, 165; introduction 3, 4; Marylanders fight on 167, 168; preparing for war 7, 9, 11, 12, 13, 14, 15, 17, 18, 19
Washington, Lund 9
Washington, Martha 9–10
Washington County, MD 100, 108, 111, 136, 147, 152
Washington, DC 60, 64, 67, 77, 82, 86, 95, 99, 104, 133, 159
Wathen, Joseph 133
Wathen, Susanna (Mrs. Edward Edelen) 58
Watkins, Gassaway (Gazaway), Cpl. 91–93, 96
Watkins, Leonard, Pvt. 110
Watkins, Mary (Mrs. Leonard Watkins) 111
Wayne, Anthony, Gen. 82, 137, 142
Weilling, Zachariah 96
Weller, John 112
Weller (Wellen), Philip, Pvt. 96, 112
Weltner, Ludwick, Lt. Col. 146, 147
West Virginia 84, 143
Wheatley, Samuel, Pvt. 73

Wheatley, William, Pvt. 73
Wheeler, Ignatius, Jr., Esq. 123
Whetcroft, William 67
White Plains, Battle of 13, 53–54, 64, 66, 73, 75, 84, 91, 92, 93, 94, 103, 104, 111, 114, 139, 142, 143, 145, 146, 147, 148, 154, 162, 163, 164, 165, 166, 168, 179
Whiteaker, James 122
Whitman, Walt 4, 23
Whittier, John Greenleaf 131
Wilcoxon (Coxon), Levin, Sgt. 112
Willey, John, Pvt. 93
Williams, Elie 132
Williams, Otho Holland, Brig. Gen. 33, 100, 111, 132, 133, 158–159
Williams, Thomas, Pvt. 128
Willing, Zachariah, Pvt. 112
Willis, Cornelius 124
Willis, Margaret 124
Wilson, John 97
Windham, Charles 113
Windham, Eleanor 113
Windham, George Washington 113
Windham (Wyndham, Windom), Thomas, Pvt. 112
Witner, William, Pvt. 155
Wollaston (Wolleston) Manor 66
Wood, John, Pvt. 114
Woodward, Benedict, Cpl. 113
Woolford, Thomas, Capt. 62
Worcester County, MD 101
Workman, Samuel, Pvt. 155
Wright, Alexander, Pvt. 129
Wright, Bozely 93
Wright, George, Pvt. 113
Wurteh (Mrs. Nathaniel Gist) 48

Yankee Doodle 13
Yates, Jane (Mrs. Charles Bruce) 136
York Island, Battle of 111, 114
Yorktown, VA 3, 11, 55
Young, Henry, Pvt. 155

www.ingramcontent.com/pod-product-compliance
Ingram Content Group UK Ltd.
Pitfield, Milton Keynes, MK11 3LW, UK
UKHW050526150426
5217IPUK00026B/1812